# THE HUNDRED LANGUAGES OF CHILDREN:

## The Reggio Emilia Approach to Early Childhood Education

### Carolyn Edwards, Lella Gandini, and George Forman

ABLEX PUBLISHING CORPORATION
NORWOOD, NEW JERSEY

Sixth Printing 1995

Printed in the United States of America.

### Library of Congress Cataloging-in-Publication Data

Edwards, Carolyn P.
    The hundred languages of children : the Reggio Emilia approach to early childhood education / by Carolyn Edwards, Lella Gandini, and George Forman.
        p.   cm.
    Includes bibliographical references (p.   ) and index.
    ISBN 089391-927-6; 0-89391-933-0 (ppb)
    1. Early childhood education—Italy—Reggio Emilia.  2. Early childhood education—United States—Case studies.  I. Gandini, Lella.  II. Forman, George E., 1942–   .  III. Title.  IV. Title: 100 languages of children.
LB1139.3.I8E38   1992
372.21'0945'43—dc20                                            92–33268
                                                                    CIP

Ablex Publishing Corporation
355 Chestnut Street
Norwood, New Jersey 07648

# Table of Contents

*Invece il cento c'é.*

No way. The hundred *is* there.*

| | |
|---|---|
| *Il bambino* | The child |
| *é fatto di cento.* | is made of one hundred. |
| *Il bambino ha* | The child has |
| *cento lingue* | a hundred languages |
| *cento mani* | a hundred hands |
| *cento pensieri* | a hundred thoughts |
| *cento modi di pensare* | a hundred ways of thinking |
| *di giocare e di parlare* | of playing, of speaking. |
| *cento sempre cento* | A hundred always a hundred |
| *modi di ascoltare* | ways of listening |
| *di stupire di amare* | of marveling of loving |
| *cento allegrie* | a hundred joys |
| *per cantare e capire* | for singing and understanding |
| *cento mondi* | a hundred worlds |
| *da scoprire* | to discover |
| *cento mondi* | a hundred worlds |
| *da inventare* | to invent |
| *cento mondi* | a hundred worlds |
| *da sognare.* | to dream. |
| *Il bambino ha* | The child has |
| *cento lingue* | a hundred languages |
| *(e poi cento cento cento)* | (and a hundred hundred hundred more) |
| *ma gliene rubano novantanove.* | but they steal ninety-nine. |
| *La scuola e la cultura* | The school and the culture |
| *gli separano la testa dal corpo.* | separate the head from the body. |
| *Gli dicono:* | They tell the child: |
| *di pensare senza mani* | to think without hands |
| *di fare senza testa* | to do without head |
| *di ascoltare e di non parlare* | to listen and not to speak |
| *di capire senza allegrie* | to understand without joy |
| *di amare e di stupirsi* | to love and to marvel |
| *solo a Pasqua e a Natale.* | only at Easter and Christmas. |
| *Gli dicono:* | They tell the child: |
| *di scoprire il mondo che già c'é* | to discover the world already there |
| *e di cento* | and of the hundred |
| *gliene rubano novantanove.* | they steal ninety-nine. |
| *Gli dicone:* | They tell the child: |
| *che il gioco e il lavoro* | that work and play |
| *la realtà e la fantasia* | reality and fantasy |
| *la scienza e l'immaginazione* | science and imagination |
| *il cielo e la terra* | sky and earth |
| *la ragione e il sogno* | reason and dream |
| *sono cose* | are things |
| *che non stanno insieme.* | that do not belong together. |
| | |
| *Gli dicono insomma* | And thus they tell the child |
| *che il cento non c'é.* | that the hundred is not there. |
| *Il bambino dice:* | The child says: |
| *invece il cento c'é.* | No way. The hundred *is* there. |

—LORIS MALAGUZZI

—LORIS MALAGUZZI

*Translated by Lella Gandini

# Contributors

**Meg Barden,** Lecturer, School of Education, University of Massachusetts, Amherst

**Nora Cannon,** Artist, Art Educator, Boston, MA

**Patricia Corsaro,** Art Specialist, Early Childhood Learning Center, North Andover, MA

**Betsy Damian,** Follow-Through Kindergarten Teacher, Cambridge Public Schools, Cambridge, MA

**Carolyn Pope Edwards,** Professor, College of Human Environmental Sciences, University of Kentucky, Lexington

**Tiziana Filippini,** *Pedagogista*, Department of Early Education, Comune of Reggio Emilia, Italy

**George Forman,** Professor, School of Education, University of Massachusetts, Amherst

**Lella Gandini,** Liaison to the U.S. for the Department of Early Education, Reggio Emilia; and Adjunct, School of Education, University of Massachusetts, Amherst

**Howard Gardner,** Professor, Graduate School of Education, Harvard University, Cambridge, MA

**David Hawkins,** Professor Emeritus, University of Colorado, Boulder

**Lilian Katz,** Professor, ERIC Clearinghouse on Elementary and Early Childhood Education, University of Illinois, Urbana

**Paul Kaufman,** Writer and Television Producer, P.K. Inc., New York

**Joan Langley,** Teacher, Amherst Public Schools, Amherst, Massachusetts

**Moonja Lee,** Doctoral Student, School of Education, University of Massachusetts, Amherst

**Debbie LeeKeenan,** Teacher, Amherst Public Schools, Amherst, Massachusetts

**Loris Malaguzzi,** Founder and Past Director; Director, *Bambini* (journal), Department of Early Education, Reggio Emilia

**Rebecca New,** Assistant Professor, Department of Education, University of New Hampshire, Durham

**John Nimmo,** Assistant Professor, Faculty of Education and Human Development, Pacific Oaks College Outreach, Bellevue, WA

**Eunice Shaw Perry,** Associate Professor, Director of Child Study, Mount Ida College, Newton, MA

**Baji Rankin,** Doctoral Student, Boston University, Boston, MA, Adjunct Faculty, Wheelock College, Institute for Self-Active Education

**Carlina Rinaldi,** *Pedagogista*, Department of Early Education, Reggio Emilia

**Diane Rollo,** Education Supervisor, Head Start, Boston, MA

**Irene Rochwarg,** Director, Early Childhood Learning Center, North Andover, MA

**Sergio Spaggiari,** Director, Department of Early Education, Reggio Emilia

**Vea Vecchi,** *Atelierista*, Department of Early Education, Reggio Emilia

**Lynda Wrisley,** Teacher, Amherst Public Schools, Amherst, Massachusetts

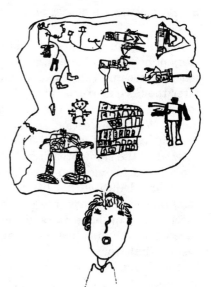

"I think about my life." Drawing by 5-year-old, Diana School.

# Foreword: Complementary Perspectives on Reggio Emilia

## Howard Gardner

Midst the multitude of books about education issued these days, few stand out. This book that you hold in your hands does. An integrated set of essays on a unique approach to early childhood education, *The Hundred Languages of Children* documents the remarkable set of schools that have evolved over the last 30 years in Reggio Emilia in Northern Italy. At the same time the book constitutes a profound meditation on the nature of early human nature, and the ways in which it can be guided and stimulated in different cultural milieus. Anyone with an interest in the education of children should read it; few who do so will remain unaffected by the experience.

In the opening pages of this book, you will read the remarkable story of how Loris Malaguzzi, an intellectually oriented young Italian teacher, became interested in the building of a new school directly after the Second World War, and how a momentary infatuation with this new construction turned into a lifelong love affair with young pupils. Without question, Malaguzzi (as he is universally called) is the guiding genius of Reggio—the thinker whose name deserves to be uttered in the same breath as his heroes Froebel, Montessori, Dewey, Piaget. But far more so than most other educational thinkers, Malaguzzi has dedicated his life to the establishment of an educational community: a remarkable group of teachers of various stripes and specialties who have worked together for years, even decades, with parents, community members, and thousands of children, to set up a system that works.

The Reggio system can be described succinctly as follows: It is a collection of schools for young children in which each child's intellectual, emotional, social, and moral potentials are carefully cultivated and guided. The principal educational vehicle involves youngsters in long-term engrossing projects, which are carried out in a beautiful, healthy, love-filled setting. Dewey wrote about progressive education for decades but his school lasted a scant four years. In sharp contrast, it is the Reggio community, more so than the philosophy or method, that constitutes Malaguzzi's central achievement. Nowhere else in the world is there such a seamless and symbiotic relationship between a school's progressive philosophy and its practices.

Just as Reggio represents the achievement of many individuals and groups, each of which brings to bear its own special gifts, so, too, the present volume is distinguished by the range of individuals who have reflected about Reggio from their own distinctive and complementary perspectives. Within the Reggio family, there are essays by individuals who represent the teaching, the architectural design and layout, the community relations, and the rich curricula of projects. From the American perspective, there are the impressions of a philosopher, a film maker, a progressive educator, and several researchers who have explored the cognitive, affective, and social dimensions of the projects carried out by the children of Reggio and their teachers. Of special note is that cohort of educator-researchers who have traveled back and forth between Reggio and Massachusetts during the 1980s, sharing experiences and developing their own transoceanic network. These individuals and others have helped to make Reggio Emilia known around the world, even as they have sought to explicate its special nature to interested audiences on both sides of the Atlantic.

Words are necessarily the prime medium in a book. The writers have done a splendid job of recreating the special atmosphere of Reggio, and the various photos and diagrams presented here add the essential visual element to the portrait. The various exhibitions about Reggio that have been mounted have helped to convey its special flavor, and there are now several film and video treatments as well. Of course, there is no substitute for a visit to Reggio Emilia, and without a doubt, the publication of this book will increase traffic to the lush and civilized Emilia Romagna area. Yet, even for those who are quite familiar with the Reggio scene, this book provides a wealth of additional information. As one who had the privilege of visiting in Reggio several years ago, and has remained in touch ever since, I can say that I learned something on nearly every page of this gritty volume.

In reading *The Hundred Languages of Children* I was struck—or struck anew—by many messages, of which I shall mention just a few. So much has been written about progressive methods in education, but so rarely are the ideals of progressive education actually realized. Perhaps one reason why is that one needs a team that is willing to work together for decades in the service of a set of energizing ideas; the team needs to evolve procedures for attaining an education of quality while still encouraging growth for all who participate. So much has been written about the powers of the young mind, and yet so rarely can they be seen in full action. In Reggio, the teachers know how to listen to children, how to allow them to take the initiative, and yet how to guide them in productive ways. There is no fetish made about achieving adult standards, and yet the dedication exemplified by the community insures that work of quality will result. The effect comes about because of the infinite care taken with respect to every aspect of existence, whether it be the decision to constitute groups of two as compared with three children, the choice of brush or color, or the receptivity to surprises and to surprise. Reggio successfully challenges so many false dichotomies: art vs. science, individual vs. community, child vs. adult, enjoyment vs. study, nuclear family vs. extended family; by achieving a unique harmony that spans these contrasts, it reconfigures our sclerotic categorical systems.

As an American educator, I cannot help but be struck by certain paradoxes. In America we pride ourselves on being focused on children, and yet we do not pay sufficient attention to what they are actually expressing. We call for cooperative learning among children, and yet we rarely have sustained cooperation at the level of teacher and administrator. We call for artistic works, but we rarely fashion environments that can truly support and inspire them. We call for parental involvement, but are loathe to share ownership, responsibility, and credit with parents. We recognize the need for community, but we so often crystallize immediately into interest groups. We hail the discovery method, but we do not have the confidence to allow children to follow their own noses and hunches. We call for debate, but often spurn it; we call for listening, but we prefer to talk; we are affluent, but we do not safeguard those resources that can allow us to remain so and to foster the affluence of others. Reggio is so instructive in these respects. Where we are often intent to invoke slogans, the educators in Reggio work tirelessly to solve many of these fundamental—and fundamentally difficult—issues.

It is tempting to romanticize Reggio Emilia. It looks so beautiful, it works so well. That would be a mistake. It is clear from the essays in this book that Reggio has struggled much in the past and that, indeed, conflict can never be absent from the achievements of any dynamic entity. The relationships to the Catholic Church have not been easy; the political struggles at the municipal, provincial, and national levels never cease; and even the wonderful start achieved by the youngsters is threatened and perhaps undermined by a secondary and tertiary educational system that is far less innovative. Reggio is distinguished less by the fact that it has found permanent solutions to these problems—because, of course, it has not—than by the fact that it recognizes such dilemmas unblinkingly and continues to attempt to deal with them seriously and imaginatively.

No matter how ideal an educational model or system, it is always rooted in local conditions. One could no more transport the Diana School of Reggio to New England than one could transport John Dewey's New England schoolhouse to the fields of Emilia Romagna. But just as we can now have "museums without walls," which allow us to observe art work from all over our world, so, too, we can now have "schoolhouses without walls" which allow us to observe educational practices as they have developed around the globe.

I have had the privilege of visiting centers of early childhood education in many lands, and have learned much from what I've observed in these diverse settings. Like other educational tourists, I have been impressed by the stimulating children's museums in the big cities of the United States, the noncompetitive classroom environments in Scandinavia, the supportive and sensitive training of artistic skills in China, the well-orchestrated engagement of joint problem-solving activity in Japan, and the sincere efforts now underway in many lands to develop sensitivity in young children to diverse ethnic and racial groups. In its own way each of these educational environments has to struggle with and find its own comfortable point of repose between the desires of the individual and the needs for the group; the training of skills and the cultivation of creativity; the respect for the family and the involvement in a wider community; attention to cognitive growth and concern with matters of temperament, feelings, and spirit.

There are many ways of mediating among these human impulses and strains. To my mind, no place in the contemporary world has succeeded so splendidly as the schools of Reggio Emilia. When the American magazine *Newsweek*, in typically understated fashion, chose "The Ten Best Schools in the World" in December 1991, it was entirely fitting that Reggio Emilia was its nominee in the Early Childhood category. Reggio epitomizes for me an education that is effective and humane; its students undergo a sustained apprenticeship in humanity, one which may last a lifetime.

Thanks to the efforts of Carolyn Edwards, Lella Gandini, and George Forman, this remarkable educational enterprise can now become better known within—and more effectively emulated by—the community of concerned citizens of our troubled world.

"Difficult, zig-zagging, intricate, important discussions." Drawing by 5-year-old, Diana School.

# Remarks:
# Malaguzzi's Story,
# Other Stories

## David Hawkins

The extraordinary story told by Loris Malaguzzi, in his interview with Lella Gandini, has reminded me vividly of my first meeting with him. That was at the great Reggio Emilia conference of March 1990, when he spoke so incisively on the conference theme—the Potentials and Rights of Children. His story has reminded me also of other stories that have been told, or could be told, from different times and places. All speak of successful efforts to create new patterns of educational practice—patterns that can at least begin to match the manifold talents of young children. Most of these other successes have been limited in scale and often, sadly, in duration. Yet brought together, they spin a golden thread through many decades of adult neglect and preoccupation with other matters. Although education is among the oldest and most vital parts of human praxis, the successes typically have been supported only through a minority tradition, ignored by mainstream society, even by the mainstream of scientific curiosity and research. That this should be true is a paradox. Such a brilliant exception as is the case of Reggio Emilia should, therefore, bring with it much joy.

I think it is worth reminding ourselves of a few of those other stories. Malaguzzi refers in passing to some of them, mainly to the theorists. Let me mention others. In the field of education, as in many others, good theory—I boldly say—has come mostly as a harvest, a reflection of successful practice. Harvested from past practice, theory in turn can, then, bring new practical guidance. An outstanding example of this twofold relation was the part played by John Dewey.

In Dewey's time, almost a century ago, a minority tradition of excellent practice in childhood education already existed in the United States. That tradition had evolved, in turn, from the experience of the Froebel Kindergartens. My own mother received a basic part of her education in a Froebel Kindergarten during the 1870s, when the number of such schools in the United States grew by two or three orders of magnitude. Strong women teachers had been supported by Froebel's basic insight into the learning process, but had outgrown the quaint rigidity of his pioneering "system." (Something similar was true, later, of Montessori's influence.) The pioneering teachers involved in this development were looking for new theoretical recognition and guidance. They found it in John Dewey, already a deeply perceptive philosopher and psychologist. But they had to educate him first, a pupil of profound aptitude! Dewey's own practice was that of a university lecturer, deeply reflective but dry as dust except to those who already shared something of his spirit and insight. Though many contemporaries were profoundly moved by his clarity of understanding, his influence has largely been lost in my country as part of the attrition of childhood education. I am happy that this great educational philosopher is still alive and well in Italy. I associate his vitality most with the names of Lydia Tronatore and Nando Filograsso, among several others.

Looking further back, Froebel linked himself theoretically to Hegel, and for practice and commitment to his mentor, Johann Pestalozzi. Not far north of Reggio Emilia, but nearly two centuries ago, Pestalozzi rescued children tragically orphaned in the wake of Napoleon's armies, developing deep insights concerning the nurturance of their life and their talents.

Coming forward again in time, one sees that the fruition of this long development has been irregular. Its practical influences have grown also in Canada and in continental Europe, developing differently in

Germany and the low countries, in France and Scandinavia. In the United States it was once powerful but has largely been co-opted by the schools, in which "Kindergarten," for the most part, survives in name only. This whole international story needs to be rescued. Here I shall only add a note about England, where their major developments had a history similar in some ways to that of the United States, starting also from 19th-century small beginnings under such influences as those of Froebel and, later, of Dewey and the McMillian sisters. Whereas in the United States this evolution suffered from neglect or rejection after World War II, in England it flourished. In some regions a large proportion of the Infant Schools (ages 5–7 + ) were radically transformed, as were smaller proportions of Junior Schools (ages 7–11 + ). Visitors to some of those good classrooms could find much to delight in and reflect upon. Political idealogues, more recently, have suppressed or ignored these forward steps. But the new ways of learning and teaching have not been wholly reversed. They are successful, they persist, and one still can learn from them.

I mention this English phase of our joint history because it attracted great attention from many of us in the United States, suffering from the loss of our own best traditions. The result was a fashion, a seeking to emulate "The English Infant School." This was a kind of emulation that ignored a long history of development, a well-rooted tree that could not simply be put in an airplane and transported. We have our own very strong traditions, and we need to rescue them.

After this circuit of history I come back, finally, to the fascinating history of Reggio Emilia and the other Italian communities in which childhood education has similarly evolved and prospered. We who labor in this particular vineyard have much to learn from the history of Reggio and its still-evolving practice. An evolution with such communal support is an achievement that Americans, in particular, will carefully study. But it can be a great mistake for us, as it was in the case of our desire to emulate the English Infant Schools, to think that we can somehow just import the Reggio experience. By reputation we are prone to look for the "quick fix." Such an attitude would deprecate the very achievement it professes to admire. Among many other institutional and cultural differences, we in the United States do not know such solidarity, such sustaining communality, reshaping itself in the ways Malaguzzi describes, demanding better education for children. Our social landscape is different, so must our battles be.

Though many of us still lack acquaintance with the obvious profusion of Reggio practice, I hazard the opinion that we—we being the United States, England, and elsewhere—have contributions both to receive and to give. I shall mention particularly the practice of developing "projects" for children's inquiry and invention. It is similar to a strategy that we saw well developed, years ago, in California. Frances Hawkins (my co-author of these remarks) taught there and contributed to that strategy, often a great advance over dreary daily "lessons." When based in part on the interests some children revealed in play and discussion, such projects could enlist their commitment and enthusiasm. Yet fundamental questions still remained open: about the degree to which such enthusiasms might support, or merely mask, the more hidden and less-developed talents of other children. To recognize and encourage these less articulate ones, on their diverse trajectories of learning, remains a constant challenge.

Such questions and challenges, we learned, must always permeate our intellectual curiosity about the earliest years of learning. We came to see the need to evolve a style of classroom practice that would support a greater simultaneous diversity of work than our project methods, even at their best, could easily maintain. Out of this more pluralistic and richer ambiance, ideas and inventions could, at times (though not often), be shared by all. Out of this sharing, projects did indeed sometimes evolve, with great vitality. But the definition and duration of these projects was always a dependent and restricted variable.

I mention this specific topic—projects—because as I read the very open and charming reflections of Loris Malaguzzi, I thought not only of the wider history of childhood education, but also about the details, the debate, the problems, that must have been involved at every step. I have tried to suggest, as an example, that the etiology and uses of the "project" may still be in that problematic state. For our own benefit, we need to know more of the debate, the retrospective valuations, the successive approximations. We need to join in the debate!

In the meantime, it is quite enough that we salute the achievement and devotion revealed in this remarkable story of a devoted teacher-theorist and a devoted community.

# Part I
# Starting Points

"Tigers." Drawing by 5-year-old,
Anna Frank School.

# 1

# Introduction

### Carolyn Edwards
### Lella Gandini
### George Forman

Reggio Emilia is a city of 130,000 people in the prosperous and progressive Emilia Romagna region of northern Italy. Its municipal early childhood system has become recognized and acclaimed as one of the best systems of education in the world (*Newsweek*, December 2, 1991). Currently the city finances and operates 22 preprimary schools for children aged 3–6, as well as 13 infant-toddler centers for children aged 0–3. Over the past 30 years, the system has evolved a distinctive and innovative set of philosophical assumptions, curriculum and pedagogy, method of school organization, and design of environments which, taken as a unified whole, we are calling the Reggio Emilia approach. This approach fosters children's intellectual development through a systematic focus on symbolic representation. Young children are encouraged to explore their environment and express themselves through all of their natural "languages," or modes of expression, including words, movement, drawing, painting, building, sculpture, shadow play, collage, dramatic play, and music. Leading children to

3

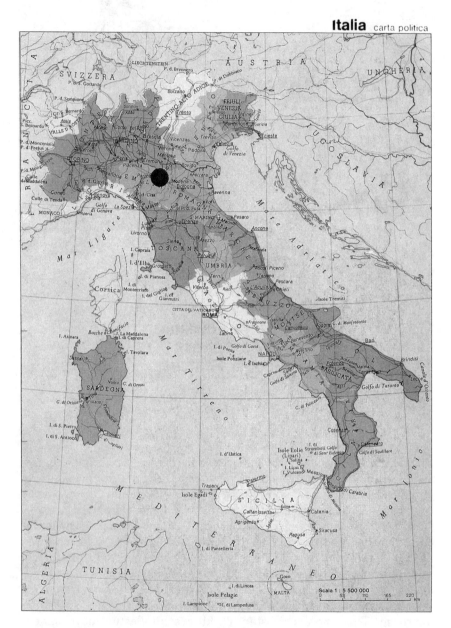

**Figure 1.1.   Map of Italy with indication of the city of Reggio Emilia.**

surprising levels of symbolic skills and creativity, the approach takes place, not in an elite and sheltered setting of private education, but rather in a municipal system of full-day child care open to all, including children with special needs. Because the system grew out of a parent cooperative movement, there has been from the beginning an explicit recognition of the relationship or partnership among parents, educators, and children. Classrooms are organized to support a highly collaborative problem-solving approach to learning. Other important features are the use of small groups in project learning, the teacher/ child continuity (two co-teachers work with the same class group for three years), and the community-based management method of governance. In Reggio Emilia, education is seen as a communal activity and sharing of culture through joint exploration between children and adults who together open topics to speculation and discussion. The approach provides us with new ways to think about the nature of the child as learner, the role of the teacher, school organization and management, the design and use of physical environments, and curriculum planning which guides experiences of joint, open-ended discovery and problem solving. Because of all these features, the Reggio Emilia approach is important and exciting to Americans. We can learn much from the Reggio story, as we wrestle with our own enormous problems: uneven quality, poor coordination, and lack of access and affordability of early childhood services; coupled with universal recognition of the need for high-quality early childhood education programs to boost children's chances for later school success.

**Figure 1.2. One of the main squares in the city of Reggio Emilia.**

**Table 1.1.   Schedule and Staffing of the Preprimary Schools in Reggio Emilia**

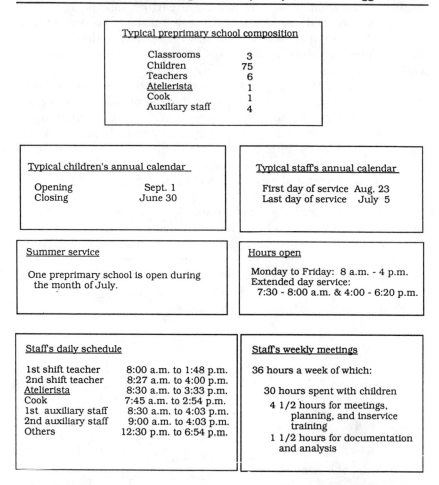

Typical preprimary school composition

| | |
|---|---|
| Classrooms | 3 |
| Children | 75 |
| Teachers | 6 |
| Atelierista | 1 |
| Cook | 1 |
| Auxiliary staff | 4 |

Typical children's annual calendar

| | |
|---|---|
| Opening | Sept. 1 |
| Closing | June 30 |

Typical staff's annual calendar

| | |
|---|---|
| First day of service | Aug. 23 |
| Last day of service | July 5 |

Summer service

One preprimary school is open during the month of July.

Hours open

Monday to Friday: 8 a.m. - 4 p.m.
Extended day service:
    7:30 - 8:00 a.m. & 4:00 - 6:20 p.m.

Staff's daily schedule

| | |
|---|---|
| 1st shift teacher | 8:00 a.m. to 1:48 p.m. |
| 2nd shift teacher | 8:27 a.m. to 4:00 p.m. |
| Atelierista | 8:30 a.m. to 3:33 p.m. |
| Cook | 7:45 a.m. to 2:54 p.m. |
| 1st auxiliary staff | 8:30 a.m. to 4:03 p.m. |
| 2nd auxiliary staff | 9:00 a.m. to 4:03 p.m. |
| Others | 12:30 p.m. to 6:54 p.m. |

Staff's weekly meetings

36 hours a week of which:

30 hours spent with children

4 1/2 hours for meetings, planning, and inservice training
1 1/2 hours for documentation and analysis

Source: "An Historical Outline, Data, and Information," page 29, published by the Municipality of Reggio Emilia, Department of Education, December 1990. Reprinted by permission.

This book is actually the second major work to appear in the English language about the Reggio Emilia approach. However, the first is not, like this one, a book, but rather an exhibit, which has been touring the United States since 1987. "The Hundred Languages of Children" Exhibit is a beautiful and intriguing display that describes the educational process through photographs; samples of children's paintings, drawings, collages, constructive structures; and explanatory scripts and panels. Created by the educators of Reggio Emilia to tell American audiences about their work[1], the exhibit in certain notable ways exemplifies the essence of the educational approach. As a medium of communication, the exhibit is wonderfully suited to the story the educators want to tell, in five important ways.

First of all, the exhibit was authored and designed not individually but rather collectively. Loris Malaguzzi, founder and for many years Director of the Reggio Emilia system of municipal early childhood education, led the task of preparing the exhibit, but (demonstrating the quality of results coming from group effort) many of the administrators and teachers from throughout the city contributed time, labor, ideas, and the results of recording project work in their classrooms. Reggio educators believe, as we shall see in detail, that reciprocity, exchange, and dialogue lie at the heart of successful education.

Second, the exhibit plunges the visitor into a form of learning that is multileveled and multimodal. Looking at the large, highly detailed panels, densely embedded with words and images, the mind and senses are overwhelmed with information and impressions coming in on multiple channels all at once. This gives visitors the immediate and tangible experience of learning through "one hundred languages." As Malaguzzi (1984) put it, the exhibit creates "a place of uninterrupted condensation of hundreds of subjective and objective experiences" (p. 20/22).

Third, wandering at will through the exhibit, visitors find themselves on a circular path as they retrace their steps and return repeatedly to favorite panels or themes, each time with deeper understanding. In just this way, education in Reggio Emilia is anything but linear; it is, instead, an open-ended spiral. Young children are not marched or hurried sequentially from one different activity to the next, but instead encouraged to repeat key experiences, observe and reobserve, consider and reconsider, represent and rerepresent.

Fourth, the exhibit as a form of communication grew directly out of what Reggio Emilia educators call "documentation." Early in their history (Malaguzzi, Chapter 3, this volume), the educators realized that systematically documenting the process and results of their work with children would simultaneously serve three key functions: provide the children with a concrete and visible "memory" of what they have said and done in order to serve as a jumping-off point for the next steps in learning; provide the educators with a tool for research and a key to

---

[1] The exhibition and the accompanying catalog (*The Hundred Languages of Children: Narrative of the Possible,* 1987) are the property and publication of the Region of Emilia Romagna and the City of Reggio Emilia, Department of Education.

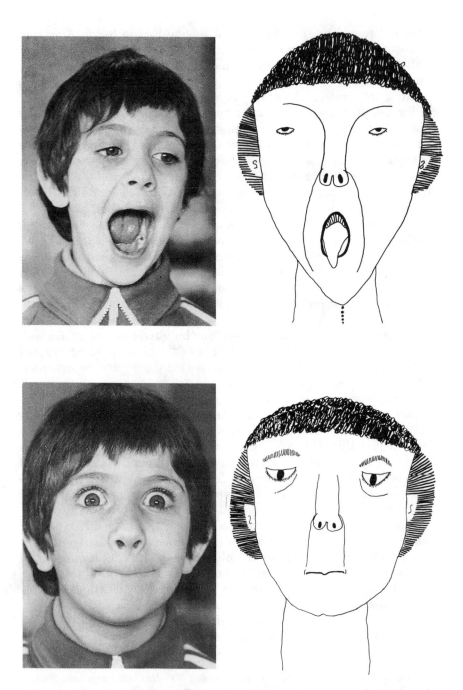

**Figure 1.3.** Silvia looks at herself in the mirror and draws self-portraits. She comments, "When I look at myself, it is as if I saw another child." From the exhibit, *The Hundred Languages of Children*: "The Importance of Looking at Ourselves."

continuous improvement and renewal; and provide parents and the public with detailed information about what happens in the schools as a means of eliciting their reactions and support. This bold insight led the development of documentation into a professional art form in Reggio Emilia, involving the use of slide shows, posters, and increasingly, videotapes, to record children's project experiences.

Finally, the exhibit is never completed; it never reaches a state in which the Reggio educators say, "Now, it is prefect." Instead, it undergoes transformations and emerges in one after another of separate versions or editions. The first exhibit opened in 1981 and began to travel in Europe under the name, "L'Occhio se Salta il Muro" ("When the Eye Jumps Over the Wall"). The title became "I Centro Linguaggi dei Bambini" ("The Hundred Languages of Children") for the third and fourth editions. In just such a way, the educational work in Reggio Emilia never becomes set and routine but instead is always undergoing reexamination and experimentation. For this reason, the Reggio educators refuse the term "model," when talking about their approach, and instead speak of "our project" and "our experience."

Yet, the exhibit does not accomplish everything. Unlike a book, it cannot be taken home for study and reflection. Furthermore, the exhibit does not answer all of our questions about the history and philosophy of the program, curriculum, planning, and teacher behavior, or the administrative organization and structure. Thus, the need for this book was born. It allows for a more extended and analytic treatment of the Reggio Emilia approach in all of its aspects, and it provides a forum for both Italians and North Americans to tell what they know about the Reggio Emilia approach. Other books will surely follow, by ourselves and others, about particular issues, especially regarding curriculum. This book represents the starting point, the general treatment of the whole system and approach, as we can at best define and understand it now.

## THE AUTHORS AND THEIR CHAPTERS

### The American Network

This book represents a combined effort of many individuals and groups. First there is the introductory chapter by the editors, who originally worked together on the exhibit and conference, "The Hundred Languages of Children," held at the University of Massachusetts in Amherst in December 1988. As we worked on these tasks in collaboration with our Italian friends, we formed the network of authors whose work is presented in Part II. Major networks have also been established by Baji Rankin, host of the 1989 exhibit and conference in Boston and leader of delegations to Reggio Emilia, and by Rebecca New, host of the 1988 exhibit in Syracuse and leader of several major delegations to Reggio. Lilian Katz, Howard Gardner, and David Hawkins have each been honored guests in Reggio Emilia, and all remaining authors have either been to Reggio Emilia with an American delegation or worked with one of the editors. Lella Gandini first started bringing information about Reggio Emilia to the United States 12 years ago; Carolyn Edwards and George Forman have observed and studied the Reggio Emilia preprimary schools intensively over the past nine years.

## The Flow of Chapter Topics

Chapter 2, by Lilian Katz, maintains the reflective mood begun by Howard Gardner and David Hawkins. As a world traveler and current President of the National Association for the Education of Young Children, she better than anyone can tell us what can be learned from the work of Reggio Emilia. She compares and contrasts these ideas with aims and principles she has discovered to be true of education in the United States, where she has been a professional leader since the days of compensatory education in the late 1960s.

Beginning with Part II, we turn quickly to what the Italians say about themselves. It is surprising and welcoming that Loris Malaguzzi (Chapter 3) saw this book as an opportunity to undertake, for the first time, a comprehensive review of his work and the history of the municipal early childhood system in Reggio Emilia. Sergio Spaggiari, as current director of the municipal early childhood system, lays out the organizational structure and how it functions in Chapter 4. Carlina Rinaldi (Chapter 5), lifelong resident of Reggio Emilia and first partner with Loris Malaguzzi in curriculum theory, explains the constructivist base of classroom practice, particularly its foundation in dialogue, communication, and joint problem solving. Tiziana Filippini, who studied for a year in the United States, explains the role and rationale for the *pedagogista (pedagogical coordinator)*, a level of staffing uncommon in the United States in Chapter 6. The *pedagogista* links the systems of schools and parents into a coherent whole in terms of values, educational objectives, and educational practices. Likewise, Vea Vecchi, the original *atelierista (resource teacher)*, explains, in Chapter 7, how the presence of the *atelier* (studio/workshop) makes possible a deepening of the instruction via the use of many diverse media.

Part III contains chapters whose authors analyze the specifics of classroom practice in Reggio Emilia. This analysis draws from principles both avowed by the Reggio teachers or latent in their practice. The chapters lay out these principles in the American idiom and theoretical constructs. Lella Gandini (Chapter 8), Reggio Emilia's liaison in the United States and consultant to early childhood systems throughout Italy, describes the way that school environments in Reggio have been built to maximize quality social encounters, the use of light, and the use of displays for documentation of the children's work. Carolyn Edwards (Chapter 9), through her video-ethnographic research on teacher behavior and meaning systems in Reggio Emilia, describes the multiple roles of the teacher and presents commentary on transcripts of actual teacher–child interactions. She helps us understand the finesse of teaching by listening and learning along with the children. George Forman (Chapter 10) presents an abridged report on his videotape, produced with Lella Gandini, on a single project, "The Long Jump," done in 1985 at the Diana School. His commentary emphasizes the role of symbol making and communication as a means to help young children construct their own knowledge. And finally, Baji Rankin (Chapter 11), who spent most of an academic year in Reggio Emilia, walks us through a project on dinosaurs conducted at the Anna Frank School. Describing how children can be challenged to build a dinosaur nine feet tall, she quickly dispels any initial skepticism that such a topic could have strong academic content!

In Part IV we shift to American authors who have applied their respective interpretations of Reggio Emilia in American classrooms. Rebecca New introduces this section from a cross-cultural perspective in Chapter 12. By considering a contemporary issue in American education, that of developmentally appropriate practice, she takes what we know from Reggio Emilia as a challenge to what we assume to be best practice—in teacher education, teaching strategies, and teacher–parent relations. In Chapter 13, a group of teachers from an elementary school in Amherst, Massachusetts, transform a well-known project from Reggio Emilia, "The City in the Rain," into a New England version, "The City in the Snow." The chapter is organized around cycles of symbolization to highlight how children need to cycle again and again through the same object of representation. Next, Debbie LeeKeenan and John Nimmo (Chapter 14), working with university-level student teachers, present the only applications of the Reggio approach to work with children as young as two and three years old. This chapter helps us understand how the project approach can be extended down the developmental range. The next chapter (Chapter 15) takes the form of a circular interview among Baji Rankin and colleagues in the Boston area. These educators, members of a dissemination team, tell how their general attitudes toward collegiality, children, and environments were influenced by visits to Reggio Emilia and how they have used these ideas in their own educational settings. Chapter 16, by Meg Barden, a long-time participant in changes in American early childhood education and child care, asks us to consider whether the message from Reggio Emilia is different from that of the progressive education movement inspired by the philosophy of John Dewey. The final chapter in Part IV (Chapter 17) is a lyrical piece by Paul Kaufman about the ambiance of Reggio Emilia and the aesthetics of a typical school day. Kaufman, a video producer, spent a week in Reggio Emilia with his film crew talking with Malaguzzi, conveying his insights on children's power to create images and filming the children exploring the poppy fields—all captured for a segment of the PBS television series, *The Creative Spirit*.

## Acknowledgments

Beyond all of the authors listed above, who generously contributed time and advice beyond writing their chapters, we would also like to thank several people for their valued help. Lester Little, Victoria Poletto, Rose Pennington, and Alison Rogers read portions of manuscript and made excellent suggestions. Deans Marilyn Haring-Hidore, Murray Schwartz, and other administrators at the University of Massachusetts, Amherst, made possible the first U. S. academic conference about the Reggio Emilia approach, including a memorable visit and lecture by Loris Malaguzzi. The Comune of Reggio Emilia provided permission to reproduce photographs from their files and exhibit catalog; Vea Vecchi proved particularly helpful in finding and selecting wonderful materials. And finally, we wish to thank our three families for their support and encouragement.

## THE HISTORICAL CONTEXT OF THE REGGIO APPROACH

As we begin to examine the experience of young children in Reggio Emilia, we need to place this experience in perspective, to inquire into the context that made it possible for this educational approach to come together. Doing so will help us better understand those factors that are common to other educational programs in Italy, those that pertain to the Emilia Romagna region, and those that are unique products of the dedication and vision of the educators of Reggio Emilia.

Historically, early education in Italy has been caught in the tangled web of relations between Church and State. The enormous power conflicts between the centuries-old Catholic Church and the young Italian state (formed only in 1860) have affected many modern outcomes, including early childhood education.

Around 1820 in the northern and central parts of Italy, charitable institutions began to emerge. These were offshoots of a concern for the poor, emerging throughout Europe at that time, with the intention of improving the lives of the urban populace, reducing crime, and forming better citizens (Cambi & Ulivieri, 1988). For young children, there came into being institutions that were, to some extent, forerunners to the two major public early education programs currently offered in Italy: the infant-toddler centers (*Asili Nido*) serving infants aged four months to three years; and preprimary schools (*Scuole dell'Infanzia*) serving children three to six years old (Ross, 1982).

Among the first type, forerunners to infant-toddler centers, were crèches (*presepi*) for breast-fed or newly weaned infants of working mothers. Industrialists set these up at their factories. For example, in Pinerolo, Piedmont, one was started in the silk mill where the cradles were rocked by the mill's hydraulic engine. Other similar institutions were promoted by the public administrations of the small, separate states that shared the Italian peninsula prior to unification. Still others resulted from initiatives by private benefactors (Della Peruta, 1980).

After the unification of the Italian state, these institutions continued to develop, but with difficulties. It was only toward the beginning of the 20th century that some of the private initiatives began to be supported by public funding, mostly municipal. The idea was to move away from charitable assistance, dispensed only by private means, toward programs combining prevention and assistance and funded by both private and public sectors. For example, next to crèches or shelters for infants there would be a center for dispensing medical instruction and aid to mothers with the goal of educating them on child care and diminishing infant mortality. All these initiatives eventually culminated in 1925 with the passage of a national law for the "Protection and Assistence of Infancy," which provided for the National Organization for Maternity and Infancy. This organization, ONMI as it was called, was to expand and organize infant centers under the Ministry of the Interior.

The Fascist regime, which had taken over Italy in 1922, took upon itself all the merits of this innovation, while still trying to keep alive the connection with private, philanthropic support. ONMI centers adopted a medical-hygienic model of child care, which was the prevailing trend of the time, and took up the Fascist ideology of motherhood, which in turn was tied to the regime's policy of population growth. Rosalyn Saltz (1976) visited ONMI centers in Rome in 1975 and subsequently remarked:

> Psycho-social aspects of an infant's development are assumed to be adequately served if the psychological atmosphere of the center is not harsh, if children are not in obvious distress and if caregivers appear to be reasonably fond of children. (p. 130)

The ONMI organization remained in place with some ideological changes for 50 years, even through the social upheavals of the 1960s and early 1970s. In December 1971, however, the major national law instituting a new kind of infant-toddler center was finally passed with the strong support of working women and the women's movement. The new centers were intended to provide a social service for families and guarantee the harmonious development of infants. The Emilia Romagna Region was ahead of the rest of the nation; the city of Reggio Emilia had opened its first municipal infant-toddler centers in 1970. Thus, in December 1975, the 604 ONMI centers were officially transferred to city administrations all over Italy (Lucchini, 1980).

Among the second type, forerunners to preprimary schools, there stands out the institution, devoted to children aged 2–6, founded by Abbot Ferrante Aporti in 1831 in Cremona and subsequently widely imitated. Here teaching and learning were important, and play was often replaced by crafts for little boys and domestic activities for little girls (Della Peruta, 1980).

After 1867, the influence of Froebel's Kindergarten started to take root. At the beginning of the 20th century, as Italy became industrialized and the Socialist Party with its progressive agenda emerged and grew, the needs of working women and the care and education of children came into focus. Progressive educators became involved. Pistillo (1989) describes the years around 1904–1913 as particularly fertile for early childhood education. During this period, a national law established a training school for teachers of young children; the sisters, Rosa and Carolina Agazzi, developed a new philosophy and method of early education; and the first Children's House was founded by Maria Montessori.

However, the Ministry of Education did not directly assist the growth of preprimary education; and while initiative remained in the private sector, it became increasingly controlled by the Catholic Church. After 1922, the Fascist regime dismissed the Montessori method and promoted only those school reforms compatible with the monopoly of the Church. The Agazzi method, favored by the Catholic Church, was proclaimed the state method of early childhood education. In 1933, over 60 percent of preprimary schools were run by religious orders (Pistillo, 1989).

After all of the years under Fascism, people were ready for change. In 1945–46, for a short period right after the Second World War, people took many initiatives into their own hands. The state government was undergoing reorganization, and the Catholic Church was in no position to intervene. It was in this very period that, in localities with a strong tradition of local initiative, there arose spontaneous attempts to establish parent-run schools, such as Loris Malaguzzi (Chapter 3) describes so vividly for Reggio Emilia.

By the 1950s, many educators and parents had become aware of the critical need for more and better early childhood education. They also knew that the dominant Christian Democratic Party had no intention of changing the status of early childhood education. New ideas about education were entering Italy: the "popular school" movement coming from France and the newly translated writings of progressive educators such as Celestin Freinet and John Dewey. A feverish debate fed people's determination to change education at all levels. In 1951, the Movement of Cooperative Education (MCE) was formed. This organization of elementary teachers had the goal of applying the techniques of Freinet; they achieved cooperation through an Italian style of critical debate. The leader of the MCE was a charismatic educator named Bruno Ciari, who was invited by the left-wing administration of Bologna to organize and direct their city school system. Indeed, it was only in cities with left-wing administrations that progressive municipal early childhood systems were established in the 1960s and 1970s. In cities in which the centrist Christian Democratic Party was dominant, the Catholic Church's monopoly on early education tended to prevail.

Ciari introduced many educational innovations, both in his writings and through the meetings he organized for teachers in Bologna. Like others in the MCE, he was convinced that a more just society could be achieved through the right kind of early childhood education. His books became classics.

The build-up of energy, enthusiasm, and thoughtful concern generated the take-off of early childhood education in Italy. The debates initiated by Ciari activated people, and in turn helped Ciari formulate many of his key ideas. Loris Malaguzzi participated in these lively debates; through them he came to know Ciari. Deeply inspired by Ciari, Malaguzzi (Chapter 3) recalls him as a fabulous friend and as "the most lucid, passionate and acute intelligence in the field of childhood education." The group around Ciari believed that education should liberate childhood energy and capacities and promote the harmonious development of the whole child in all areas—communicative, social, affective, and with respect to critical and scientific thinking. Ciari urged educators to develop relationships with families and encourage participatory committees of teachers, parents, and citizens. He argued there should be two rather than one teacher in each classroom, and that teachers and staff should work collectively, without hierarchy. He thought children should be grouped by age for part of the day, but mix openly during another part, and he wanted to limit the number of children per classroom to 20. Finally, he gave much attention to the physical setting of education (Ciari, 1972).

In 1967 there appeared an explosive pamphlet, *Letter to a Teacher*, by the Scuola di Barbiana. This was a passionate but solidly documented denunciation of selectivity and social class discrimination in the national school system. Widely quoted, the *Letter* became a manifesto in the fight for educational reform. In 1968, the student movement erupted; students occupied the universities and demonstrated in the streets. The next year saw mass mobilization of workers; widespread strikes in the cities arose over the national labor contract negotiations. Women's groups became outspoken and led the protests for better social services, schools, and child care (New, in press). Oftentimes all of these groups marched together through the streets, putting concerted pressure on the political parties and government (Corsaro & Emiliani, 1992).

The 10-year period from 1968 to 1977 saw the enactment of many key pieces of social legislation. During this same period, women were entering the labor force in ever increasing numbers and vigorously pressing their demands. The most important of the new laws were as follows:

1968   Establishment of government-sponsored preprimary education
1971   Establishment of maternity leave (12 weeks of paid leave at 70% of earnings and a further 6 months of leave at 30%)
1971   Establishment of government-sponsored *Asili Nido* (infant-toddler centers)
1975   Institution of a new family law
1977   Institution of work parity (equal pay for equal work) between men and women

In this changing social landscape, with its notable legislative accomplishments, the educators were rewarded for their visions about education and care, responsive to new expectations.

The Emilia Romagna Region remained one of the most innovative, but many other regions also established high-quality municipal preprimary and infant-toddler systems. Among these were Tuscany, Lombardy, Trentino, Piedmont, Veneto, and Liguria. By the middle of the 1980s, however, many cities had reached a plateau in their level of preprimary services and were expending more innovative energy on their infant-toddler centers. One city noted for the excellence of its infant-toddler centers is Pistoia in Tuscany; this city is also known for its *Area Bambini* (Children's Places) providing after-school programs, part-time infant-toddler education, and other programs to respond to the needs of contemporary families (Edwards & Gandini, 1989).

For Reggio Emilia, the distinguishing feature over the years has been its continuing high investment and involvement in education for children aged 3–6, even while attending to the age group 0–3. In the chapters to follow, the principal aspects of this achievement will be spelled out. These include the *atelier* and *atelierista*, the complex functions of the pedagogical team, the continuous dialogue between administrators, teachers, and elected officials, and participation of the whole city in development of the early childhood system. Most of all, though, the achievement consists of a unique and magnificent combination of commitment and determination, research and experimentation, renewal and openness—all strengthened by years of work in refining skills of communication and documentation. Let us go to that story and ask of its implications and possibilities for ourselves.

## REFERENCES

Cambi, F., & Ulivieri, S. (1988). *Storia dell'infanzia nell'italia liberale (Childhood history in liberal italy)*. Florence: La Nuova Italia.

Ciari, B. (1961). *Le nuove tecniche didattiche (The new teaching techniques)*. Rome: Editori Riuniti.

Ciari, B. (1972). *La grande disadattata (The great maladjusted)*. Rome: Editori Riuniti.

Corsaro, W.A., & Emiliani, F. (1992). Child care, early education, and children's peer culture in Italy. In M.E. Lamb, K.J. Sternberg, C.P. Hwang, & A.G. Broberg (Eds.), *Child care in context* (pp. 81–115). Hillsdale, NJ: Erlbaum.

Della Peruta, F. (1980). Alle origini dell'assistenza alla prima infanzia in Italia (At the origins of early childhood assistance in Italy). In L. Sala La Guardia & E. Lucchini (Eds.), *Asili nido in Italia (Infant-toddler centers in Italy)* (pp. 13–38). Milan, Italy: Marzorati.

Edwards, C.P., & Gandini, L. (1989). Teachers' expectations about the timing of developmental skills: A cross-cultural story. *Young Children, 44*(4), 15–19.

Lucchini, E. (1980). Nasce l'asilo nido di tipo nuovo (The birth of the new type of infant-toddler centers). In L. Sala La Guardia & E. Lucchini (Eds.), *Asili nido in Italia* (pp. 13–38). Milan, Italy: Marzorati.

Malaguzzi, L. (1984). *L'occhio se salta il muro.* Catalog of the Exhibit, "L'occhio se salta il muro," published by the Comune di Reggio Emilia, Assesserato Istruzione, Regione di Emilia Romagna.

New, R. (in press). Italian child care and early education: *Amor maternus* and other cultural contributions. In M. Cochran (Ed.), *International handbook of child care policies and programs.* Westport, CT: Greenwood Press.

Pistillo, F. (1989). Preprimary education and care in Italy. In P. Olmstead & D. Weikart (Eds.), *How nations serve young children: Profiles of child care and education in 14 countries* (pp. 151–202). Ypsilanti, MI: High/Scope Press.

Rizzini, M. (1980). Asilo nido e sviluppo sociale dal primo presepe all'ONMI (Infant-toddler centers and social development from the first shelter to ONMI). In L. Sala La Guardia & E. Lucchini (Eds.), *Asili nido in Italia* (pp. 13–38). Milan: Marzorati.

Saltz, R. (1976). Infant day care Italian style. In M.L. Hanes, I.J. Gordon, & W.F. Breivogel (Eds.), *Update: The first ten years of life* (pp. 128–144). Gainesville, FL: University of Florida.

Ross, H. (1982). Infants in Italy: An evaluation of other than mother care. *Early Child Development and Care, 9,* 121–154.

Scuola di Barbiana. (1967). *Lettera a una professoressa (Letter to a teacher).* Florence, Italy: Libreria Editrice Fiorentina.

The 10 best schools in the world, and what we can learn from them. (1991, December 2). *Newsweek,* pp. 50–59.

"Shopper." Drawing by child of the Ada Gobetti School.

# 2

# What Can We Learn From Reggio Emilia?

## Lilian Katz

The ideas explored in this chapter are based on three brief visits to six of the Reggio Emilia municipal preprimary schools, discussions with educators there and with American colleagues knowledgeable about them, plus examination of the printed and videotaped materials describing their work. While such brief exposure to these rich and complex pedagogical practices can yield only a limited understanding of them, it nevertheless advanced my own thinking about several aspects of early childhood education in the U.S. that are outlined as six lessons below.

### PROJECT WORK AND THE VISUAL ARTS
### FOR PREPRIMARY CHILDREN

As can be seen from the other chapters in this volume, there are many features of the Reggio Emilia approach of great interest to early childhood educators. However, my own particular interest is in the inclusion of projects into the curriculum for children three to six years old.

In the book *Engaging Children's Minds: The Project Approach* (1989), written before the Reggio Emilia approach had come to our attention, Sylvia Chard and I presented our rationale for including *project work* in early childhood programs and guidelines for its implementation. We use the term project work to refer to in-depth studies of particular topics undertaken by small groups of young children (Katz & Chard, 1989). From our point of view, project work is designed to help young children make deeper and fuller sense of events and phenomena in their own environment and experience that are worthy of their attention. Projects provide the part of the curriculum in which children are encouraged to make their own decisions and choices, usually in cooperation with their peers, about the work to be undertaken. We assume that such work increases childrens' confidence in their own intellectual powers, and strengthens their dispositions to go on learning (see Katz & Chard, 1989, especially Chapter 2).

In the course of a project, for example, on a topic such as "What Happens at the Supermarket," or "How Houses are Built," children explore the phenomena first hand, and in detail over an extended period of time. The activities of the children include direct observation, asking questions of relevant participants and experts, collecting pertinent artifacts, representing observations, ideas, memories, feelings, imaginings, and new understandings in a wide variety of ways, including through dramatic play.

Most preschoolers—at least at age three or four—are not yet able to represent their observations and thoughts very well in writing. They may, of course, dictate their thoughts and observations to others to write them down. However, a major lesson from Reggio Emilia is the way preprimary school children can use what they call *graphic languages* (Rinaldi, 1991) to record their ideas, observations, memories, feelings, and so forth. Observations of the children at work reveal how these graphic languages are used to explore understandings, to reconstruct previous ones, and to co-construct revisited understandings of the topics investigated.

Certainly, most early childhood educators in the U.S. have long acknowledged that young children can explore and express their feelings and understandings verbally, visually, and through dramatic play, and typically encourage children to do so. The Reggio Emilia experience demonstrates that preprimary schoolers can use many graphic media to communicate the information gained and ideas explored in project work and can do so much more readily and competently than typically assumed in the U.S. and probably in many other countries as well. The Reggio Emilia childrens' work suggested to me that many of us in the U.S. seriously underestimate preprimary school children's graphical representational capabilities and the quality of intellectual effort and growth it can stimulate.

By way of example, a group of 4- and 5-year-olds in one of the preprimary schools undertook an extended study of an exceptionally large cooperative supermarket in their neighborhood. A study of a store is a fairly popular topic in many preschools and kindergartens in the U.S. as well. But several features of the project as conducted by the children of the "Ada Gobetti" school in Reggio Emilia are especially noteworthy. First, the children made several visits to the market, including one when it was closed! (see Figure 2.2). In this way they were able to get a close look at various features of it, to sketch many of the objects and elements that impressed them, and to run up and down the aisles undisturbed by shoppers, noting anything of interest about the facility, including how their voices sounded in such a large interior space. Detailed drawings of the supermarket (see Figure 2.1), the rows of baskets, the counters, shoppers with or without baskets, with or without children under foot, the cashiers, and so forth, are captured in remarkable detail in the drawing of the supermarket scene.

But the drawings alone would mean relatively little without the teachers' documentation of what the children said about what they observed and experienced. The children's recorded comments and discussions provided teachers with knowledge of the children's levels of understanding and misunderstandings of these everyday phenomena (see Figures 2.3 and 2.4).

The children also shopped at the supermarket, giving due attention to preparing the shopping list, paying for their purchases, receiving change, and then using the items for cooking upon their return to the school. Some of the children interviewed the manager and put a barrage of questions to him about what is involved in being the "boss" (see Figures 2.5 and 2.6).

The children also submitted their "wish list" to the manager reflecting what they thought should be added to the facility: a television viewing room, comfortable restroom facilities, a playground, a place to play with dolls, and so forth. Many of the desired additions are beautifully illustrated by a combination of drawings superimposed on photographs of furnishings apparently cut out of newspapers or magazines. In addition, many children developed their own designs of packages of cereal, crackers, detergent boxes, and the like. The children also constructed a market in the classroom and enjoyed the dramatic play greatly enriched by their close observation of the objects, people, and events they observed at the market.

Of course, one could ask why teachers should bother to undertake a project on such a mundane topic as the local supermarket—something

Figure 2.1. Part of children's collective drawing of their experience at the supermarket. (From the booklet, *Noi Bimbi e Lui Gulliver*, Ada Gobetti School, 1984, Education Department, Reggio Emilia. Reprinted by permission.)

**Figure 2.2.    Children's comments following a visit to the closed supermarket.**

It is as large as a forest.
You could get lost in it, just like on the Via Emilia.
It is as huge as the whale of Pinocchio.
It looks like a swimming pool.
The man in the supermarket divides things in half, half on one shelf and half on another one.

which children experience frequently and directly. After all, in a year or two all the children will know that the cashiers do not take the money home, and that they do not decide the price of an item on the basis of their own personal tastes! So why not study something outside of the children's daily experiences? Many U.S. teachers prefer to introduce esoteric topics with which they hope to "capture" or excite the children's interests, presumably under the assumption that everyday objects and events are uninteresting. However, the work of preprimary schoolers in Reggio Emilia indicates that the processes of "unpacking" or defamiliarizing everyday objects and events can be deeply meaningful and interesting to them.

Furthermore, when the topic of a project is very familiar to the children, they can contribute to the project from their own knowledge, and suggest questions to ask and lines of investigations to pursue; the children themselves can take leadership in planning, can assume responsibilities for specific observations and for information and artifacts to collect. Such projects investigating real phenomena offer children the opportunity to be the "natural anthropologists" they seem born to be! On the other hand, if the topic of a project is exotic and outside of the children's direct experience they are dependent upon the teacher for most of the questions, ideas, information, thinking, and planning. Young children are dependent on adults for many aspects of their lives and their learning experiences; however, project work is that part of the curriculum in which their own interests, ideas, preferences, and choices can be given relatively free reign.

Another value of project work is that extended studies of particular phenomena undertaken in project work give young children an early experience of knowing and understanding a topic in depth. As Inagaki (in press) points out, having the experience of knowing a topic in depth can be highly rewarding for young children. Such early experiences of feelings of mastery may also lay the foundation of a lifelong disposition to seek in-depth understandings of topics worthy of their attention.

It should also be noted that sometimes the teachers in Reggio Emilia undertake a project on a topic of unpredictable or uncertain value. Willingness to explore a topic that might not work very well is part of their commitment to experimentation, and to exploring together with

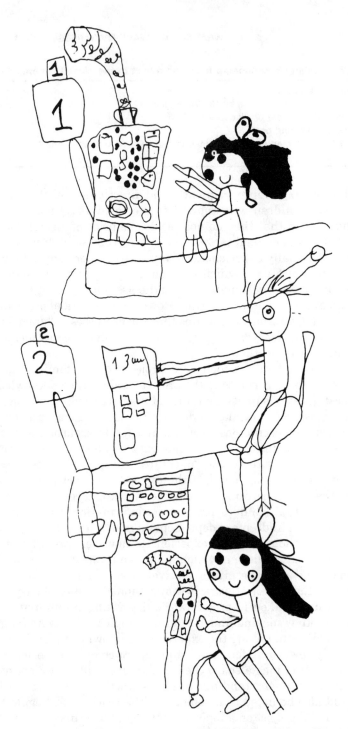

Figure 2.3. "The Mystery of the Cashier's" Detail from Figure 2.1.

**Figure 2.4  Children's comments and drawing of the supermarket.**

**What do you like to do at the supermarket?**

Push the carts.
Touch the merchandise.
Climb on the shelves.
Run up and down.
Ask questions to everybody.
Eat pieces of cheese.
To know what is behind the closed doors.
Buy everything.
Look at myself in the mirror.

the children what kinds of experiences and ideas might emerge from an experiment. In one of the Reggio Emilia preprimary schools the children engaged in an extended project about the solar system and space travel—phenomena hardly in children's direct or immediate experience! The topic grew out of the children's animated response to a large poster of the solar system brought to the school by one of the children. The children's great interest in various "star wars" characters seen in films, television, and their toys was evidently partly responsible for their positive reactions to the poster. The paintings, drawings, clay work, and large complex space station made by the children suggest that their understandings of the solar system remained substantially pre-Galilean! But their imaginings about life on a space station, space travel, rocket launching, space vehicles, space creatures, and so forth, were richly and skillfully depicted in drawings, paintings, clay, and papier-mâché, including the large space station constructed with a wide variety of materials.

It seems to me, then, that a first lesson from Reggio Emilia practices is that preprimary school children can communicate their ideas, feelings, understandings, imaginings, and observations through visual representation much earlier than most U.S. early childhood educators typically assume. The representations the children create with such impressive skill can serve as a basis for hypotheses, discussions and arguments, often leading to further observations and fresh representations. Using this approach we can see how children's minds can be engaged in a variety of ways in the quest for deeper understanding of the familiar world around them.

## TREATING CHILDREN'S WORK SERIOUSLY

Observing the care children give to their drawings suggested a lesson about the possible effects of the treatment of children's work on its quality. It seems to me that the Reggio Emilia children approach the

**Figure 2.5.   Children's comments related to the manager and drawing.**

---

### Questions about the Manager

Who is the manager?
He is the one who gives money away.
He is a president.
He is the one who watches out to see if anyone steals the money.
He gets up early in the morning, opens the doors, and organizes everything.

---

### Questions to the Manager

Are you a boss?
How many people do you direct?
How do you become a manager?
Do you get more money than the others?

---

**Figure 2.6.   "Interview with the boss." (From the booklet, *Noi Bimbi e Lui Gulliver.*)**

task of drawing whatever they are studying purposefully and assiduously because they are accustomed to *use* their own field drawings for further work, such as making group murals, sculptures, paintings, and so forth. Unlike the custom in the U.S., the visual representations are not just decorative products to be taken home at the end of the day, most likely never to be looked at or discussed again; in Reggio Emilia they serve as resources for further exploration and deepening knowledge of the topic. Educators in Reggio Emilia, referring to these visual representations as graphic languages, speak of children "reading" their own and each others' drawings. Teachers transcribe the recorded comments and the discussions of the children at work; with this documentation, the drawings are "read" and "reread" by the teaching staff as a basis for planning next steps in the exploration of the topic.

## REALISTIC AND IMAGINATIVE REPRESENTATION

A third lesson from the Reggio Emilia preprimary schools' experience is that children's extensive experience of drawing from observation does not appear to inhibit their desire or ability to draw, paint, and so on, from the imagination. Contrary to fears of many U.S. early childhood educators, the work of the Reggio Emilia children suggests that an either/or choice is unnecessary: The children appear to be competent in representative and unrepresentative, realistic and abstract visual expression. In other words, experience of the former does not necessarily damage the competence or desire to engage in the latter. Because of the high level of competence in evidence in the Reggio Emilia preprimary schools, it is understandable that many U.S. educators label it as art education, or art instruction; some even assume that the preprimary schools are art schools! But such characterizations seem to miss the point: Visual and graphic languages provide a way of exploring and expressing understandings of the world easily available to most preschoolers. The visual arts are integrated into the work simply as additional "languages" available to young children not yet very competent in conventional writing and reading; the arts are not taught as a subject, a discipline, as a discrete set of skills, or treated in other ways as a focus of instruction for its own sake.

This is not to suggest that the children are not given directions and guidance in the use of tools, materials, and techniques of graphic and visual representation. Of considerable interest is the way such teaching (versus instruction) invariably includes giving the child—in simple form—the principle underlying a suggested technique or approach to materials. The inclusion of the principle within a suggestion increases the chances that the child will be able to solve the problem when the adult is not there—surely a major goal of teaching at every level.

It should be kept in mind that the Reggio Emilia children—especially the younger ones—engage in many other activities besides project work. Opportunity for a whole range of spontaneous play with blocks, role play, outdoor play, listening to stories, acting out plays, cooking, housekeeping, and dress-up activities, as well as "one-shot" activities like painting, collage, and clay work are available to all the children daily. Provisions are made for all children to be involved in an extended project throughout their time in the school. Of course, some children draw, paint, and so on, more skillfully than others. But the extensiveness of early experience of expressing and communicating their ideas and observations visually during the preschool years helps explain the unexpectedly high level of competence.

In summary, a useful lesson of the Reggio Emilia approach is that there is no reason to believe that teachers must choose between encouraging realistic or imaginative visual expression as two mutually exclusive alternatives.

## THE CONTENT OF TEACHER–CHILD RELATIONSHIPS

The fourth lesson to be drawn from observations in Reggio Emilia preprimary schools concerns the content of the relationships between adults and children. My underlying assumption is that individuals cannot just relate to each other: They have to relate to each other about something. In other words, relationships have to have content of mutual interest or concern that can provide pretexts and texts for the interaction between them.

In his studies of the Oxford preschools in England, Bruner (1980) showed that the content of the teacher–child interactions was predominantly about managerial issues. He laments, for example, that of nearly 10,000 periods observed, only 20 percent contained genuine conversations, and points out that the nursery classes observed were organized so that it was difficult for connected conversations to occur (Bruner, 1980, p. 62). He also points out that "a high proportion of adult-initiated interaction with children was given over to the boring stuff of petty management—housekeeping talk about milk time, instructions about picking up, washing, and the like" (p. 61).

As far as I know, there are no comparable large-scale data on the content of interactions between preschool teachers and children in the

U.S. However, it is my general impression from observations of early childhood settings all over the U.S. that the content of teacher–child relationships seems similarly focused on the routines and the rules of classroom life, especially during informal activity periods; when children are painting or drawing, teachers seem very reluctant to engage the children in any kind of conversation at all. When children are filling in worksheets and workbooks, teachers are understandably eager to give positive feedback, and therefore frequently say things to them like "You did well!" "That's the right idea!" "Very good!" and similar general positive comments. In other words, the content of the relationships between our teachers and their pupils tends to be dominated by information about the child's conduct and level of performance. Thus it seems that the content of relationships between teachers and children in our early childhood settings, when not focused on mundane routines, is about the children themselves.

My impression of Reggio Emilia practices is, in contrast, that to a large extent the content of teacher–child relationships is focused on the work itself, rather than mainly on routines or the children's performance on academic tasks. Adults' and children's minds meet on matters of interest to both of them. Both the children and the teachers seem to be equally involved in the progress of the work, the ideas being explored, the techniques and materials to be used, and the progress of the projects themselves. The children's roles in the relationships were more as apprentices than as the targets of instruction or objects of praise.

Such relationships have several benefits. The first is that the children's minds are engaged in challenging work which includes making decisions about what to represent, how to represent it, how to coordinate the efforts and resolve conflicting views of the various contributors to the project, and so forth. Second, because the teachers' and the children's minds meet on matters of real interest to both of them, teachers' minds are also engaged. They seem more intent on listening closely to the children's suggestions and questions, probing their thinking, making suggestions, encouraging children to respond to each others' ideas, and they are especially more attentive to the risk of overassisting the children (Rabitti, 1992).

Because there are no formal prespecified lessons that all children must learn, teachers can generate activities that can contribute to developing children's more appropriate understandings of the topic. Thus, the content of the teacher–child relationship is rich with problem setting and problem solving. The work of the projects provides ample texts, pretexts, and contexts for extensive genuine conversations between the adults and the children, as well as among them.

Frances Hawkins (1986) points out that the child and his or her behavior is appropriate as the main content of a relationship between an adult and a child only if the adult is a therapist and the child is the patient! In Hawkins' words:

> A teacher has a unique role . . . It is not the role of mother or therapist or peer, but that of one who values learners and learning professionally. (p. 35)

Comparing Reggio Emilia preprimary schools and those I typically see in North America suggested to me that one way the quality of a preschool program can be evaluated is to examine the content of adult–child relationships. A program has intellectual vitality if the teacher's individual and group interactions are mainly about what the children are learning, planning, and thinking about their work, play, and each other, and only minimally about the rules and routines.

## CHILDREN'S SENSE OF WHAT ADULTS THINK IS IMPORTANT

Like most visitors to the municipal preprimary schools of Reggio Emilia and to the exhibition of their work entitled, *The Hundred Languages of Children*, I frequently wondered how such an exceptional level of competence in graphic representations was achieved. One hypothesis is that they work so studiously because, like all other young children, those in the Reggio Emilia preprimary schools sense what is important to the adults around them. They have some level of awareness of what the adults care about, what the adults think is interesting, worth doing, worth probing, or worthy of their time and serious attention. The children know what the adults take great pains to explain, to take pictures of, make notes about, to transcribe from tape recordings, to display very carefully, and so forth. The children sense what the adults talk about to each other, bring to the attention of their parents, and show to a steady stream of interested visitors. Therefore the children know—perhaps at a preconscious level—that the adults take the children's work and ideas very seriously.

If it is true that the children in the Reggio Emilia preprimary schools know what the adults really care about, then surely children elsewhere are similarly aware of what the adults who matter to them really care about. Thus, all teachers might ask: What do most of my pupils really believe I take seriously and care deeply about? Theoretically, of course, it is possible that in some cases the answer to this question might be "nothing." However, in the absence of any reliable information relevant to this question, let us assume that all teachers convey some messages to their pupils about what aspects of children's effort and behavior really catches their serious attention, deep interest, appreciation, and sometimes true delight.

By comparison, my impression is that in the U.S. we are not as likely as we could be to help children sense that their intellectual quest is of deep interest and importance to us. In many of the preschool programs I see, adults' serious attention is most likely to be stirred when something among the children is amiss or disturbs routine activities, rather than when the construction of understandings is the main focus of activity. I suspect that because, on the whole, we overestimate children academically and underestimate them intellectually, we miss moments when our attention could convey to children that their ideas are important. This is not to suggest that a sense of what teachers deem important can be conveyed explicitly by "lecturing" or "preaching" to the children about it. Rather, even very young children are most likely making inferences about what adults care about based on multiple observations of the adults' actual behavior in context.

An important lesson then from our colleagues in the Reggio Emilia preprimary schools is that when adults communicate sincere and serious interest in the children's ideas and in their attempts to express them, rich and complex work can follow, even among very young children.

## MODELS AND METAPHORS FOR EARLY CHILDHOOD PROGRAMS

In the processes of organizing and operating programs in preschools and primary schools, it is natural to use an underlying framework, model, or metaphor taken from other phenomena that have similar parameters. Similarly, in our deliberations about education and the relationships within educational settings, we use metaphors that betray the underlying models of our interpretive frameworks (Nuthall & Snook, 1973). Based on observations in the Reggio Emilia preprimary schools, discussions with the teachers, and with others involved in them, it seemed to me that the underlying model and metaphors that guide their decisions and choices are different from those we customarily use in the United States.

### The Extended Family Model

One of my strong impressions of the Reggio Emilia municipal preprimary schools is that in several ways they are modeled on the lines of extended families and communities more than most of the long-day early childhood programs seen in the U.S. To begin with, the buildings in which their preprimary schools are housed are more like large homes than most of our preschools, and certainly more so than our typical kindergartens within elementary schools. Each of the six preprimary schools I visited is exceptionally attractive in the quality of furnishings and organization of space, in the displays of the children's work, which together create a comfortable, warm, and cheerful ambiance and pleasant environment.

Although there are approximately 75 3- to 6-year-old children in each school, and about 25 in a class, the quality of life within them seems to achieve a homelike closeness and intimacy associated with family life that is especially appropriate for young children. The fact that the children stay with the same teacher throughout the three years of their participation in the program enables them, their parents, and their teachers to form strong and stable relationships with each other, as they might if they were members of extended families and small close communities. In contrast, by the time most U.S. teachers have been able to develop a real relationship with a parent and to know him or her well enough to respond meaningfully and frankly with their concerns, it is necessary to move on and get to know the next group of parents! In some of the Reggio Emilia preprimary schools the classes are organized into mixed-age groups providing more familylike environments than are possible with homogeneous groups (see Katz, Evangelou, & Hartmann, 1990).

As indicated above and elsewhere in this volume, a great deal of the work of the children in Reggio Emilia is done in small groups. No evidence was seen of all children in a class subjected to instruction at the same time, of having to create the same pictures or other art products—a common sight in our schools, especially in connection with holidays like Halloween, Valentine's Day, Mother's Day, and so forth.

The informal nature of the curriculum lends itself particularly well to cooperative work among small groups of children mixed in age. The informal communitylike atmosphere also seems to be enhanced by the comparative freedom from time pressures. The children are free to work and play without the frequent interruptions and transitions so common in most of our early childhood programs. It seems to me that the majority of our early childhood programs are organized into a rigid timetable, and are often one-shot activities started, packed up, and put away within prespecified time periods, usually counted in minutes.

The fact that Reggio Emilia children assume responsibility for some of the real chores involved in group life throughout the long day, for example, setting the tables for meals, tidying up afterwards, and frequently working with the cooking staff, and sharing responsibility for keeping the art materials in good order, and so forth, strengthens an atmosphere of communal life. The communal feeling is also enhanced by the participation of the entire staff of the preprimary schools in all aspects of the program, and the frequent long meetings of all concerned, including the parents.

Extended families are characterized by shared responsibility, intimacy, informality, and participation. The extended family seems to provide a very appropriate model upon which to design early childhood programs. Though such a model is likely to have its own problems, its appropriateness can be understood when contrasted to the corporate-industrial model that serves as a basis for education in the U.S.

## Corporations and Industries as Models

Observations in Reggio Emilia reminded me that in the U.S., the principal models and metaphors used—especially at the primary and secondary school level—come from the industrial and corporate world and its factories, rather than from the extended family or communal life. Nursery schools were developed from nurseries that were places in the home devoted to the nourishment and care of the very young. However, during the last 20 years or so, the term "nursery" in the U.S. literature related to programs for 3- to 5-year-olds has been completely replaced by the term "preschool"—as in precooked and preshrunk!

Child care centers, on the other hand, have often been compared to warehouses in which children were held in custody until their parents could resume their childrearing responsibilities. They are now increasingly referred to as child care programs, or even all-day preschools, as a way to discard the custodial and warehouse metaphor. It seems to me, however, that early childhood programs are increasingly in danger of being modeled on the corporate/industrial or factory model so pervasive at the elementary and secondary levels of education.

Schlechty (1990) points out that factories are designed to transform raw material into prespecified products by treating it to a sequence of prespecified standard processes.

> In this vision, students are viewed as raw material to be subjected to standardized processes and procedures to mold them, to be tested against rigid standards, and inspected carefully before being passed on to the next workbench for further processing. (Schlechty, 1990, p. 22)

The industrial model assigns teachers the role of technocrats who are responsible for operating the factory machinery according to a prespecified design handed down to them, and for whom "the curriculum must be articulated with the tests that will be used to inspect the students who are the products of this controlled and rational process" (Schlechty, 1990, p. 23). Concepts frequently used in educational discussion, such as delivery systems, cost-benefit ratios, prespecified specific behavioral and learning outcomes, outcome-based curriculum, curricular packages, packaging of innovations, teacher-proof materials, the child care industry, and so on, betray the application of the industrial model to the design, operation, and assessment of schooling.

In a similar way, most of our official state and school district curriculum guides reflect an assumption that virtually all children should be subjected to the same sequence of instructional treatments in lock-step fashion in the interests of creating a standard product. Schlechty sums up the implications of this trend toward the factory model as the school becomes like:

> An assembly line down which children go, differentiated on the basis of the quality of the raw material being processed. The quality of the raw material is determined primarily in terms of student family background and measured in terms of "Academic aptitude" or ability to do school work assigned. (Schlechty, n. d.)

The industrial model as a framework for designing and interpreting education is inappropriate in many ways at every level of education, but especially so for young children. During the early years of children's lives stability of relationships and the formation of attachment between children and those who care for them is highly desirable and perhaps essential. In institutions designed on the model of a factory, individuals are interchangeable; the only requirement is that the changing individuals carry out the same prespecified functions and roles in standardized ways. An industrial model also implies that education is an unidirectional process: Adults impose instructional procedures on the raw material—children—in order to change it in predictable ways.

The proliferation of numerous special categories of children and special education programs (e.g., transition classes, learning disabled and developmentally delayed children, etc.) and the high rates of retention in the early grades are analogous to the recalls of defective products common to U.S. industry (see also Skrtic, 1991).

## Optimizing the Strengths of Families and Institutions

A preschool program and pedagogical approach based on an extended family model is likely to have its own problems. While preschools are not factories or corporations, nor are they families. They are institutions staffed by professionals employed to apply specialized knowledge and skills to their work in the best interests of every client.

Institutions differ from factories in that they are designed to serve people and their needs, and not to produce standardized goods. By definition, public institutions are operated according to rules and regulations to be applied uniformly to all clients, independently of the particular individuals being served or the particular professional providing the service.

Families differ from both factories and institutions in that they are particularistic, responsive to the unique characteristics, needs, wishes, and values of its members in ways marked by a relatively high intensity of emotion, involvement, and attachment not possible or desirable in institutional settings. Similarly, the roles of parents and teachers are distinct from each other, and ideally allow each to make complementary but different contributions to the child's growth, learning, and development (Katz, 1984). Professionals are committed to a universalistic ethic that enjoins them to apply all of their specialized knowledge and skills impartially and equally to every child, whether they like the child or feel close to him or her or not. All of these considerations suggest that a preschool must optimize the special and essential benefits of family life to children, and it must do so within the constraints and standards essential to professional practice and institutional regulation.

The municipal preprimary schools of Reggio Emilia show us an optimum combination of the strengths of family relationships and the integrity of professional practices par excellence in several ways. First, the inclusion and involvement of parents in virtually every aspect of the schools' functioning is deliberate and central to the planning and operation of the preprimary schools. The quality of thought and the amount of energy given to the establishment and maintenance of strong school–parent relationships in these schools are impressive and daunting, and are consistent with the major role of parents in founding these schools.

Parent involvement is also addressed in the way the children's work is displayed. Invariably, alongside the children's work are photographs of the children at work, transcriptions of their questions, and comments made in the course of their work are also displayed. In this way, the children can easily share their actual school experiences (and not just their products) with their parents. The enthusiasm of the children and the interest of the parents in children's work helps strengthen the involvement of parents in the children's learning, provides a rich basis for parent–child discussion, and deepens parents' understanding of the nature of learning in the early years. The level of involvement of parents in the schools is reminiscent of parent-cooperative nursery schools of the U.S. and of the preschool play groups of New Zealand and Britain. Perhaps a new model of the parent cooperative nursery school as a way to optimize the needs of children, parents, and teachers should be developed in the U.S. that addresses the needs of working parents and the importance of their participation in their children's school experiences.

Second, the approach to curriculum seems to be that each individual child's characteristics, aptitude, needs, and interests are examined and monitored by extensive and detailed recordkeeping and documentation. The whole staff, including nonteaching members, meet weekly for discussions and planning, ensuring that detailed knowledge of each child is noted and shared. Finally, the quality of life and the affective and aesthetic dimensions of the preprimary schools seen in Reggio Emilia suggest that it is possible to optimize the advantages of family relationships and institutional requirements if a community is willing and able to support them financially.

## SUMMARY

I have suggested six lessons to be learned from colleagues in the Reggio Emilia municipal preprimary schools. First, children and teachers together examine topics of interest to young children in great depth and detail in project work and make excellent use of a variety of visual and graphic forms as they do so. The teachers seem to have higher expectations than most of us in the U.S. of young children's abilities to represent their thoughts, feelings, and observations with the graphic skills they already have at hand, namely drawing, painting, and other graphic arts. The teaching staff act on the assumption we often give lip service to: that children have an inherent desire to grow, to know, to understand things around them.

Second, when children have experience using their drawing, paintings, and so on, as a basis for further discussion and work, they attend to it with great care. Young children do not have to take work home every day; when they do, the work is not being used for their learning. Third, early introduction to observational and realistic representation does not necessarily inhibit children's abilities or desires to use the media for abstract, creative, and imaginative expression as well.

Fourth, the kind of work undertaken by the children in these projects provides rich content for teacher–child relationships. Fifth, many features of the adults' behavior convey to the children that all aspects of their work are taken seriously. This message is not communicated directly by pronouncement or announcement; it permeates the environment indirectly through a variety of actions, provisions, and strategies. Finally, the underlying model upon which school life is based is closer to family and community relationships than is customary in the U.S., where I believe early childhood programs are ill-served by the encroachment of an industrial/corporate model.

Much has been accomplished by early childhood educators in Reggio Emilia over a period of a generation. It should be kept in mind as we seek to learn from them and apply some of that learning at home that the schools are relatively well funded and supported by their community. They show us what can be achieved when a community makes a real commitment to its young children.

## REFERENCES

Bruner, J. (1980). Under five in Britain. *Oxford Preschool Research Project* (Vol. 1). Ypsilanti, MI: High/Scope Press.

Hawkins, F.P. (1986). *The logic of action. Young children at work*. Boulder, CO: Associated University Press.

Inagaki, K. (in press). Piagetian and post-Piagetian conceptions of development and their implications for science education in early childhood. *Early Childhood Research Quarterly*.

Katz, L.G. (1984). Contemporary perspectives on the roles of mothers and teachers. In L.G. Katz (Ed.), *More talks with teachers*. Urbana, IL: ERIC Clearinghouse on Elementary and Early Childhood Education.

Katz, L.G., & Chard, S.C. (1989). *Engaging children's minds: The project approach*. Norwood, NJ: Ablex Publishing Corp.

Katz, L.G., Evangelou, D., & Hartmann, J.A. (1990). *The case for mixed-age grouping in early childhood*. Washington, DC: National Association for the Education of Young Children.

Nuthall, G., & Snook, I. (1973). Contemporary models of teaching. In R.M.W. Travers (Ed.), *Second handbook of research on teaching* (pp. 47–76). Chicago: Rand McNally & Co.

Rabitti, G. (1992). *Preschool at "la villetta."* Unpublished Master of Arts thesis, University of Illinois, Urbana, IL.

Rinaldi, C. (1991). *The Reggio Emilia approach*. A paper presented at the Conference on the Hundred Languages of Children, Detroit, MI.

Schlechty, P. (1990). *Schools for the 21st century*. San Francisco: Jossey-Bass.

Schlechty, P. (n.d.). *Four model paradigms for schooling*. Louisville, KY: Center of Leadership in School Reform.

Skrtic, T.M. (1991). The special education paradox. *Harvard Education Review, 61*(2), 148–206.

# Part II

# Reggio Emilia's Educators Describe Their Program: Interviews with Lella Gandini

Loris Malaguzzi, founder of the
program in Reggio Emilia.

# 3

# History, Ideas, and Basic Philosophy

## An Interview with Lella Gandini*

### Loris Malaguzzi

### PART I: HISTORY

**The Year 1946: The Unbelievable Beginning of a School
Run by Parents**

**Gandini:** *I would like to know about the distant roots of your group
experience as well as of your own personal experience.*
    **Malaguzzi:** The history of our approach, and of my place in it, starts
six days after the end of the Second World War. It is the spring of 1945.

---

* Translated by Lella Gardini.

Destiny must have wanted me to be part of an extraordinary event. I hear that in a small village called Villa Cella, a few miles from the town of Reggio Emilia, people decided to build and run a school for young children. That idea seems incredible to me! I rush there on my bike and I discover that it is all quite true. I find women intent upon salvaging and washing pieces of brick. The people had gotten together and had decided that the money to begin the construction would come from the sale of an abandoned war tank, a few trucks, and some horses left behind by the retreating Germans.

"The rest will come," they say to me.

"I am a teacher," I say.

"Good," they say, "If that is true, come work with us."

It all seemed unbelievable: the idea, the school, the inventory consisting of a tank, a few trucks, and horses. They explain everything to me: "We will build the school on our own, working at night and on Sundays. The land has been donated by a farmer; the bricks and beams will be salvaged from bombed houses; the sand will come from the river; the work will be volunteered by all of us."

"And the money to run the school?"

A moment of embarassment and then they say, "We will find it." Women, men, young people—all farmers and workers, all special people who had survived a hundred war horrors—are dead serious.

Within eight months the school and our friendship had set down roots. What happened at Villa Cella was but the first spark. Other schools were opened on the outskirts and in the poorest sections of town, all created and run by parents. Finding support for the school, in a devastated town, rich only in mourning and poverty, would be a long and difficult ordeal, and would require sacrifices and solidarity now unthinkable. When seven more were added in the poor areas surrounding the city to the "school of the tank" at Villa Cella, started by women with the help of the National Liberation Committee (CLN), we understood that the phenomenon was irreversible. Some of the schools would not survive. Most of them, however, would display enough rage and strength to survive for almost 20 years.

Finally, after seven years of teaching in a middle school, I decided to leave my job. The work with the children had been rewarding, but the state-run school continued to pursue its own course, sticking to its stupid and intolerable indifference towards children, its opportunistic and obsequious attention towards authority, and its self-serving cleverness, pushing prepackaged knowledge. I went to Rome to study psychology at the National Center for Research (CNR). When I returned to Reggio Emilia I started, for the municipality, a town-sponsored mental health center for children with difficulties in school. At this time I began living two parallel lives, one in the morning at the

**Figure 3.1.  A group of children and teacher from the Villa Cella School, 1950.**

center and the other in the afternoon and evening in the small, parent-run schools.

The teachers in these small schools had exce[tion]. They were very different from one anot[her], trained in various Catholic or other private sch[ools], were ample and greedy, and their energy bou[nd] these teachers and started to work with the chil[dren] we ourselves were learning. Soon we became a[ware] were in poor health and undernourished. We [saw] the standard Italian language was to them, a[s] generations spoken a local dialect. We asked th[em] finding ways for all of us to cooperate effectiv[ely] most demanding task—not for a lack of deter[mination but a] lack of experience. We were breaking traditional patterns.

*[handwritten note: WHAT ARE THE TRADITIONAL PATTERNS THEY ARE BREAKING? NORMS OF CLASS/STATUS?]*

When we started to work with these courageous parents, we felt both enthusiasm and fear. We knew perfectly well how weak and unprepared we were. We took stock of our resources—not a difficult task. More difficult was the task of increasing those resources. And even more difficult was to predict how we would use them with the children. We were able to imagine the great challenge, but we did not yet know our own capabilities nor those of the children. We informed the mothers that we, just as the children, had much to learn. A simple, liberating thought came to our aid, namely that things about children and for children are only learned from children. We knew how this was true and at the same time not true. But we needed that assertion and guiding principle; it gave us strength and turned out to be an essential part of our collective wisdom. It was a preparation for 1963, the year in which the first municipal schools came to life.

## The Year 1963: The First City-Run School for Young Children

**Gandini:** *Will you recall that event?*

**Malaguzzi:** It was a school with two classrooms, large enough for 60 children, and we gave it the name of Robinson to recall the adventures of Defoe's hero. You will have heard how the birth of the first school in 1963 established an important landmark. For the first time in Italy, the people affirmed the right to establish a secular school for young children: a rightful and necessary break in the monopoly the Catholic Church had hitherto exercised over children's early education. It was a necessary change in a society that was renewing itself, changing deeply, and in which citizens and families were increasingly asking for social services and schools for their children. They wanted schools of a new kind: of better quality, free from charitable tendencies, not merely custodial, and not discriminatory in any way.

It was a decisive achievement, although the school was housed in a small wooden building assigned to us by the authorities. Indeed, it was difficult to find enough children to participate because of the novelty of a city-run school. Three years later, one evening it burned down. We all ran there, even the mayor, and there we stood watching until only ashes remained. Yet, one year later, the school was rebuilt in brick and concrete. We were now involved in a serious endeavor. From these early roots of civic determination and passion, widening to become part of the public consciousness, are the happenings and stories that I am now narrating to you.

We received the first expert group of teachers from the parent-run schools. Responsibilities were clear in our minds; many eyes, not all friendly, were watching us. We had to make as few errors as possible; we had to find our cultural identity quickly, make ourselves known, and win trust and respect. I remember that, after a few months, the need to make ourselves known became so strong that we planned a most successful activity. Once a week we would transport the school to town. Literally, we would pack ourselves, the children, and our tools into a truck and we would teach school and show exhibits in the open air, in the square, in public parks, or under the colonnade of the municipal theater. The children were happy. The people saw; they were surprised and they asked questions.

We knew that the new situation required continuity but also many breaks with the past. The experiences of the past we sought to preserve were the human warmth and reciprocal help, the sense of doing a job that revealed—through the children and their families—unknown motivation and resources, and an awareness of the values of each project and each choice for use in putting together entirely different activities. We wanted to recognize the right of each child to be a protagonist and the need to sustain each child's spontaneous curiosity at a high level. We had to preserve our decision to learn from children, from events, and from families to the full extent of our professional limits, and to maintain a readiness to change points of view so as never to have too many certainties.

It was a feverish time, a time of adaptation, of continuous adjustment of ideas, of selection of projects, and of attempts. Those projects and attempts were expected to produce a great deal and to do well; they were supposed to respond to the combined expectations of children and families and to reflect our competences, which were still in the making. I remember that we really got involved in a project based on Robinson Crusoe. The plan was for all of us together, including the children, to reconstruct the story, the character, and the adventures of our hero. We worked on reading and retelling the story; we used our memory as well as our skills at drawing, painting, clay, and woodworking. We rebuilt the ship, the sea, the island, the cave, and the tools. It was a long and spectacular reconstruction.

The following year, experts by now, we went on to work on a similar reconstruction of the story of Pinocchio. Then a few years later we changed gears. I had been at the Rousseau Institute and at the Ecole des Petits (School for Young Children) of Piaget in Geneva. Because we were inspired by Piaget, we opted to work with numbers, mathematics, and perception. We were then, and still are, convinced that it is not an imposition on children or an artificial exercise to work with numbers, quantity, classification, dimensions, forms, measurement, transformation, orientation, conservation and change, or speed and space, because these explorations belong spontaneously to the everyday experiences of living, playing, negotiating, thinking, and speaking by children. This was an absolutely new challenge in Italy, and our initiative rewarded us. It marked the beginning of an experimental phase that gained breadth from examining different psychological theories and looking at different theoretical sources and research coming from outside our country.

But in reflecting on that experience, a time during which we were proceeding without clear points of reference, we should also recall our excesses, the incongruity of our expectations, and the weaknesses of our critical and self-critical processes. We were aware that many things in the city, in the country, in politics, in customs, and in terms of needs and expectations were changing. In 1954 the Italian public started watching television. Migrations from the South to the North began, with the consequent abandonment of the countryside. With new work possibilities, women were developing aspirations and demands that were breaking with tradition. The baby boom modified everything, particularly the role and the aims of schools for young children, and led to a powerful, growing demand for social services. Furthermore, the request to place young sons and daughters in preschools was developing into a mass phenomenon.

From all this emerged the need to produce new ideas and to experiment with new educational strategies, in part because the municipal government was increasingly determined to institute more schools to satisfy the emerging needs of children and families. Women's groups, teachers, parents, citizens' councils, and school committees were starting to work with the municipality to support and contribute to that development.

After much pressure and battles by the people, in 1967 all the parent-run schools came under the administration of the municipality of Reggio Emilia. We had fought for eight years, from 1960 to 1968. As part of the larger political struggle all over Italy for publicly supported schools for young children as the entitlement of every child aged 3–6, we had debated the right of the state and the municipalities to establish such schools. In the national parliament confrontation, the secular forces were victorious over the side arguing for Catholic education. Our city was at the forefront: in 1968 there were 12 classes for young children run by the municipality. There would be 24 in 1970, 34 in 1972, 43 in 1973, 54 in 1974, and 58 in 1980, located in 22 different school buildings.

Today, when in Italy 88 percent of the children between ages three to six have acquired the right to go to school, and parents choose between three types of institutions—national, municipal, and private—it seems appropriate to remember those remote events, humble yet powerful, that took place in the countryside and on the urban periphery; events from which those in the city drew inspiration in order to develop an exemplary policy in favor of the child and the family.


### The Year 1976: A Hard Year—a Good Year

**Gandini:** *You said that the education of young children was a virtual monopoly of the Catholic church; how did Catholic people react to a lay school?*

**Malaguzzi:** Already, since 1970, the scenario had changed. Schools and social services had become inescapable national issues and the cultural debate around them had become more enlivened and at the same time more civil. I remember that it had not been that way when in 1963 we had organized an Italian-Czeck seminar on the subject of play. It had not been that way when in 1968 we sponsored a symposium on the relationship among psychiatry, psychology, and education—considered a dangerous, or unknown, combination at the time—nor, for that matter, when later we organized a meeting among biologists, neurologists, psychologists, and experts in education to discuss children's graphic expression. The latter meeting, because of its attention to biology and neurology, brought upon us the accusation of having placed too much emphasis on materialism.

Our experience had brought us a long way and had become a reference point for educators in many areas of the country. This was especially true for young teachers who were discovering a profession which up to then had been monopolized by nuns. Around 1965 our schools had gained two fabulous friends. The first was Gianni Rodari, a poet, writer of widely translated stories for children who dedicated his most famous book, *Grammatica della Fantastica (The Grammar of Fantasy,* 1973), to our city and its children. The second was Bruno Ciari, the most lucid, passionate, and acute intelligence in the field of childhood education. They were indeed stupendous friendships. In 1971, with notable daring, we organized a national meeting for teachers only. We expected 200 participants, but 900 showed up. It was dramatic and exalting, but at the same time it was an event that allowed us to publish the first work on the subject of early education, *Esperienze per Una Nuova Scuola dell'Infanzia (Experiences for a New School for Young Children,* Malaguzzi, 1971). After a few months we published another work, *La Gestione Sociale nella Scuola dell'Infanzia (Community-based Management in the Preprimary School,* Malaguzzi, 1971). Those two works contained everything that we had put together with the teachers of Reggio Emilia and Modena (where I was also a consultant) with regard to our ideas and experiences.

In 1972 the whole City Council, including the Catholic minority, voted in favor of the rules and regulations that we had drafted to govern the schools for young children. After years of polemics, or simply lack of acknowledgment, this event marked the legitimization of 10 years of laborious effort. We celebrated in every school.

In 1975 I was invited to be the keynote speaker at another meeting, organized this time by the regional government of Emilia Romagna, on the rights of children. It could not have come at a better time. I had just returned from a visit to the Institut Rousseau and the "Ecole des

Petits" in Geneva and was inspired with admiration for the Piagetian views and with the plans, mentioned earlier, that we would soon start to implement.

The year 1976 was a hard, unexpected year. In the month of November the government speaker for the Catholic establishment, through the government-sponsored radio network, began a defamatory campaign against the city-run schools for young children and especially against our schools. They were attacked as a model of education that was corrupting the children and as a model of a policy of harassment against private, religious schools. After seven days of this campaign, we felt that we had to react. My decision was to suspend the regular planning activities of teachers and invite the local clergy to come to an open debate inside our schools. This public discussion lasted the better part of five months. As time went by, the harsh opposition became more civil, tempered, and honest; as ideas began to emerge, a reciprocal understanding began to take shape. At the end of this adventure we were left exhausted, with the sense that the anguish had dissipated, and I believe this sense of relief was shared by everyone on both sides. What remained was a feeling of enrichment and humanity.

Reflecting upon this event in historical perspective, we can see that this ugly affair arose from the deep uneasiness felt by some Church officials over the loss of their monopoly on education. They were simultaneously being confronted with a decrease in the number of men and women choosing religious vocations, resulting in the increased need for secular teachers and a consequent increased cost of running their schools. Furthermore, the Italian Constitution forbade the use of federal funds to support religious schools; therefore, the Church was attempting to obtain financial support from local government (later this would be granted).

Still another factor, in my view, explaining the attack on our schools was the rapid growth of the cultural influence of our experience. Our work, the seminars, the meetings, and the publications had all contributed to a national recognition of our city-run schools. State schools for young children also existed, alongside the municipal ones, but their growth was slow and too controlled by the central government. Thus, our program was shining a spotlight on the limitations of the religious schools, which were, with a few exceptions, incapable of going beyond the old and outdated custodial approach to education.

One of the consequences was that a government agency called "The National Teaching Center" established ties with our group and invited me to participate in their meetings. These ties still endure. Another result was that an important publishing company entrusted me with the direction of a new journal, *Zerosei (Zero to Six,* 1976–1984), and later *Bambini (Children,* 1985–present), addressed to educators of young children. I am still involved in this enterprise.

In the end, that painful confrontation of 1976 and its favorable conclusion made us stronger and more aware of what we had built, as well as more eager to go on with it. In the 1980s we went ahead with our first flight abroad toward Sweden with the first edition of our exhibit, "When the Eye Jumps Over the Wall," and the beginning of other flights that would take us traveling around the world.

## A Professional and Life Choice

**Gandini:** *It seems that you made a choice to dedicate your life to the education and care of young children. When did you make this life choice?*

**Malaguzzi:** I could just avoid answering, as others have done before, by saying that when you don't ask me I know, but when you ask me, I do not know the answer anymore. There are some choices that you know are coming upon you only when they are just about to explode. But there are other choices that insinuate themselves into you and become apparent with a kind of obstinate lightness, that seem to have slowly grown within you during the happenings of your life because of a mixing of molecules and thoughts. It must have happened this latter way. But also World War II, or any war, in its tragic absurdity might have been the kind of experience that pushes a person toward the job of educating, as a way to start anew and live and work for the future. This desire strikes a person, as the war finally ends and the symbols of life reappear with a violence equal to that of the time of destruction.

I do not know for sure. But I think that is where to look for a beginning. Right after the war I felt a pact, an alliance, with children, adults, veterans from prison camps, partisans of the Resistance, and the sufferers of a devastated world. Yet all that suffering was pushed away by a day in spring, when ideas and feelings turned toward the future, seemed so much stronger than those that called one to halt and focus upon the present. It seemed that difficulties did not exist, and that obstacles were no longer insurmountable.

It was a powerful experience emerging out of a thick web of emotions and from a complex matrix of knowledge and values promising new creativity of which I was only becoming aware. Since those days I have often reassessed my position, and yet I have always remained in my niche. I have never regretted my choices or what I gave up for them.

**Gandini:** *What are your feelings, and how do you view your experiences when you recall the history of your program?*

**Malaguzzi:** Dear Lella, you have to agree that seeing an army tank, six horses, and three trucks generating a school for young children is extraordinary. The fact that the school still exists and continues to function well is the minimum that one could expect from such beginnings. Furthermore, its valuable history confirms that a new educational experience can emerge from the least expected circumstances.

If we continue to review those extraordinary origins, it is because we are still trying to understand the intuitions, the ideas, and the feelings that were there at the start and that have accompanied us ever since. These correspond to what John Dewey called, "the foundation of the mind," or Lev Vygotsky considered, "the loan of consciousness." Such concepts we have always kept in mind, especially in moments when we have had to make difficult decisions or overcome obstacles. Indeed, the first philosophy learned from these extraordinary events, in the wake of such a war, was to give a human, dignified, *civil* meaning to existence, to be able to make choices with clarity of mind and purpose, and to yearn for the future of mankind.

**Figure 3.2.   Loris Malaguzzi speaking to a group of educators.**

But the same events granted us something else right away, to which we have always tried to remain faithful. This something came out of requests made by mothers and fathers, whose lives and concerns were focused upon their children. They asked for nothing less than that this school, which they had built with their own hands, be a different kind of school, a school that could educate their children in a different way from before. It was the women especially who expressed this desire. The equation was simple: If the children had legitimate rights, then they also should have opportunities to develop their intelligence and to be made ready for the success that would not, and should not, escape them. These were the parents' thoughts, expressing a universal aspiration, a declaration against the betrayal of children's potential, and a warning that children first of all had to be taken seriously and believed in. These three concepts could have fitted perfectly in any good book on education. And they suited us just fine. The ideas coming from parents were shared by others who understood their deep implications. And if our endeavor has endured for many years, it has been because of this collective wisdom.

## PART II: PHILOSOPHY

### The Sources of Our Inspiration

**Gandini:** *What theories and schools of thought do you think influenced the formulation of your approach?*

**Malaguzzi:** When somebody asks us how we got started, where we came from, what the sources of our inspiration are, and so on, we cannot help but recite a long list of names. And when we tell about our humble and at the same time extraordinary origins, and we try to explain that from those origins we have extracted theoretical principles that still support our work, we notice much interest and not a little incredulity. It is curious (but not unjustified) how resilient is the belief that educational ideas and practices can derive only from official models or established theories.

We must, however, state right away that we also emerged out of a complex cultural background. We are immersed in history, surrounded by doctrines, politics, economic forces, scientific change, and human dramas; there is always in progress a difficult negotiation for survival. For this reason we have had to struggle and occasionally correct and modify our direction, but so far destiny has spared us from shameful compromise or betrayal. It is important for pedagogy not to be the prisoner of too much certainty, but instead to be aware of both the relativity of its powers and the difficulties of translating its ideals into practice. Piaget has already warned us that the errors and ills of pedagogy come from a lack of balance between scientific data and social application.

Preparing ourselves was difficult. We looked for readings; we traveled to capture ideas and suggestions from the few but precious innovative experiences of other cities; we organized seminars with friends and the most vigorous and innovative figures on the national education scene; we attempted experiments; we started exchanges with Swiss and French colleagues. The first of these groups (Swiss) gravitated around the area of active education and Piagetian tendencies, while the second (French) invented a very strange school: Every three years this French school would move to a new location where the reconstruction of old, abandoned farmhouses would be the basis of the educational work with the children. So it was that we proceeded, and gradually things began to come together in a coherent pattern.

## The Education of Children in the 1960s

**Gandini:** *We know that in the 1960s there emerged in Italy a new consciousness regarding the education of young children. What was the cultural scenario that accompanied it?*

**Malaguzzi:** In the 1960s, issues surrounding schools for young children were at the center of fiery political debates. The need for them was undeniable, but the main debate was whether schools should exist as a social service. More substantive pedagogical considerations remained on the back burner. In reality, on the entire subject of education, Italy was far behind. For 20 years under Fascism, the study of the social sciences had been suppressed and European and American theories and experiences excluded. That kind of isolation was disappearing in the 1960s. The works of John Dewey, Henri Wallon, Edward Chaparède, Ovide Decroly, Anton Makarenko, Lev Vygotsky, and later also Erik Erikson and Urie Bronfenbrenner were becoming known. Furthermore, we were reading *The New Education* by Pierre Bovet and Adolfe Ferrière and learning about the teaching techniques of Celestine Freinet in France, the progressive educational experiment of the Dalton School in New York, and the research of Piaget and colleagues in Geneva.

This literature, with its strong messages, guided our choices; and our determination to continue gave impetus to the flow of our experiences. We avoided the paralysis that had stalled left political theorists for more than a decade in a debate regarding the relationship between content and method in education. For us that debate was meaningless because it did not take into account differences that were part of our society and ignored the fact that active education involves an inherent alliance between content and method. Also strengthening our belief in active education was our awareness of the pluralism of the families, children, and teachers becoming ever more involved in our joint project. This awareness was making us more respectful of different political positions. We were becoming more free of intolerance and prejudice.

Looking back it seems to me that this choice toward respect gave strength to our autonomy as we elaborated our educational project, and helped us resist many contrasting pressures.

The Italian tradition relied on Rosa Agazzi and Maria Montessori, two important figures from the beginning of the century. Montessori was first praised and then relegated to the sidelines by the Fascist regime because of her scientific approach to pedagogy. Agazzi was adopted as a model because her pedagogy was closer to the view of the child in Catholicism. I still believe that the writings of Montessori and Agazzi should be meditated upon in order to move beyond them.

Meanwhile, in practice, the Roman Catholic Church had almost a monopoly on preschool education, concentrating its efforts on helping needy children and offering custodial services rather than responding to the social and cultural changes. The typical classroom contained 40–50 children, entrusted to one nun with no teaching degree and no salary. The situation speaks for itself through the numbers: in 1960, only about one-third of young children were in preschool where they were taught by 22,917 teachers, of whom 20,330 were nuns.

## More About the Sources of Inspiration

**Gandini:** *You have mentioned a first wave of sources that influenced you. Can you tell us more about the ideas that have been important to you?*

**Malaguzzi:** In the 1970s we listened to a second wave of scholars, including psychologists Wilfred Carr, David Shaffer, Kenneth Kaye, Jerome Kagan, Howard Gardner, and philosopher David Hawkins, and theoreticians Serge Moscovici, Charles Morris, Gregory Bateson, Heinz Von Foerster, and Francisco Varela, plus those who work in the field of dynamic neuroscience. The network of the sources of our inspiration spans several generations and reflects the choices and selections that we have made over time. From these sources we have received ideas both long and not-so-long lasting—topics for discussion, reasons to find connections, discordances with cultural changes, occasions for debating, and stimuli to confirm and expand upon practices and values. And, overall, we have gained a sense of the versatility of theory and research.

But talk about education (including the education of young children) cannot be confined to its literature. Such talk, which is also political, must continuously address major social changes and transformations in the economy, sciences, arts, and human relationships and customs. All of these larger forces influence how human beings—even young children—"read" and deal with the realities of life. They determine the emergence, on both general and local levels, of new methods of educational content and practice, as well as new problems and soul-searching questions.

## In Search of an Educational Approach for the Youngest Children

**Gandini:** *In Italy, group care of very young children (4 months to 3 years of age) in a collective environment has developed in a very successful way. How did it begin in Reggio Emilia?*

**Malaguzzi:** In Reggio Emilia, the first infant-toddler center (*Asilo nido*) for children under three years of age came to life one year before the promulgation of the 1971 national law instituting this type of service. This law was a victory for Italian women after 10 years of struggle. The new institution was an attempt to meet the joint needs of women, choosing both motherhood and work, and children, growing up in the nuclear family.

Proponents of infant-toddler centers had to deal with the polemic raised by the rediscovered writings of John Bowlby and Rene Spitz, who right after World War Two studied the damage resulting from the separation of the mother–child pair. Furthermore, they had to address the resistance of the Catholic world, which feared risks and pathologies in a breakdown of the family. It was a very delicate question. Our experience with children 3–6 years of age was a useful point of reference, but at the same time not a complete answer. Rather than thinking in terms of custodial care, we argued that their education demanded professional expertise, strategies of care, and environments that were appropriate and unique to their developmental level.

We had many fears, and they were reasonable ones. The fears, however, helped us; we worked cautiously with the very young teachers and with the parents themselves. Parents and teacher learned to handle with great care the children's transition from a focused attachment on parents and home to a shared attachment which included the adults and environment of the infant-toddler center.

It all went much better than expected. We had the good fortune to be able to plan the environment of the first center with an excellent architect. The children understood sooner than we had expected that their adventure in life could flow between two agreeable and comfortable places—home and the center. In both they could express their previously overlooked desire to be and mature with peers and to find in them points of reference, understanding, surprises, affective ties, and merriment that could dispel shadows and uneasiness.

For us, the children, and the families, there now opened up the possibility of a very long and continuous period of living together, from the infant-toddler center through the preprimary school, that is, five or six years of reciprocal trust and work. This time, we discovered, was a precious resource, capable of making synergistic potentials flow among educators, children, and families.

Today, in my city about 40 percent of eligible children are served by our municipal infant-toddler centers, and about 10–20 percent more would be if there were space. What have we learned from this experience? Twenty years of work have convinced us that even the youngest children are social beings. They are predisposed; they possess from birth a readiness to make significant ties with other caretakers besides their parents (who do not thereby lose their special responsibilities and prerogatives).

The obvious benefit that the children obtain from interactive play with peers is a most reassuring aspect of the group experience, the potential of which has wide implications not yet appreciated. In consequence, we agree with the American psychologists (e.g. Ellen Hock, Urie Bronfenbrenner) that it is not so important whether the mother chooses the role of homemaker or working mother, but rather that she feels fulfillment and satisfaction with her choice and receives support from her family, the child care center, and at least minimally, the surrounding culture. The quality of the relationship between parent and child becomes more important than the sheer quantity of time they spend together.

## PART III: BASIC PRINCIPLES

### The Structural Combination of Educational Choices and Organization

**Gandini:** *What kind of organization helped you to realize the innovative ideas in your schools for young children?*

**Malaguzzi:** We think of a school for young children as an integral living organism, as a place of shared lives and relationships among many adults and very many children. We think of school as a sort of construction in motion, continuously adjusting itself. Certainly we have to adjust our system from time to time while the organism travels on its life course, just as those pirate ships were once compelled to repair their sails all the while keeping on their course at sea.

It has also always been important to us that our living system of schooling expands toward the world of the families, with their right to know and to participate. And then it expands toward the city, with its own life, its own patterns of development, its own institutions, as we have asked the city to adopt the children as bearers and beneficiaries of their own specific rights.

### Is it Possible to Create an Amiable School?

**Gandini:** *A visit to your schools always gives a sense of discovery and serenity. What are the ingredients that create such an atmosphere and level of positive tension?*

**Malaguzzi:** I believe that our schools show the attempt that has been made to integrate the educational program with the organization of work and the environment so as to allow for maximum movement, interdependence, and interaction. The school is an inexhaustible and dynamic organism: It has its difficulties, controversies, joys, and capacities to handle external disturbances. What counts is that there be an agreement about what direction the school should go, and that all forms of artifice and hypocrisy be kept at bay. Our objective, which we always will pursue, is to create an amiable environment, where children, families, and teachers feel at ease.

To start with, then, there is the environment. There is the entrance hall, which informs and documents, and which anticipates the form and organization of the school. This leads into the dining hall, with the kitchen well in view. The entrance hall leads into the central space, or *piazza*, the place of encounters, friendships, games, and other activities that complete those of the classrooms. The classrooms and utility rooms are placed at a distance from but connected with the central area. Each classroom is divided into two contiguous rooms, picking up one of the very few practical suggestions by Piaget. His idea was to allow children either to be with teachers or stay alone; but we use the two spaces in many ways. In addition to the classrooms, we have established the *atelier,* the school studio and laboratory, as a place for manipulating or experimenting with separate or combined visual languages, either in isolation or in combination with the verbal ones.

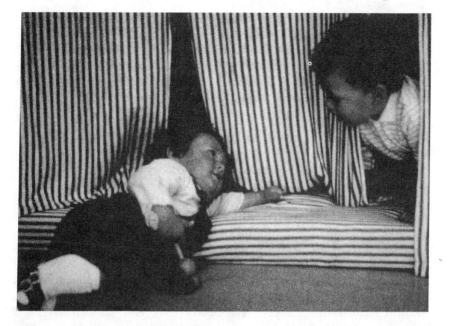

**Figure 3.3.    A place to hide or to be with a friend. Infant-Toddler Center Arcobaleno.**

We have also the *mini-ateliers* next to each classroom, which allow for extended project work. We have a room for music and an archive, where we have placed many useful objects both large and small, and noncommercial, made by teachers and parents. Throughout the school the walls are used as spaces for both temporary and permanent exhibits of what the children and teachers have created: Our walls speak and document.

The teachers work in co-teaching pairs in each classroom, and they plan with other colleagues and the families. All the staff members of the school meet once a week to discuss and broaden their ideas, and they participate together in in-service training. We have a team of *pedagogisti* to facilitate interpersonal connection and to consider both the overall ideas and the details. The families meet by themselves or with the teachers, either in individual meetings, group meetings, or whole school meetings. Families have formed an Advisory Council for each school that meets two or three times a month. The city, the countryside, and the nearby mountains serve as additional teaching sites.

Thus, we have put together a mechanism combining places, roles, and functions that have their own timing, but that can be interchanged with one another in order to generate ideas and actions. All this works within a network of cooperation and interactions that produces for the adults, but above all for the children, a feeling of belonging in a world that is alive, welcoming, and authentic.

## For an Education Based on Interrelationships

**Gandini:** *How do you create and sustain interaction, relationships, and cooperation among all parties connected with the schools?*

**Malaguzzi:** In our system we know it is essential to focus on children and be child-centered, but we do not feel that is enough. We consider also teachers and families as also being central to the education of children. We therefore choose to place all three components at the center of our interest.

Our goal is to build an amiable school, where children, teachers, and families feel at home. Such a school requires careful thinking and planning concerning procedures, motivations, and interests. It must embody ways of getting along together, of intensifying relationships among the three central protagonists, of assuring complete attention to the problems of education, and of activating participation and research. These are the most effective tools for all those concerned—children, teachers, parents—to become more united and aware of each other's contributions. They are the most effective tools to use in order to feel good about cooperating and to produce, in harmony, a higher level of results.

Anyone who starts a program thinks about actions that will transform existing situations into new, desired ones. In our approach, then, in order to proceed, we make plans and reflections connected with the cognitive, affective, and symbolic realms; we refine communication skills; we are very active in exploring and creating along with many other participants, while remaining open to change. In this manner, while all the goals are shared, still the most valuable aspect is interpersonal satisfaction.

Even when the structure we have in mind (the centrality of children, teachers, and families) reveals flaws and difficulties, and the participation shows different levels of intensity, the stimulating atmosphere of the school provides a sense of positive receptiveness to all concerned. That happens because the school invites an exchange of ideas; it has an open and democratic style, and thereby it tends to open minds.

The aspects of isolation, indifference, and violence that are more and more a part of contemporary social life are so contrary to our approach that they make us even more determined to proceed. The families feel the same way; the alienating aspects of modern life become a reason to be even more eager and open to our offerings.

All this contributes to structure an education based on relationship and participation. On the practical level, we must continuously maintain and reinvent our network of communication and encounters. We have meetings with families to discuss curriculum. We ask for their cooperation in organizing activities, setting up the space, and preparing the welcoming of new children. We distribute to each child the telephone numbers and addresses of all the other children and their teachers. We encourage visits, including snacks among the children at their homes, and visits to parents' workplaces. We organize with parents excursions, for example, to swimming pools and gymnasiums. We work with parents in building furnishings and toys. We meet with them to discuss our projects and our research, and we meet to organize dinners and celebrations in the school.

This type of approach with parents reveals much about our philosophy and basic values. These include the interactive and constructivist aspects, the intensity of relationships, the spirit of cooperation, and individual and collective effort in doing research. We appreciate different contexts, pay careful attention to individual cognitive activity within social interactions, and establish affective ties. As we learn two-way processes of communication, we acquire a wider awareness of political choices regarding infancy, encourage mutual adaptation among children and adults, and promote growth of adult educational competencies. We have truly left behind a vision of the child as egocentric, focused only on cognition and physical objects, and whose feelings and affectivity are underestimated and belittled.

## Relationship and Learning

**Gandini:** *In what particular way do you see children's learning take place within the context of the rich relationships that you describe?*

**Malaguzzi:** In my view, relationships and learning coincide within an active process of education. They come together through the expectations and skills of children, the professional competence of adults, and more generally, the educational process.

We must embody in our practice, therefore, reflections on a delicate and decisive point: *What children learn does not follow as an automatic result from what is taught. Rather, it is in large part due to the children's own doing as a consequence of their activities and our resources.*

It is necessary to think about the knowledge and skills that children construct independently of and prior to schooling. This knowledge base does not belong to the "pre-history" mentioned by Vygotzky (as if it were a separate experience), but to the children's social development in process. In any context, children do not wait to pose questions to themselves and form strategies of thought, or principles, or feelings. Always and everywhere children take an active role in the construction and acquisition of learning and understanding. To learn is a satisfying experience, but also, as the psychologist Nelson Goodman tells us, to understand is to experience desire, drama, and conquest.

So it is that in many situations, especially when one set up challenges, children show us they know how to walk along the path to understanding. Once children are helped to perceive themselves as authors or inventors, once they are helped to discover the pleasure of inquiry, their motivation and interest explode. They come to expect discrepancies and surprises. As educators we have to recognize their tension, partly because, with a minimum of introspection, we find the same within ourselves (unless the vital appeal of novelty and puzzlement has faded or died). The age of childhood, more than the ages that follow, is characterized by such expectations. To disappoint the children deprives them of possibilities that no exhortation can arouse in later years.

**Figure 3.4.   Glass walls separate *atelier* and *piazza* at the Diana School.**

Yet, in so praising the child, we do not intend to return to the naïveté of the 1970s, when discovery of the child's active role in structuring events and the two-way causality in child–adult interaction resulted in a strange devaluation of the role of the adult. Nor do we wish to overvalue the child's control of this interaction. In reality, the two-way direction of interaction is a principle hard to miss. We imagine the interaction as a ping-pong match. (Do you remember the badminton games between two boys, splendidly recounted by the great Gestalt psychologist, Max Wertheimer, in *Productive Thinking* (1945)?) For the game to continue, the skills of the adult and child need appropriate adjustments which allow the growth through learning of the skills of the child.

All of these considerations remind us that the way we get along with children influences what motivates them and what they learn. Their environment must be set up so as to interface the cognitive realm with the realms of relationship and affectivity. So also there should be

**Figure 3.5.  A structure, lined with mirrors and built by parents and teachers, invites children to interact and play with their images.**

connection between development and learning, between the different symbolic languages, between thought and action, and between individual and interpersonal autonomies. Value should be placed on contexts, communicative processes, and the construction of a wide network of reciprocal exchanges among children and between children and adults.

Yet, what is most central to success is to adhere to a clear and open theoretical conception which guarantees coherence in our choices, practical applications, and continuing professional growth.

## The Widening of Communication Networks

**Gandini:** *You have described in great detail the importance of relationships in your approach. But is your approach based only on relationship?*

**Malaguzzi:** No, of course not. Relationship is the primary connecting dimension of our system, however, understood not merely as a warm, protective envelope, but rather as a dynamic conjunction of forces and elements interacting toward a common purpose. The strength of our system lies in the ways we make explicit and then intensify the necessary conditions for relations and interaction. We seek to support those social exchanges that better insure the flow of expectations, conflicts, cooperations, choices, and the explicit unfolding of problems tied to the cognitive, affective, and expressive realms.

Among the goals of our approach is to reinforce each child's sense of identity through a recognition that comes from peers and adults, so much so that each one would feel enough sense of belonging and self-confidence to participate in the activities of the school. In this way we promote in children the widening of communication networks and mastery and appreciation of language in all its levels and contextual uses. As a result, children discover how communication enhances the autonomy of the individual and the peer group. The group forms a special entity tied together through exchange and conversation, reliant on its own ways of thinking, communicating, and acting.

The approach based on relationship best reveals how a classroom is composed of independent individuals as well as subgroups and alliances with different affinities and skills. The communicative landscape becomes variegated; we notice children who communicate less than others. The teachers, participant observers, respond to what they see by asking questions, initiating face-to-face exchanges, redirecting activities, and modifying the way or the intensity of their interaction with particular children. Small-group activities, involving two to four children, are modules of maximum desirability and communicative efficacy. They are the type of classroom organization most favorable to education based on relationship. They facilitate fruitful conflicts, investigations, and activities connected to what each child has previously said and self-regulatory accommodations.

It might help to look at this in systemic terms. The system of relationship in our schools is simultaneously real and symbolic. In this system each person has a formal role relationship with the others. Adult and child roles are complementary: They ask questions of one another, they listen, and they answer.

As a result of these relationships, the children in our schools have the unusual privilege of learning through their communications and concrete experiences. I'm saying that the system of relationships has in and of itself a virtually autonomous capacity to educate. It is not just some kind of giant security blanket (the "transitional object" of D.W. Winnicott). Nor is it some kind of flying carpet that takes the children to magic places. Rather, it is a permanent living presence always on the scene, required all the more when progress becomes difficult.

## What Is Needed to Make an Alliance Succeed

**Gandini:** *One of the many questions that comes up when talking about your program is how you succeed in enlisting and maintaining the participation of families at such a high level?*

**Malaguzzi:** That is one of the first questions we are usually asked. Let me answer without reference to philosophy, sociology, and ethics. Family participation requires many things, but most of all it demands of teachers a multitude of adjustments. Teachers must possess a habit of questioning their certainties, a growth of sensitivity, awareness, and availability, the assuming of a critical style of research and continually updated knowledge of children, an enriched evaluation of parental roles, and skills to talk, listen, and learn from parents.

Responding to all of these demands requires from teachers a constant questioning of their teaching. Teachers must leave behind an isolated, silent mode of working that leaves no traces. Instead, they must discover ways to communicate and document the children's evolving experiences at school. They must prepare a steady flow of quality information targeted to parents but appreciated also by children and teachers. This flow of documentation, we believe, introduces parents to a quality of knowing that tangibly changes their expectations. They reexamine their assumptions about their parenting roles and their views about the experience their children are living and take a new and more inquisitive approach toward the whole school experience.

With regard to the children, the flow of documentation creates a second, and equally pleasing, scenario. They become even more curious, interested, and confident as they contemplate the meaning of what they have achieved. They learn that their parents feel at home in the school, at ease with the teachers, and informed about what has happened and is about to happen. We know we have built a solid friendship when children readily accept one of their parents saying, "This evening I am going to school to talk with the teachers," or "I am going to the meeting of the Advisory Council," or when parents help prepare school excursions and celebrations.

Finally, it is important for parents and children to realize how much work teachers do together. They must see how often teachers meet to discuss, sometimes peacefully and other times more loudly. They must see how teachers cooperate on research projects and other initiatives, how they document their work with patience and care, how skillfully they wield their cameras and videocameras, with what kindness they hide their worries, join children's play, and take responsibility. All of this represents for the children a range of models that make a deep impression. They see a world where people truly help one another.


## PART IV: TEACHERS

### The Collegial Work of Teachers

**Gandini:** *In your schools there seems to be no hierarchy among teachers. Is this really the case?*

**Malaguzzi:** Co-teaching, and in a more general sense, collegial work, represents for us a deliberate break from the traditional professional and cultural solitude and isolation of teachers. This isolation has been rationalized in the name of academic freedom, yet wrongly understood. Its results, certainly, has been to impoverish and desiccate teachers' potential and resources and make it difficult or impossible for them to achieve quality.

I remember, however, that the archetype, one teacher per classroom, was so strongly rooted when we began our work that our proposal of co-teaching pairs, which should have been seen as a welcome liberation from excessive stress, did not at first find ready acceptance among teachers. The ones who did accept it, however, soon discovered the evident advantages, and this cleared up the uncertainty. The work in pairs, and then among pairs, produced tremendous advantages, both educationally and psychologically, for adults as well as for children. Furthermore, the co-teaching pairs constituted the first building block of the bridge that was taking us toward community-based management and partnership with parents.

Community-based management has always been an important part of our history and supporting beam of our work. At times, it has been a decisive force for revitalization, unification, or cultural education. At other times it has played a key mediating role with the town administration and political institutions. It has always been essential in strengthening our position.

One regret that has remained constant over the years—shared also by the children—has been our inability to offer a significant number of male teachers. Until a few years ago Italian law forbade males to teach preprimary children—an immensely stupid law that we openly transgressed, ignoring the warnings and reprimands from the Ministry of Education. Now this prohibition has been lifted, yet other reasons still make it difficult to hire male teachers in the schools for young children. To make matters worse, in Italy as in several other European countries, today there are fewer women choosing to become teachers of young children. Those who do, tend to leave this type of job more easily for something else. The reasons for this phenomenon are many and should be studied carefully. But the results are clear in terms of the costs, paid by children, in loss of dignity for schools, teachers, and the entire culture.

## The Questionable Training of Teachers

**Gandini:** *Tell me about the training of the teachers of young children.*

**Malaguzzi:** The preparation of teachers to work with young children is, I believe, a sort of legally sanctioned farce, really unspeakable. It is, and has been, dominated by the Roman Catholic Church. Since 1923 the Italian government has run only six preparatory schools for preprimary teachers—all located in small, country towns with the naive, idealistic belief that the purest source of teachers of young children would be adolescent girls untouched by the moral disorders of the city.

In 1960 there were 129 preparatory schools for preprimary teachers under private Catholic auspices with 21,621 students, versus the six state schools with only 2,531 students. Today the same proportions hold true. All of these schools are at the secondary school level but are less rigorous than the regular secondary schools that train teachers for the elementary level. They do not, and never have had, a common program of studies; indeed, the only thing they have in common is the final examination. The training lasts but three years. A student can enroll after finishing middle school and, therefore, obtain a diploma at age 17. The preparation is founded on nothing, in terms of either a liberal arts foundation or appropriate professional studies. There is in the works a major reform that would include a university preparation for teachers of young children, but achieving that reform will be difficult.

Even in Reggio Emilia, our teachers come out of these preparatory secondary schools. Therefore, you can see why their professional formation and development must take place while on the job working with the children.

## Formation and Reformation of Teachers

**Gandini:** *How do you now go about supporting teacher development in your schools?*

**Malaguzzi:** We have no alternatives but in-service training. As the intelligence becomes stronger through use, so does the teachers' role, knowledge, profession, and competence become stronger through direct application. Teachers—like children and everyone else—feel the need to grow in their competences; they want to transform experiences into thoughts, thoughts into reflections, and reflections into new thoughts and new actions. They also feel a need to make predictions, to try things out, and then interpret them. The act of interpretation is most important. Teachers must learn to interpret ongoing processes rather than wait to evaluate results. In the same way, their role as educators must include understanding children as producers, not as consumers. They must learn to teach nothing to children except what children can learn by themselves. And furthermore, they must be aware of the perceptions the children form of the adults and their actions. In order to enter into relationships with the children that are at the same time productive, amiable, and exciting, teachers must be aware of the risk in expressing judgments too quickly. They must enter the time frame of the children, whose interests emerge only in the course of activity or negotiations arising from that activity. They must realize how listening to children is both necessary and expedient. They must know that activities should be as numerous as the keys of a piano, and that all call forth infinite acts of intelligence when children are offered a wide variety of options to chose from. Furthermore, teachers must be aware that practice cannot be separated from objectives or values and that professional growth comes partly through individual effort, but in a much richer way through discussion with colleagues, parents, and experts. Finally, they need to know that it is

**Figure 3.6.   A discussion about the weights of different objects.**

possible to engage in the challenge of longitudinal observations and small research projects concerning the development or experiences of children. Indeed, education without research or innovation is education without interest.

Already this is no small task! However, it is not possible even to begin if teachers do not have a basic knowledge about different content areas of teaching in order to transform this knowledge into 100 languages and 100 dialogues with children. We have at present limited means to prepare teachers as we would like, but we try to look within ourselves and find inspiration from the things we do.

## The *Atelier* as a Place of Provocation

**Gandini:** *How did the idea and the establishment of the atelier work into your educational project?*

**Malaguzzi:** I will not hide from you how much hope we invested in the introduction of the *atelier*. We knew it would be impossible to ask for anything more. Yet, if we could have done so we would have gone further still by creating a new type of school typology with a new school made entirely of laboratories similar to the *atelier*. We would have constructed a new type of school made of spaces where the hands of children could be active for "messing about," (in the sense that David Hawkins was going to tell us better, later). With no possibility of boredom, hands and minds would engage each other with great, liberating merriment in the way ordained by biology and evolution.

Although we did not come close to achieving those impossible ideals, still the *atelier* has always repaid us. It has, as desired, proved to be subversive—generating complexity and new tools for thought. It has allowed rich combinations and creative possibilities among the different (symbolic) languages of children. The *atelier* has protected us not only from the long-winded speeches and didactic theories of our time (just about the only preparation received by young teachers!), but also from the behavioristic beliefs of the surrounding culture, reducing the human mind to some kind of "container" to be filled.

The *atelier* has met other needs as well. One of the most urgent problems was how to achieve effective communication with the parents. We wanted to always keep them informed about the goings-on in the schools, and at the same time establish a system of communication that would document the work being done with the children. We wanted to show parents how the children thought and expressed themselves, what they produced and invented with their hands and their intelligence, how they played and joked with one another, how they discussed hypotheses, how their logic functioned. We wanted the parents to see that their children had richer resources and more skills than generally realized. We wanted the parents to understand how much value we placed in their children. In return, then, we felt it would be fair to ask parents to help us and be on our side.

The *atelier,* a space rich in materials, tools, and people with professional competences, has contributed much to our work on documentation. This work has strongly informed—little by little—our way of being with the children. It has also, in a rather beautiful way, obliged us to refine our methods of observation and recording so that the processes of children's learning became the basis of our dialogue with parents. Finally, our work in the *atelier* has provided us with archives that are now a treasure trove of children's work and teachers' knowledge and research. Let me emphasize, however, that the *atelier* was never intended to be a sort of secluded, privileged space, as if there and only there the languages of expressive art could be produced.

It was, instead, a place where children's different languages could be explored by them and studied by us in a favorable and peaceful atmosphere. We and they could experiment with alternative modalities, techniques, instruments, and materials; explore themes chosen by children or suggested by us; perhaps work on a large fresco in a group; perhaps prepare a poster where one makes a concise statement

**Figure 3.7.  As the school year ends, parents, children, and teachers celebrate with outside games.**

through words and illustrations; perhaps even master small projects on a reduced scale, stealing their skills from architects! What was important was to help the children find their own styles of exchanging with friends both their talents and their discoveries.

But the *atelier* was most of all a place for research, and we expect that it will continue and increase. We have studied everything, from the affinities and oppositions of different forms and colors, to the complex aims of narrative and argumentation, from the transition of expressing images in symbols to decoding them, from the way children have been contaminated by exposure to mass media, to sex differences in symbolic and expressive preferences. We have always found it a privilege to be able to encounter the fascinating multiple games that can be played with images: turning a poppy into a spot, a light, a bird in flight, a lighted ghost, a handful of red petals within a field of green and yellow wheat. So positive and confirming were our experiences that they eventually led us to expand the use of the *atelier* into the centers for the youngest children in the infant-toddler centers.

## Genesis and Meanings of Creativity

**Gandini:** *The creative behavior and creative production by children has been an elusive theme, about which pages and pages have been written. What is your own view on the subject?*

**Malaguzzi:** We were all very weak and unprepared in the 1950s when the theme of creativity, just landed from the United States, crossed our path. I remember the eagerness with which we read the theories of J.P. Guilford and Paul Torrance. I also remember how later on those theories could be reread and reinterpreted through the perspectives of Bruner, Piaget, and the Cognitivists, the neo-Freudians, Kurt Lewin, the last of the Gestalt psychologists, and the humanistic psychologists Carl Rogers and Abraham Maslow.

It was a difficult but exciting period; we felt that those proposals had great vigor and potential. The work on creativity seemed disruptive to many (almost too many) things, for example, the philosophical dimension of man and life and the productivity of thought. These proposals went so far as to suggest complicity with the unconscious, chance and the emotions with feelings, and so on. Yet, despite their brilliant attractiveness, we have to say frankly that after many years of work, the progress of our own experience, plus our observation and study of children and adults, have suggested to us much caution and reflection.

As we have chosen to work with children we can say that they are the best evaluators and the most sensitive judges of the values and usefulness of creativity. This comes about because they have the privilege of not being excessively attached to their own ideas, which they construct and reinvent continuously. They are apt to explore, make discoveries, change their points of view, and fall in love with forms and meanings that transform themselves.

Therefore, as we do not consider creativity sacred, we do not consider it as extraordinary but rather as likely to emerge from daily experience. This view is now shared by many. We can sum up our beliefs as follows:

1. Creativity should not be considered a separate mental faculty but a characteristic of our way of thinking, knowing, and making choices;
2. Creativity seems to emerge from multiple experiences, coupled with a well-supported development of personal resources, including a sense of freedom to venture beyond the known;
3. Creativity seems to express itself through cognitive, affective, and imaginative processes. These come together and support the skills for predicting and arriving at unexpected solutions;
4. The most favorable situation for creativity seems to be interpersonal exchange, with negotiation of conflicts and comparison of ideas and actions being the decisive elements;
5. Creativity seems to find its power when adults are less tied to prescriptive teaching methods, but instead become observers and interpreters of problematic situations;

6. Creativity seems to be favored or disfavored according to the expectations of teachers, schools, families, and communities as well as society at large, according to the ways children perceive those expectations;

7. Creativity becomes more visible when adults try to be more attentive to the cognitive processes of children than to the results they achieve in various fields of doing and understanding;

8. The more teachers are convinced that intellectual and expressive activities have both multiplying and unifying possibilities, the more creativity favors friendly exchanges with imagination and fantasy;

9. Creativity requires that the *school of knowing* finds connections with *the school of expressing,* opening the doors (this is our slogan) to the hundred languages of children.

Starting with these ideas, we have been trying to understand how they should be revised, yet without letting the myths of spontaneity, which often accompany the myths of creativity, mislead us. We are convinced that between basic intellectual capacities and creativity, a theme preferred by American research, there is not opposition but rather complementarity. The spirit of play can pervade also the formation and construction of thought.

Often when people come to us and observe our children, they ask us which magic spell we have used. We answer that their surprise equals our surprise. Creativity? It is always difficult to notice when it is dressed in everyday clothing and has the ability to appear and disappear suddenly. Our task, regarding creativity, is to help children climb their own mountains, as high as possible. No one can do more. We are restrained by our awareness that people's expectations about creativity should not weigh upon the school. An excessive widening of its functions and powers would give to the school an exclusive role that it cannot have.

## PART V: IMAGES OF CHILDHOOD

### Sweeping Childhood Under the Rug

**Gandini:** *The predicament of childhood today is the subject of much writing. What are your views on this?*

**Malaguzzi:** The dramatic contradictions that characterize the education of children are constantly on my mind. I am speaking about what we know of children versus what we do not know, as well as what we know but fail to do with them and for them. But the problem is wider still, for it involves the human race and the waste of its intelligence and humanity. I think David Hawkins says it best, "In its organization, in its choices, in its ways to come into relation with learning and knowledge, the educational system badly represents the nature and the potential of human capability" (personal communication; also see Hawkins 1966).

All people—and I mean scholars, researchers, and teachers, who in any place have set themselves to study children seriously—have ended up by discovering not so much the limits and weaknesses of children but rather their surprising and extraordinary strengths and capabilities linked with an inexhaustible need for expression and realization.

But the results of those learned inquiries, describing new aspects of development and opening endless possibilities for practical application and ethical and philosophical consideration, have not been sufficiently seized upon by educators. Instead, during this delay, metaphors and images reemerge portraying childhood in one of two extreme ways: as blank, powerless, and entirely shaped by adults; or on the other hand, as autonomously capable of gaining control of the adult world. We have not correctly legitimized a culture of childhood, and the consequences are seen in all our social, economic, and political choices and investments. It is a typical, frightening example of offense and betrayal of human resources.

Specific instances are clearly visible in Europe and the rest of the Western World. We see budgetary cuts, lack of policy and planning, a general lowering of prestige for those who teach or study children, with consequent loss of young people from the profession and the growth of child abuse. We can speak of all of this bad news for children without even mentioning the disasters of war and epidemics that still ravage our planet and conscience.

It is a painful story. John Dewey confronted this same situation earlier in the century and was inspired to urge a method of education combining pragmatic philosophy, new psychological knowledge, and—on the teaching side—mastery of content with inquiring, creative experiences for children. He envisioned all this, also seeking a new relationship between educational and sociocultural research. This last aspect, I believe, is part of the unfinished business of the democratic process, but represents the genuine cultural achievement that childhood and coming generations have a right to expect. As Dewey said, "Human institutions ought to be judged by their educational influence, and by the measure of their capacity to extend the knowledge and competence of man."

I know all this could take place in such a moment as the present, when science, history, and the public conscience appear unanimous in recognizing the child as endowed with the virtues, resources, and intrinsic rights that we mentioned above. But a child so endowed paradoxically explodes in the hands of his creators; such a child becomes too overwhelming for philosophy, science, education, and political economy. The incapacity of societies to respond to such a child would seem to cast doubt on the nobility of our motives regarding children.

Others, too, have sometimes masked their true interests, perhaps even from themselves. Queen Elizabeth (Horace Walpole tells us in his *Anecdotes of Painting,* 1762–1771) was a great collector, yet there is no proof that she admired or loved the art of painting. What is absolutely certain is that she loved, with passion, the paintings that portrayed herself!

## The Differences Among Children

**Gandini:** *One aspect that the visitors of your schools find puzzling is how you can respond to children's different capabilities and needs when you give such importance to social relationships and group work?*

**Malaguzzi:** We certainly recognize differences in the make-up of children along with differences that can be reduced or widened by the favorable or unfavorable influences of the environment. But children have—this is my conviction—a common gift, namely, the potential and competencies that we have described above. We hold this to be true for children who are born in any culture in any place on our planet. Yet, recognizing the universality of children's potential opens up new questions with which so far we in Reggio Emilia have had little familiarity, but which the multicultural events of our time press upon us with urgency.

I would be very cautious concerning differences in cognitive style and strategies. People are too quick to attribute them to one season of life, especially when looking at infants, whose minds undergo many rapid reorganizations and changes in development. The styles we observe are an objective fact about individuals. Beyond that, however, they also reflect the historical and cultural context.

The wider the range of possibilities we offer children, the more intense will be their motivations and the richer their experiences. We must widen the range of topics and goals, the types of situations we offer and their degree of structure, the kinds and combinations of

**Figure 3.8.   One of the teachers' regular meetings to plan and discuss their work.**

resources and materials, and the possible interactions with things, peers, and adults. Moreover, widening the range of possibilities for children also has consequences for others. It renders teachers to be more attentive and aware, and makes them more capable of observing and interpreting children's gestures and speech. Teachers thereby become more responsive to children's feedback, take more control over their own expressive feedback to children (correcting excessive monotony or excitement), and make their interventions with children more personal. All of this will make it easier for teachers to pause and make self-evaluations.

The more we distance ourselves from quick and temporary solutions, from responding to individual differences in a hurried way, the wider will be the range of hypotheses open to us. The more we resist the temptation to classify children, the more capable we become to change our plans and make available different activities. This does not eliminate the responsibility or usefulness of noting differences among children. Let us take them into account, let us keep an eye on them. But let us always exercise caution and learn to observe and evaluate better without assigning levels or grades. Let me add that in reading the specialized literature on evaluation, I have not found the factor of time to be treated correctly. Ferdinando Pessoa (1986) says that the measure of the clock is false. It is certainly false concerning the time of children—for situations in which true teaching and learning take place, for the subjective experience of childhood. One has to respect the time of maturation, of development, of the tools of doing and understanding, of the full, slow, extravagant, lucid, and ever-changing emergence of children's capacities; it is a measure of cultural and biological wisdom.

If nature has commanded that of all the animals, infancy shall last longest in human beings—infinitely long, says Tolstoy—it is because nature knows how many rivers there are to cross and paths to retrace. Nature provides time for mistakes to be corrected (by both children and adults), for prejudices to be overcome, and for children to catch their breath and restore their image of themselves, peers, parents, teachers, and the world. If today we find ourselves in an era in which the time and rhythm of machines and profits dominate those of human beings, then we want to know where psychology, education, and culture stand.

## PART VI: THEORIES OF LEARNING

### The Construction of Meanings

**Gandini:** *One debate in education that seems never to be settled concerns the role of the adult in children's learning. What are your thoughts about this?*

**Malaguzzi:** I would not want to minimize the determining role of adults in providing children with semantic structures/systems of meaning that allow minds to communicate. But at the same time, I would like to emphasize children's own participation: They are autonomously capable of making meaning from their daily life experiences through mental acts involving planning, coordination of ideas, and abstraction. Remember, meanings are never static, univocal, or final; they are always generative of other meanings. The central act of adults, therefore, is to activate, especially indirectly, the meaning-making competencies of children as a basis of all learning. They must try to capture the right moments, and then find the right approaches, for bringing together, into a fruitful dialogue, their meanings and interpretations with those of the children.

### Our Piaget

**Gandini:** *You have mentioned Piaget's influence on your work, and at the same time you have mentioned that your views differ from his on various points. Can you tell us more about this influence and the differences?*

**Malaguzzi:** We maintain intact our sense of gratitude toward Piaget. If Jean Jacques Rousseau invented a revolutionary conception of childhood without ever dealing with children, Piaget was the first to give them an identity based on a close analysis of their development, by observing and talking to children over extended periods of time.

Howard Gardner describes Piaget as the first to take children seriously; David Hawkins describes him as the one who dramatized children splendidly; while Jerome Bruner credits Piaget with demonstrating that those internal principles of logic guiding children are the same principles as those that guide scientists in their inquiries. In fact, in Reggio we know that children can use creativity as a tool for inquiring, ordering, and even transgressing the given schemes of meaning (which Piaget attributed also to the very young in the last years of his life). They can also use creativity as a tool for their own progress in the worlds of necessity and possibility.

With a simple-minded greed, we educators have tried too often to extract from Piaget's psychology things that he did not consider at all usable in education. He would wonder what use teachers could possibly have for his theories of stages, conservation of matter, and so on. In fact, the richest potentiality of Piagetian thought lies in the domain of epistemology, as seen in his major opus, *The Biology of Knowledge* (1971, the University of Chicago Press). Nevertheless, many suggestions can be taken directly or indirectly from his works to reflect and elaborate upon the meaning of education.

Barbel Inhelder, Piaget's most devoted disciple, told friends after the death of the Maestro: "Write freely about his work, make corrections, try to render his thought more specific; still, it will not be easy for you to overturn the underlying structure of his ingenious theories." We in Reggio have followed her advice. Our interest in him increased once we understood that his concern was with epistemology, and that his main goal was to trace the genesis of universal invariant structures. Piaget sacrificed many things to that audacious research; yet he also managed to open other paths of research, such as the study of moral judgment, that he did not pursue, as if a fever was burning in him to simultaneously explore many directions. Some of these paths he later rediscovered after they had been casually abandoned.

Now we can see clearly how Piaget's constructivism isolates the child. As a result we look critically at these aspects: the undervaluation of the adult's role in promoting cognitive development; the marginal attention to social interaction and to memory (as opposed to inference); the distance interposed between thought and language (Vygotsky criticized this, and Piaget, 1962, responded); the lock-step linearity of development in constructivism; the way that cognitive, affective, and moral development are treated as separate, parallel tracks; the overemphasis on structured stages, egocentrism, and classificatory skills; the lack of recognition for partial competencies; the overwhelming importance given to logicomathematical thought; and the overuse of paradigms from the biological and physical sciences. After making all of these criticisms, however, we must go on to note that many constructivists today have turned their attention to the role of social interaction in cognitive development.

## The Dilemma of Learning and Teaching

**Gandini:** *Learning and teaching do not always go together, but in your program you have found ways to help children construct their learning. How did you balance this equation?*

**Malaguzzi:** After all we have said about children, we have to discuss more fully the role that children assume in the construction of self and knowledge, and the help they get in these matters from adults. It is obvious that between learning and teaching, we honor the first. It is not that we ostracize teaching, but that we declare, "Stand aside for a while and leave room for learning, observe carefully what children do, and then, if you have understood well, perhaps teaching will be different from before."

Piaget (1974) warned us that a decision must be made about whether to teach schemes and structures directly or to present the child with rich problem-solving situations in which the active child learns from them in the course of exploration. The objective of education is to increase possibilities for the child to invent and discover. Words should not be used as a shortcut to knowledge. Like Piaget, we agree that the aim of teaching is to provide conditions for learning.

Sometimes discussions about education treat teaching and learning as almost synonymous. In reality, the conditions and goals of the one who teaches are not identical to the conditions and goals of the one who learns. If teaching is monodirectional and rigidly structured according to some "science," it becomes intolerable, prejudicial, and damaging to the dignity of both teacher and learner.

But even where teachers assume themselves to be democratic, their behavior still too often is dominated by undemocratic teaching strategies. These include directives, ritualized procedures, systems of evaluation (which Benjamin Bloom believed should be properly guiding models of education), and rigid cognitivistic curriculum packages, complete with readymade scripts and reinforcement contingencies. All of these strategies provide a professional justification for waste and suffering, and at the same time create the illusion of an impressive system that reassures adults at an unthinking level. Official adoption is easy. By the time the shortcomings of such a package or system do emerge, it is already too late and the damage is done.

Figure 3.9. "A leaf can become. . . ." Drawings by children of the Diana School.

**Figure 3.10.   A small group of children share ideas and discoveries on the computer.**

To conclude, learning is the key factor on which a new way of teaching should be based, becoming a complementary resource to the child and offering multiple options, suggestive ideas, and sources of support. Learning and teaching should not stand on opposite banks and just watch the river flow by; instead, they should embark together on a journey down the water. Through an active, reciprocal exchange, teaching can strengthen learning how to learn.

## Our Vygotsky

**Gandini:** *You have mentioned the importance of the teacher's being able to capture the delicate moment in which the child is ready to take a step toward learning. Could you elaborate on that?*

**Malaguzzi:** At this point the intervention of Vygotsky, our own Vygotsky, becomes indispensable for clarifying this and other points raised in the previous paragraphs. Vygotsky reminds us how thought and language are operative together to form ideas and to make a plan for action, and then for executing, controlling, describing, and discussing that action. This is a precious insight for education.

But upon penetrating the adult–child relationship, and thus returning to the theme of teaching and learning, the Russian psychologist (1978) tells us about the advantages of the *zone of proximal development*, that is, the distance between the levels of capacities expressed by children and their levels of potential development, attainable with the help of adults or more advanced contemporaries.

The matter is somewhat ambiguous. Can one give competence to someone who does not have it? The very suggestion seems to readmit the old ghosts of teaching that we tried to chase away. But we can dispel any risk of returning to traditional teaching by holding to our principle of "circularity" (a term not seen in Vygotsky's writings). Put more simply, we seek a situation in which the child is about to see what the adult already sees. The gap is small between what each one sees, the task of closing it appears feasible, and the child's skills and disposition create an expectation and readiness to make the jump. In such a situation, the adult can and must loan to the children his judgment and knowledge. But it is a loan with a condition, namely, that the child will repay.

It is useless to assert that the readiness of children is too hard to observe. It can indeed be seen! We need to be prepared to see it, for we tend to notice only those things that we expect. But also we should not be in a hurry. We tend all too often today to become slaves of the clock, an instrument that falsifies the natural and subjective time of children and adults.

Vygotsky's suggestion maintains its value and legitimates broad interventions by teachers. For our part in Reggio, Vygotsky's approach is in tune with the way we see the dilemma of teaching and learning and the ecological way one can reach knowledge.


## PART VII: FROM THEORY TO PRACTICE

### A Profession that Does Not Think Small

**Gandini:** *How have you gone about putting into practice the many ideas and inspirations that you have either generated or encountered?*

**Malaguzzi:** The effect of theories can be inspiring and onerous at the same time. This is especially so when it is time to roll up our sleeves and proceed with educational practice. The first fear is to lose the capacity or the ability to connect the theories with the objective problems of daily work, which in turn are generally complicated by administrative, legal, or cultural realities.

But there are further fears, such as those of getting lost in a blind empiricism that can lead to a break with the connections to the necessary theoretical, ideal, and ethical principles; being troubled by the challenge of new theories and approaches that can bring into question your own training and choices; and, last but not least, missing out on the promise that the schools provide as best as possible for all the children as well as meet the expectations and needs of their families. These fears are unavoidable because in our task we cannot be satisfied with approximate results and because our choice was to set up a school with a critical and reforming function. We did not want to be only perfunctory caretakers.

Our theories come from different fields and we meditate on them as well as on the events that take place in our very hands. But a unifying theory of education that sums up all the phenomena of educating does not (and never will) exist. However, we do indeed have a solid core in our approach in Reggio Emilia that comes directly from the theories and experiences of active education and finds realization in particular images of the child, teacher, school, family, and community. Together these produce a culture and society that connect, actively and creatively, both individual and social growth.

And still Ferrière, Dewey, Vygotsky, Bruner, Piaget, Bronfenbrenner, and Hawkins are very much present for us, along with the latest suggestions from Kaye on the tutorial role of the adult, Shaffer on the relationship between language and social interaction, Serge Moscovici and Gabriel Mugny on the genesis of representation and the importance of the interpersonal cognitive constructions, and Gardner on the forms of intelligence and open minds. In the same way we look to the sociolinguistic work on how adults and children jointly construct contexts of meaning, as well as to cognitive research founded on constructivist, symbolic interactionist, and social constructivist perspectives. Altogether, this literature counteracts the behaviorist theories that reduce the creative and protagonistic force of human action to simple, unreadable behavior.

## The Success of a Theory Comes Out in the Practice

**Gandini:** *But how, concretely, do all these theories connect with what goes on in the schools?*

**Malaguzzi:** It is well known how we all proceed as if we had one or more theories. The same happens for teachers: Whether they know it or not they think and act according to personal theories. The point is how those personal theories are connected with the education of children, with relationships within the school, and with the organization of work. In general, when colleagues work closely together and share common problems, this facilitates the alignment of behaviors and a modification of personal theories. We have always tried to encourage this.

When we start speaking about the theory and practice of education, we can go on and on. I agree with Wilfred Carr (1987) when he says that it is good to avoid discussing theories too much because the risk is to deprive them of their practical aspect. In truth, a theory is legitimate only if it deals with problems that emerge from the practice of education and that can be solved by educators. The task of theory is to help teachers understand better the nature of their problems. This way practice becomes a necessary means for the success of theory. In this vein, taking this thought even further, David Hawkins has observed, "The knowledge of practitioners is meaningfully deeper than any found in the thought of many academic researchers; therefore, the teacher must be treated not as an object of study but as an interpreter of educational phenomena" (personal communication; also see Hawkins, 1966).

This validation of the practical work of the teacher is the only rich "textbook" on which we can count to aid us in developing our educational reflections. Moreover, the work of the teachers, when not abandoned to itself, when not left without the support of institutions and alliances with colleagues and families, is capable not only of producing daily educational experiences but is also capable of becoming subject and object of critical scrutiny.

## Getting from Research to Action

**Gandini:** *You said that teachers should also be researchers. How do you promote this?*

**Malaguzzi:** To learn and relearn together with the children is our line of work. We proceed in such a way that the children are not shaped by experience, but are the ones who give shape to it. There are two ways in which we can look into children's learning processes and find clues for supporting them: One is the way children enter into an activity and develop their strategies of thought and action; the other is the way in which the objects involved are transformed. Adults and children go about their learning differently: They use different procedures, honor different principles, make different conjectures, and follow different footprints.

Our teachers do research either on their own or with their colleagues to produce strategies that favor children's work or can be

**Figure 3.11.    Five-year-old children take their time playing checkers.**

utilized by them. They go from research into action (and vice versa). When all the teachers in the school are in agreement, the projects, strategies, and styles of work become intertwined and the school becomes a truly different school. Some of our teachers proceed in this research with more intentionality and better methods than others; the records and documentaries that result from their endeavors are significant beyond the immediate needs for action and become common objects of study, at times with so much substance as to become of interest to a wider audience. As a result, these teachers feel, and help others to feel, more motivation to grow and attain a much higher level of professionalism. In the process our teachers realize that they must avoid the temptation of expecting children to give them back what they already know, but that instead they must retain the same sense of wonder that children live through in their discoveries.

This whole approach causes children to be better known by their teachers. Therefore, they feel more open to challenge, more able to work with their peers in unusual situations, and more persistent

**Figure 3.12.   The children's activities are supported by teachers.**

because they realize that what they have in mind can be tried out. Children know that when pursuing their goals, they can make their own choices, and that is both freeing and revitalizing. It is, indeed, what we had promised the children, their families, and ourselves.

Our way of working makes possible the choice among different modes of interaction. Small groups of children work simultaneously and can be found all around the school setting, organized so as to facilitate social, cognitive, verbal, and symbolic constructions. Our children in fact have many choices: they have places where they can be alone, in a small number, in a large group, with the teachers or without them, in the *atelier*, in the *mini-atelier*, in the large *piazza*, or, if the weather is good, in the outside courtyard, rich with small and large play structures. But the choice to work in a small group, where they explore together, pleases both them and us. Because of that, the classroom is transformed into one large space with market stalls, each one with its own children and its own projects and activities. This arrangement permits good observations and organically developing research about cooperative learning as well as about the bartering and marketing of ideas.

We like this arrangement of our school. We live in the tradition of a city, with its squares and porticoes, which provide an irreplaceable model for meetings, negotiations, and dialogues of various human encounters; moreover, the central square of our city transforms itself twice a week into the hundred stalls of the market. This market has the same function as the *forum*, of which Bruner (1986) wrote, and whose echo resounds in our schools.

## No Planning, Much Reconnaissance

**Gandini:** *People often ask what kind of curricular planning, if any, you have in Reggio Emilia?*

**Malaguzzi:** No, our schools have not had, nor do they have, a planned curriculum with units and subunits (lesson plans), as the behaviorists would like. These would push our schools towards teaching without learning; we would humiliate the schools and the children by entrusting them to forms, dittos, and handbooks of which publishers are generous distributors.

Instead, every year each school delineates a series of related projects, some short range and some long. These themes serve as the main structural supports, but then it is up to the children, the course of events, and the teachers to determine whether the building turns out to be a hut on stilts or an apartment house or whatever.

But, of course, infant-toddler and preprimary teachers do not start off each school year at square one. They have standing behind them a patrimony of talent, knowledge, experiments, research, documentation, and examples showing successes and failures. The teachers follow the children, not plans. The goals are important and will not be lost from sight, but more important are the why and the how of reaching them.

"Reconnaissance" is a strong word in our vocabulary. Our schools start off with a reconnaissance flight over all the human, environmental, technical, and cultural resources. Then more reconnaissance missions will be made to get a full overview of the situation: within and among schools, to families and Advisory Councils, to the pedagogical team, and to the town administration and elected officials. Also, teachers do reconnaissance trips through workshops, seminars, and meetings with experts in various fields.

What educators acquire by discussing, proposing, and launching new ideas is not only a set of professional tools, but also a work ethic that gives more value to being part of a group and to having interpersonal solidarity, while at the same time strengthening intellectual autonomy. The support resulting from *an itinerant reconnaissance education* gives us great strength and help. Its task is to startle and push us along new roads. There is not a better evaluation of our work than this.

## If the Curricula Are Found In the Children

**Gandini:** *Children are the ones who shape their school experience rather than being shaped by them. How does this principle influence your choices about what experiences to offer to children?*

**Malaguzzi:** If the school for young children has to be preparatory and provide continuity with the elementary school, then we as educators are already prisoners of a model that ends up as a funnel. I think, moreover, that the funnel is a detestable object, and it is not much appreciated by children either. Its purpose is to narrow down what is big into what is small. This choking device is against nature. If you put it upside down, it serves no purpose.

Suffice it to say that the school for young children has to respond to the children: It should be a giant rodeo where they learn how to ride 100 horses, real or imaginary. How to approach a horse, how to stroke it, and how to stay close to it are all aspects of an art that can be learned. If there are rules, children will learn them. If they fall off, they will get back on. If special skills are called for, they will watch their more expert contemporaries carefully, and they will even discuss the problem or ask to borrow the adults' experience.

It is true that we do not have planning and curricula. It is not true that we rely on improvisation, which is an enviable skill. We do not rely on chance either, because we are convinced that what we do not yet know can to come extent be anticipated. What we do know is that to be with children is to work one-third with certainty and two-thirds with uncertainty and the new. The one-third that is certain makes us understand and try to understand. We want to study whether learning has its own flux, time, and place; how learning can be organized and encouraged; how situations favorable to learning can be prepared; which skills and cognitive schemes are worth bolstering; how to advance words, graphics, logical thought, body language, symbolic languages, fantasy, narrative, and argumentation; how to play; how to pretend; how friendships form and dissipate; how individual and group identities develop; and how differences and similarities emerge.

All this wisdom does not compensate for what we do not know. But not knowing is the condition that makes us continue to search; in this regard we are in the same situation as the children. We can be sure that the children are ready to help us. They can help by offering us ideas, suggestions, problems, questions, clues, and paths to follow; and the more they trust us and see us as a resource, the more they give us help. All these offerings, merged with what we ourselves bring to the situation, make a handsome capital of resources.

In the last few years we have undertaken many experiments: how children five years old approach the computer; the differences between graphics by boys and girls; the symbolic meanings of drawings; the constructive capacities of logical-organizational thought (which led to a documentary now revisited with George Forman); the acquisition of reading and writing in a communicative context; the forms of thought

**Figure 3.13.  Exploring measurement in the school-yard.**

used in learning about measurement and numbers; cooperative learning through play (in collaboration with Carolyn Edwards, Lella Gandini, and John Nimmo); and the behavior of infants aged two in partially structured situations. The results of these studies guide us in the formulation of flexible projects. But there is another reason for experimenting and documenting, namely the necessity to reveal in full light the image of a competent child. This, in turn, bolsters our position against detractors and the mystification of official programs and practices.

In our documentaries, archives, and exhibits, which now tour the world, there is the entire story. It is a history of grown-ups, projects, curricula that are emerging, but above all, it is about the children.

## CONCLUSION

**Gandini:** *We are at the end of our conversation; you have offered much food for thought but not spoiled our appetite for learning more. We are eager to have other opportunities for exchanges with you and the wonderfully competent and warm people who work side by side with you. The host of bright and hopeful ideas and experiences you have been bringing to children in Reggio Emilia now travels far beyond the confines of your city.*

**Malaguzzi:** This experience and my account of it have no leave-taking. My words instead carry a greeting to our American friends who, like us, are interested in helping children hold their heads high, our friends moreover toward whom we are culturally indebted.

If at the end any message is still needed, it is a message of reflection. I do not know how adult the world of adults really is. I know that the rich, adult world hides many things, while the poor one knows neither how nor what to hide. One of the things that it hides with the most rigor and callousness is the condition of children. I will refrain from detailing the data about death and desperation. I know that my account is a luxury; it is a privilege because the children of whom I speak live in the rich world.

But also in this world, deception continues, at times cynical and violent, at times more subtle and sophisticated, laced with hypocrisy and illiberal theories. Deception infiltrates even the institutions of early education. The continuing motivation for our work has in fact been an attempt to oppose, albeit with modest means, this deception and to liberate hopes for a new human culture of childhood. It is a motive that finds its origin in a powerful nostalgia for the future and for mankind.

And now, if you will indulge a weakness on my part, I propose a toast to Benjamin, the youngest child of Howard Gardner and Ellen Winner. Gardner (1989) tells of his trip to China in his book, *To Open Minds,* which I have just finished reading, and not without emotion. Why Benjamin? Because with the key that he earnestly tries to insert in a lock, he can in a way stand for all the children of whom we have been talking. Let us come closer, observe his action, and join in his adventure. It is his, and our, hope.

## REFERENCES

Bruner, J. (1986). *Actual minds, possible worlds.* Cambridge, MA: Harvard University Press.

Carr, W. (1986). *Becoming critical: Education, knowledge, and action research.* Philadelphia, PA: Falmer Press.

Gardner, H. (1989). *To Open Minds: Chinese clues to the dilemma of contemporary education.* New York: Basic Books.

Hawkins, D. (1966). Learning the unteachable. In L. Shulman & E. Keislar (Eds.), *Learning by discovery: A critical appraisal.* Chicago, IL: Rand McNally.

Malaguzzi, L. (1971). *Esperienza per una nuova scuola dell 'infanzia.* Rome, Italy: Editori Riuniti.

Malaguzzi, L. (1971). *La gestione sociale nella scuola dell 'infanzia.* Rome, Italy: Editori Riuniti.

Pessoa, F. (1986). *Il libro dell' inquietudine*. Milano, Italy: Fertrinelli.

Piaget, J. (1962). *Comments on Vygotsky's critical remarks*. Cambridge, MA: MIT Press.

Piaget, J. (1971). *Biology and knowledge*. Chicago, IL: The University of Chicago Press.

Piaget, J. (1974). *To understand is to invent*. New York: Grossman.

Rodari, G. (1973). *Grammatica della fantasia*. Torino, Italy: Einaudi.

Vygotsky, L.S. (1978). *Mind in society: The development of higher psychological processes*. Cambridge, MA: Harvard University Press.

Wertheimer, M. (1945). *Productive Thinking*. New York: Harper and Row.

Sergio Spaggiari, Director of
Early Childhood Education in
Reggio Emilia.

# 4

# The Community–Teacher Partnership in the Governance of the Schools

## An Interview with Lella Gandini*

### Sergio Spaggiari

This is how the children at the Michelangelo School see the Advisory
Council:

> "It is a committee where people ask questions."
> "Somebody asks a question and somebody else answers."
> "They make long speeches, like this . . blah . . blah . . blah."
> "I think it is a kind of Parliament."
> "Yes, yes a Parliament!"

---

* Translated by Victoria Poletto and Lella Gandini.

**Gandini:** *One of the most difficult organizational concepts to under-stand in the educational approach for young children at Reggio Emilia is that of "social" (or community) participation. Could you describe how this concept came into being?*

**Spaggiari:** It is a long story. Let me begin by emphasizing that from the 1970s on, the idea of community participation in education has had official backing. It has been viewed as a means of fostering innovation, protecting educational institutions against the dangers of excessive bureaucracy, and stimulating cooperation between educators and parents. This participation has evolved into two different forms: first, through the system of community-based management (what we call *gestione sociale*) in the infant-toddler centers and preprimary schools run by the city; and second, through committees in the public schools, with wide representation at every level—primary, middle, and secondary. I am going to speak about the first.

Community-based participation in infant-toddler centers and preprimary schools goes back a long way. We can trace its roots back to the extraordinary educational experiences which developed immediately after the Liberation of Italy in 1945 in certain regions of Italy (Emilia Romagna and Tuscany), thanks to the initiative and participation of women's groups, ex-resistance fighters (ex-partisans), unions, and cooperatives—all directly involved in promoting educational and welfare services. These initiatives embraced people across the social spectrum and from the very beginning emphasized the values of cooperation and involvement.

The first examples of this involvement were the "school-city" committees which were specifically formed to democratically administer schools for young children, and involved both the people who were connected with the school and those periferal to it. These organizations were created with the specific purpose of "inventing" a school that would involve parents, teachers, citizens, and neighborhood groups not only in the running of the school but also in defending the rights of children.

Furthermore, although the most active and vibrant models of participation were begun by municipal administrations led by political progressives and leftists, we should point out that there is also a clear link between these models and traditional Catholic support for the role of the family and the community, as evidenced through the extended network of parochial preschools.

**Gandini:** *What exactly is the role of community-based management, and how was it developed and formalized?*

**Spaggiari:** In 1971, the idea of participation was finally formalized with the passage of national laws governing infant-toddler centers.

This concept was one that had gradually evolved over several decades, and finally led to the legal formalization of community-based management. It was in large part the concrete realization of the sustaining slogans of many union and political battles dating back to earlier times. The demand was for the national government to provide public funding, the regional governments to take care of overall planning, and the municipal governments to be responsible for community-based management.

Therefore, in order for the experience of participation to remain valid and vital and not be left to the whims and fancies of the moment, it must be guided by clear and thoughtful pedagogical considerations. Such guidance comes from the municipal administration and the continuity of experience provided to the children and families by the system of infant-toddler centers and preprimary schools.

In the last 15 years, in our country, this experience of community-based management has been consolidated both in infant-toddler centers and preprimary schools. It now encompasses, in both its organizational and educational form, all the processes of participation, democracy, collective responsibility, problem solving, and decision making—processes all integral to an educational institution. Community-based management embodies the theoretical and practical synthesis of the interrelationships forged between children, families, service providers, and society at large.

The experience of community-based management has shown its true worth in its ability to adapt to new cultural and social situations such as the influx of newcomers and the recent tendency of parents to view the world in individual rather than political or ideological terms.

**Gandini:** *How does the idea of community-based management fit in with your overall educational approach in Reggio?*

**Spaggiari:** At this point the goals of community-based management are an integral part of the content and methods of our educational approach. They are central to the educational experience in the infant-toddler centers and preprimary schools here in Reggio Emilia.

The community-based management in these centers and schools seeks to promote strong interaction and communication among educators, children, parents, and community. Community-based management enhances the worth of an educational approach that has its origins and objectives in the principles of communication and solidarity. The participation of the families is just as essential as is the participation of children and educators.

Obviously, such a "three-party" system is part of the community at large, which in turn becomes the fourth component, having its own particular influence and worth.

In short, community-based management is not so much a system of governing as it is a philosophical ideal permeating all aspects of the entire educational experience.

Seen in this context, participation in general, and community-based management in particular, are central to the educational experience. That is, you cannot separate them from the choices of content and method in the infant-toddler centers and in the preprimary schools. They carry equal importance and weight in the individual growth of all children, particularly in this age group. The years between birth and six must be seen as a precious resource of human potential, in which a forward-looking society must be prepared to invest responsibly.

**Gandini:** *In the last 10 years in Italy there has been a drop in the birth rate, which has brought with it a change in the structure of young families. What effect has this phenomenon had on participation?*

**Spaggiari:** As a consequence of this drop in the birth rate, today's child is perceived as a rare and precious object. However, in an aging society like ours, a child is also considered a disruptive presence, almost an intruder, in a world not in tune with the child's needs and rights. For these very reasons, the education of children in this age group presents a most difficult and complex task. The enormous responsibilities of this task cannot be undertaken single handedly by either the family or the school.

There is a much stronger awareness on the part of parents today that the job of educating a child involves much support and solidarity, much sharing of ideas, many encounters, a plurality of views, and above all different competencies. It is precisely because families with only one child feel isolated that they will take the initial step toward meeting and working with others. The types of group support that come from participation and community-based management provide a response to the psychological needs of such families. They facilitate a dialogue between the parent and the child, between educators and parents, between groups of educators and different families, and eventually extending to involve the whole community. The idea of seeking solutions collectively, as is done in many municipal education programs in Italy, is contrary to the popular notion that families tend to see problems in narrow, private terms.

**Gandini:** *What are the duties of the Advisory Council in community-based management?*

**Spaggiari:** In light of the above-mentioned changes, the role of the Advisory Council has evolved over time. Besides continuing to support the needs of the city, the main role of the Advisory Council has shifted from administrative concerns (e.g., enrollment, fees) and political choices (e.g., new centers) to expressly addressing the needs of families and educators. The Advisory Council has therefore become the initiator and main vehicle of participation in all its complex aspects.

**Gandini:** *Who serves on the Advisory Council?*

**Spaggiari:** Every two years the parents, educators, and townspeople elect representatives to the Advisory Council from among themselves for each infant-toddler center and preprimary school. There are 33 such schools in the town of Reggio Emilia and consequently there are 33 Advisory Councils. Two or three representatives from each Advisory Council are elected to sit on the Municipal Board on Infant-Toddler and Preprimary Education, together with the Administrative Director of Early Education (myself), the team of *Pedagogisti*, and the elected city official in charge of education (the *Assessore*), and the Mayor.

In recent years 66 percent of the parents have voted in the elections for the Advisory Councils. And many have served. For example, in 1988, out of 2,215 families using our municipal early childhood services, 611 parents were elected; that means that one out of three families participated in the running of the infant-toddler centers and preprimary schools.

The Advisory Council in a preprimary school with an enrollment of 75 children might be composed of 19 parents, 13 educators, and 7 townspeople. Within each Advisory Council a group of volunteers takes care of administration: They draw up agendas and emergency plans, they process parental concerns and proposals, and so on. Other members serve on different committees with specific objectives. For example, they study and implement strategies to maximize parental participation; they organize meetings on special subjects such as children's sleep problems or the need to repaint the dining hall of a school; they consider activities to facilitate the transition between infant-toddler center and preprimary school, or between preprimary and primary school; and so on. They also coordinate work sessions, monitor implementation, and assess the results of the work done.

This shift in the role of the Advisory Council over the last few years has proved to be particularly effective within the framework of the individual classes in each school.

**Gandini:** *In what specific ways do infant-toddler centers and preprimary schools involve parents?*

**Spaggiari:** First of all, since discussion and decision making are done collectively within each school, parents are highly involved. In addition, by widening the field of participation, the educators who par-

**Table 4.1.  Organizational Chart of the Early Childhood Education System in Reggio Emilia, Italy**

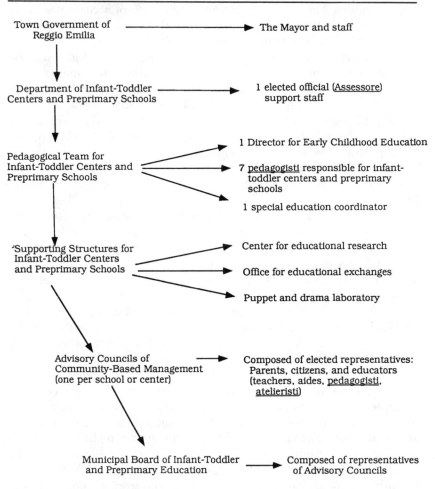

Source: "An Historical Outline, Data, and Information," page 24, published by the Municipality of Reggio Emilia, Department of Education, December 1990. Reprinted by permission.

ticipate in community-based management include all types of adults working in the schools—teachers, cooks, aides—all of whom must share the responsibility which stems from being part of a community of educators. The ideas and skills that the families bring to the school and, even more importantly, the exchange of ideas between parents and teachers, favors the development of a new way of educating, and helps teachers to view the participation of families not as a threat but as an intrinsic element of collegiality and as the integration of different wisdoms.

In order to achieve this, it is necessary, long before a child ever comes to school, to provide children, parents, and teachers with many different opportunities for interaction, as Loris Malaguzzi has suggested (Chapter 3). Carlina Rinaldi (1985) has listed and described the main opportunities for participation once the school year has begun:

1. *Meetings at the individual classroom level.* Classroom teachers meet with the parents to discuss such things as the happenings within that particular group of children, the pedagogical and practical directions of the group, examples of activities which have taken place (through slides, displays of work, and so on), and the assessment of the educational experiences. Preferably, these meetings should take place in the evening or at a time which is convenient for the majority of families. The agenda should be

**Figure 4.2. Parents and teachers voting to elect representatives to the Advisory Council of the Diana School.**

agreed upon and parents notified well in advance. This type of meeting should be repeated at least five or six times a year.

2. *Small group meetings.* Teachers meet with a small group of parents from their class. The limited number of participants allows for a closer and more personalized discussion of the needs and problems of specific families and particular children. It is useful for the teacher to hold such meetings until all the families have participated at least once during the year.

3. *Individual parent/teacher conferences.* These are usually requested by a family or suggested by the educators and can either deal with specific problems related to a particular family or child or offer the opportunity for in-depth discussion regarding the development of the personality of the child.

4. *Meetings around a theme.* These meetings are initiated and conducted by parents and educators and are open to all those connected with the center or the school who are interested in discussing or widening their knowledge of a specific subject. Such themes might include the role of the father, children's fears, and so on. The topic in question is debated and analyzed by all the people present, thus providing everybody with the opportunity to exchange ideas and points of view.

5. *Encounters with an expert.* These encounters take the form of a lecture or round table discussion and might involve many schools. They are tailored to increase everybody's knowledge of problems or issues of common interest, for example, fairytales, children's sexuality, books for young children, children's diet, and so on.

6. *Work sessions.* These are opportunities to contribute in a concrete way to the improvement of the school. Parents and teachers come together to build furnishings and equipment, rearrange the educational space, improve the school yard, and maintain classroom materials.

7. *Labs.* In these "learning by doing" meetings, parents and teachers acquire techniques with a strong educational potential, such as working with paper (origami), making puppets, working with the shadow theater, using photographic equipment, and so on. One such example is "the cooking practicum" where the cook and parents of new children together prepare dishes on the menu which may be hitherto unfamiliar to them.

8. *Holidays and celebrations.* These are group activities where children, parents, grandparents, friends, and townspeople come together. Sometimes they involve the whole school, sometimes just a particular class. Examples of celebrated events include children's birthdays, a grandparent's visit, the end of the year, seasonal occurrences, and so on.

**Figure 4.3.** "Meeting of the Advisory Council." Drawing by children of the Michelangelo School.

9. *Other meeting possibilities.* Trips into town, picnics, excursions, short holidays at the seaside or in the mountains, staying in city-owned hostels, are possibilities. One special event is "a day at the school" when a parent spends the whole day with his or her child's class. Other activities involve small groups visiting each other homes, or the whole group spending some time in a specific place, for example, the gym, swimming pool, main city square, or the market.

**Gandini:** *So, to conclude, could you summarize what you think are the key requirements for sustaining a successful program of participation?*

**Spaggiari:** Yes, the cardinal elements that support a rich network of meetings include these two things: (a) a diversity of activities which meet the various interests, needs, and aspirations of different families; and (b) a focus on the classroom unit as the natural place of encounter for those who are interested in the educational experience of the school, and the starting point to becoming involved in the wider life of the community. Within this diversified context, the Advisory Council takes on a new and wider significance. It can be seen as the driving force behind participation, making possible those infinite ways of coming together presented above. In an educational experience that is truly shared, choices and decisions have to be made with the widest possible consensus, and with a deep respect for a plurality of ideas and viewpoints.

## REFERENCES

Rinaldi, C. (1985). L'elaborazione comunitaria del progetto educativo. In R. Vianello (Ed.), *Stare con i bambini: Il sapere degli educatori.* Bergamo, Italy: Juvenilia.

**Carlina Rinaldi,** *pedagogista.*

# 5

# The Emergent Curriculum and Social Constructivism

## An Interview with Lella Gandini*

### Carlina Rinaldi

In recent years educators in Italy have been involved in a debate about planning curriculum and activities with children under six years of age. Two contrasting points of view have been put forward. The first defines planning as a method of work that establishes in advance general educational objectives along with specific objectives for each activity. The second defines planning as a method of work in which the teachers lay out general educational objectives, but do not formulate the specific goals for each project or each activity in advance. They

---

* Translated by Lella Gandini and Baji Rankin.

formulate instead hypotheses of what could happen on the basis of their knowledge of the children and of previous experiences. Along with these hypotheses they formulate objectives that are flexible and adapted to the needs and interests of the children. These interests and needs include those expressed by children at any time during the project as well as those the teachers infer and bring out as the work proceeds. This second type of planning we call "emergent curriculum."

Carlina Rinaldi, who for 20 years has worked side by side with Loris Malaguzzi, has participated in this Italian debate over curriculum planning, and along with her colleagues in Reggio Emilia, has championed this second type of planning—emergent curriculum. She describes the ample basis upon which planning is designed and how it is constructed, with regards to the education of children in their schools.

**Gandini:** *Could you describe to me your basic principles in working with young children in your schools:*

**Rinaldi:** To better understand why and how we in Reggio Emilia have made certain choices on an educational, political, and didactic organizational level, and in particular with regard to planning using an "emergent curriculum," it is necessary to clarify some fundamental paradigms we refer to in constructing our educational approach in Reggio Emilia, known in the United States as the "Reggio Emilia Approach." First of all, I want to state that our experience and the processes connected with it have been shared not only with the children and teachers, but also with the families. Everything has been accomplished within the context of a city that was and is still able to plan ahead, but most importantly has been able to provide a coherent direction for schools, making occasionally difficult choices that involve both quantity and quality as an inseparable pair. The schools are not, therefore, "experimental" schools. They are, rather, part of a public system that has strived to combine the child's welfare and the social needs of families with the fundamental human rights of the child. This approach combines the concepts of social services with those of education, as we do not see these two as antithetical. In fact, schooling for us is a system of relations and communications embedded in the wider social system.

One point among many appears to us to be fundamental and basic: the image of the children. The cornerstone of our experience, based on practice, theory, and research, is the image of the children as rich, strong, and powerful. The emphasis is placed on seeing the children as unique subjects with rights rather than simply needs. They have potential, plasticity, the desire to grow, curiosity, the ability to be amazed, and the desire to relate to other people and to communicate. Their need and right to communicate and interact with others emerges

**Figure 5.1.  A 3-year-old child involved in exploration with Giovanni Piazza, *atelierista* of the Villetta School.**

at birth and is essential element for survival and identification with the species. This probably explains why children are so eager to express themselves within the context of a plurality of symbolic languages, and why children are also very open to exchanges and reciprocity as deeds and acts of love which they not only want to receive but also want to offer. These form the basis of their ability to experience authentic growth, dependent on the elements listed above, as well as on conflict and error.

All of these potentials are expressed and achieved first and foremost within a group learning context. This fact has involved us in a continuous search for an educational approach that breaks rank with traditional education. We are talking about an approach based on listening rather than speaking, where doubt and amazement are welcome factors along with scientific inquiry and the deductive method of the detective. It is an approach in which the importance of the unexpected and the possible are recognized, an approach where educators know how to waste time, or better yet, know how to give back to the children all of the time that they need. It is an approach which protects originality and subjectivity without creating isolation of the individual and offers to children the possibility of confronting special situations and problems as members of small peer groups. This approach requests that adults—both teachers and parents—offer themselves as resource people to whom the children can (and want to) turn. The task of these resource people is not simply to satisfy or answer questions, but instead to help children discover answers and, more importantly still, to help them ask themselves good questions.

**Gandini:** *I see how this attitude on the part of educators can make your interventions with the children rewarding and stimulating. Could you describe some aspects of the work of teachers as they plan together a curriculum adaptable to the evolving ideas and explorations of children?*

**Rinaldi:** In our work, we speak of planning, as being understood in the sense of preparation and organization of space, materials, thoughts, situations, and occasions for learning. These allow for exchange and communication between the three protagonists and interactive partners of the school: children, educators, and families. The educational institution is, in fact, a system of communication and interaction among the three protagonists, integrated into the larger social system.

Given this system in its complexity, it can be understood why the potential of children is stunted when the endpoint of their learning is formulated in advance. Instead, at the initiation of a project, the teachers should get together and discuss fully all the possible ways that the project should be anticipated to evolve, considering the likely ideas, hypotheses, and choices of children. By so doing they prepare themselves for all the subsequent stages of the project—even should the unexpected occur.

To carry out its primary task, however, the school must sustain the children's total welfare, as well as the welfare of parents and teachers. The system of relationships is so highly integrated that the well-being of each of the three protagonists depends on the others. There must be mutual awareness of rights, needs, and pleasures and attention paid to the quantity and quality of social occasions that create a system of permanent relations. The full participation of families is thus an integral part of the educational experience. Indeed, we consider the family to be a pedagogical unit that cannot be separated from the school.

Thus, because educational institutions, like the infant-toddler centers and the preprimary schools, are complex ecological systems, rich in bonding and resources, with the potential for self-regulation, they would be asphyxiated by before-the-fact planning.

**Gandini:** *You have described your educational experience as containing these strong elements of social interaction and at the same time as being constructivist. In fact, you have described the child as "a social constructivist." Could you tell me more about these concepts?*

**Figure 5.2.   A parent visits the school with her children.**

**Rinaldi:** The emphasis of our educational approach is placed not so much upon the child in an abstract sense, but on each child in relation to other children, teachers, parents, his or her own history, and the societal and cultural surroundings. Relationships, communications, and interactions sustain our educational approach in its complexity; they are powerful terms characterized by two important elements: action and group socialization. We consider them to be fundamental structuring elements toward the construction of each child's identity.

It is our belief that all knowledge emerges in the process of self- and social construction. Therefore, the teacher must establish a personal relationship with each child and ground this relationship in the social system of the school. Children, in turn, do not just passively endure their experience, but also become active agents in their socialization, co-constructed with their peers. Their actions can be understood as more than just responses to the social environment, they can also be considered as mental structurings developed by the child through social interaction. Obviously, there is a strong cause and effect relationship between social and cognitive development, a sort of spiral which is sustained by cognitive conflict that modifies both the cognitive and social system.

Conflict is an essential element, in our view. Conflict transforms the relationships a child has with peers—opposition, negotiation, taking the other's point of view, and reformulating an initial premise—as part of the processes of assimilation and accommodation into the group. We see these dynamics, until a short time ago considered part of the socialization process, to be also substantially cognitive procedures.

Now you can see the issues in their full richness but also in their complexity. The adults' difficulty is to initiate and nurture situations that stimulate this kind of educational process, where conflict and negotiation appear as the "driving forces" for growth. An emergent curriculum is the one that allows for this social constructivist process to develop.

**Gandini:** *Planning without preconceived objectives is connected, therefore, to the relationships between teachers, children, and the social network. The goal is to allow for the child to make choices, communicate those choices, and receive feedback from others. And all that contributes to the construction of knowledge. Is that correct?*

**Rinaldi:** Yes. And I would like to clarify another important issue that I feel deserves special attention. This concerns the role of the adult. The challenge for the adult is to be present without being intrusive in order to best sustain cognitive and social dynamics while they are in progress. At times, the adult must foster productive conflict by challenging the responses of one or several children. At other times, the adult must step in to revive a situation where children are losing interest because the cognitive map that is being constructed is either beyond or beneath the child's present capabilities. Always the teacher remains an attentive observer, and beyond that, a researcher. The teacher's observations and transcribed tapes are taken to colleagues for group reflection. They produce discussion and conflict within each educator's self and the group at large, and these are as important as the preceding conflicts and discussions among the children. The teachers' reflections then modify, at times radically, their thoughts and hypotheses about the children and, even more importantly, their interactions with the children. With all this, it should not be forgotten how important the role of the adult is in providing the children with a stimulating environment, materials, and equipment.

**Gandini:** *You spoke before about the value of working with a small group of children. Could you elaborate further on the size of the group that is working on a project?*

**Rinaldi:** It is another aspect very important to us. Loris Malaguzzi, the founder of our program, has considered carefully what aspects are affected by group size. A group of two children produces extraordinarily rich dynamics in both a social and cognitive sense. The younger the child, the more beneficial is the dyadic situation, and both children and adults can fully take advantage of its benefits. It offers the child

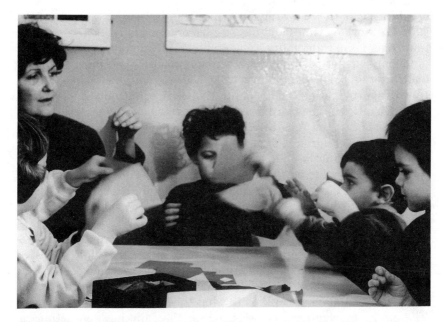

**Figure 5.3.   A teacher and a group of children engaged with colored paper.**

the possibility of really understanding the rhythm of the communication and the task of adjusting oneself to another. The child can learn to recognize changes in styles of communication, as well as changes in topic. The teachers observing will also acquire the same understanding and learning. A group of three children produces very different dynamics. Due in part to the uneven number of children, there are many possibilities not only for solidarity and alliance, but also for separation and conflict. In a similar way, a group of four offers different possibilities than does a group of five. After much consideration we have concluded that in order to maximize the cognitive learning process, group size should be limited to five. Beyond this number, group dynamics become too complex and the sheer number of interactors too many to allow each child to evaluate and transform his or her knowledge and identity through a constantly changing knowledge of others' identities.

To do all this, and make all our concepts become real, requires strong, constant willingness and availability by the organization as a whole. We must also engage in a continuous process of evaluation and adaptation of our methodology and our political choices, because they are also part of our educational approach. In our view everything is connected and influences the system. We have to see to *planning and organization* of the following four aspects: first, there is *the work of the staff*. We work on times and modes of communication, always striving toward ideals of collegiality, competence, professionalism, and teacher autonomy, and stressing growth through in-service training. The second factor is *participation*. We believe in the value of school-family rapport, participation, and community-based management (see Spaggiari, Chapter 4). The third factor concerns *the environment:* the architecture, spaces, the furniture. The last factor concerns *the activities* involving the children. Of course, all of these aspects are interdependent. There cannot be, for example, a planning of activities without professional rapport between adults, and without environment being organized and enriched so as to sustain our educational approach.

   **Gandini:** *Could you give us an example of your emergent curriculum planning and tell us about a specific project?*

   **Rinaldi:** A project, which we view as a sort of adventure and research, can start through a suggestion from an adult, a child's idea, or from an event, such as a snowfall or something else unexpected. But every project is based on the attention of the educators to what the children say and do, as well as to what they do not say and do not do. The adults must allow enough time for the thinking and actions of children to develop.

   An example of one of the projects is the one called "The Crowd" (a project carried out at the Scuola Diana, documented by Vea Vecchi, overseen by Loris Malaguzzi). It began at the end of a school year in a classroom of 4–5-year-olds. The teachers, in preparation for the long summer vacation ahead, discussed with the children the idea of saving memories and fragments of their upcoming experiences during the holidays. Although the summer marks an interruption of the school year, our commitment to the children remains in force and we try to find ways to keep their interest in learning alive during the vacation months. So the teachers discuss with children ideas and also propose them to the parents. In this case, each family agreed to take along on their vacation sites a box with small compartments in which their child could save treasures, be it a shell from the beach or a tiny rock from the mountains or a leaf of grass. Every fragment, every piece collected would become a memento of an experience imbued with a sense of discovery and emotion.

   In the fall, therefore, when the children returned to school, the teachers were ready to revive those memories with questions such as: "What did your eyes see?" "What did your ears hear?" and so on. The teachers expected to hear stories about days spent at the beach or hiking, and to learn about the sight of boats, waves, and sunsets, but instead the children in this classroom brought a very different perspective. Because the children could express themselves vividly, and because the teachers could ask the right questions, an adventure in learning began quite unexpectedly. What happened was this. A little boy, Gabriele, sharing his experience said, "Sometimes we went to the pier. We walked through a narrow long street, called 'the gut,' where one store is next to another, and where in the evening it is full of people. There are people who go up, and people who walk down. You cannot see anything, you can only see a crowd of legs, arms, and heads."

The teachers immediately caught the word "crowd" and asked other children what it meant to them. By doing so the adventure in learning, a project, was launched. The word "crowd" turned out to be fantastically rich, almost explosive, in the meanings it contained for these children. The teachers immediately apprehended an unusual excitement and potential in this word. Here what some of the children said:

*Stefano:*   "It is a bag full of people all crowded in."
*Nicola:*    "It is a bunch of people all attached and close to one another."
*Luca:*      "There are people who jump on you and push you."
*Clara:*     "It is like a congested place when it is a holiday."
*Giorgia:*   "There are lots of people who are going to see a soccer game . . . who are going to see the game, really they are all males."
*Ivano:*     "It is a bunch of people all bunched up together just like when they go to pay taxes."

After the group discussion, the teachers asked the children to draw their thoughts and words about the crowd. But upon looking at the children's drawings they observed that the level of representation in their drawings was discrepant from the level of their verbal descriptions. The project was put on hold for a couple of days, during which time the teachers asked themselves: What's going on here? How can we help the children to integrate their different symbolic languages? How can we make the children become aware of their own process of learning? So the teachers waited for a couple of days and then gave the children a chance to listen to their earlier comments (which had been taped and transcribed, so they could be read aloud, while they looked at the drawings and commented on each other's work).

The teacher now noticed a further growth in the children's vocabulary as they expanded on their stories. And the images prepared in a second set of drawings became more elaborate and detailed. For example, Teresa, thinking back on her memory of the "crowd" said, "It goes left, right, forward, and when they forget something, they go back." But Teresa then confronted a puzzle: She noticed that her statements

**Figure 5.4.   Three children construct together a building out of folded paper.**

did not match her drawing, for the figures on her paper were all facing forward. She seemed uncomfortable, and then before all her friends, came up with a marvelous explanation. She said that in the drawing she had shown only a piece of the crowd with people who did not forget anything, and that is why they were all walking forward. Also Federico had a problem with his drawing because in it everyone faced forward except the dog who was in profile. He admitted he was only able to draw dogs this way. Ivano expressed concern about his drawing saying that if people kept walking forward, as he had drawn them, they would smash against the wall.

At this point, there was unanimous desire expressed by the children to learn more about how to draw people from the rear and their profile. The teachers' role was to sustain and support this process. They asked one girl, Elisa, to stand in the middle of the room surrounded by small groups of children placed at different vantage points where they could observe her, describe her body and position, and draw her from four angles: front, back, right, and left. Through this process the children learned a great deal about the difficult concept of point of view. One child concluded: "We put ourselves in a square, and Elisa has four sides just like us."

The teachers also wanted to take the children outside the school—a typical step in our project work. Children and teacher went to the center of town where they observed and photographed people coming and going in the busy streets. Children mingled with the people, becoming, once again, "the crowd." A few days later the slides of that day were projected on the classroom wall, and the children enjoyed those images, moving through their reflections. Then they made more drawings, and Teresa proudly came up with a picture of herself, her boyfriend, and a dog all in profile! At this point the children, as they often do, cut out the figures to add, as in a collage, to their earlier drawings. This evoked many questions. "Can we put together in a crowd people undressed for the beach and people dressed up for the promenade?" "Can we put together people of different sizes?" In this latter instance children remembered that they had used the photocopy machine to reduce drawings and they decided they should now use it again to make people bigger or smaller so they could look "normal." The teachers also encouraged the children to use the cut-out figures for puppet play, dramatization, and shadow play. They also sculpted figures from clay. Finally, the children concluded their exploration with a collective project in which they superimposed in a box many of their figures to create "a crowd" just as Teresa had said, "that goes left, right, forward and when they forget something, they go back."

Looking at this one example of the extraordinary capacity of children, it will be understandable how in my work with children I have come to the conclusion that it is very important to be able to grow with them. We reinvent and reeducate ourselves along with the children. Not only does our knowledge organize theirs, but also the children's ways of being and dealing with reality likewise influences what we know, feel, and do.

Tiziana Filippini, *pedagogista.*

# 6

# The Role of the *Pedagogista*
## An Interview with Lella Gandini*

**Tiziana Filippini**

**Gandini:** *We would like to hear, from your own perspective and experience, how the role of the pedagogista has taken shape. How is the pedagogista a supporting part of the system in Reggio Emilia?*

**Filippini:** I've been working as a *pedagogista* since about 1978. The word, *pedagogista* cannot really be translated into English. One could say coordinator or "educational advisor," but neither of these is exactly right. Another reason the role is difficult to explain is that it has to be understood in terms of the image we hold of the child, the role of the

---

* Translated by Lella Gandini and Carolyn Edwards.

teacher, the place of the families and community, and all other basic premises and principles described by Loris Malaguzzi (Chapter 3).

In Italy, the role of *pedagogista* is quite a new professional position. It is difficult to define precisely because it has evolved differently in different places. But, in general, the role of *pedagogista* emerged when during the 1960s and 1970s a few municipalities began to open pre-primary schools and to run them directly. As the establishment of city-run infant-toddler centers (starting in 1971) and preprimary schools took place slowly and unevenly across the towns and cities of Italy, *pedagogista* appeared first and most predominantly in Northern Italy, with somewhat different definitions of duties in various locales.

In Reggio Emilia, we have a city administration running a complex system of centers and schools for children aged 0–6 years, all under the municipal government. We have an elected official at the head. Then, serving under this Assessore, we have appointed directors, including a Director of Early Childhood Education (for many years Loris Mala-guzzi, but presently Sergio Spaggiari), who coordinates a staff of nine including seven *pedagogisti*, a coordinator of special education, and a curriculum specialist in theater.

**Gandini:** *You said before that—as with all aspects of work in Reggio—the role of pedagogista is based on a certain image of the child.*

**Filippini:** Our image of the child has evolved out of our collective experience and a continually reexamined understanding of education-al philosophy and psychological theory. For us, each child is unique and the protagonist of his or her own growth. We also note that children desire to acquire knowledge, have much capacity for curiosity and amazement, and yearn to create relationships with others and to communicate. Children are so open to exchange and reciprocity. From early in life they negotiate with the social and physical world—with everything the culture brings to them. And starting with this idea, we have tried to create the school as a system in which everything is connected.

The *pedagogista* is included in this system of relations. The func-tions of the *pedagogista* in Reggio Emilia are multiple. I cannot inter-act with just one part of the system and leave the rest aside, because that would injure the system.

In my work I deal with city administrators and employees of many kinds: elected officials, civil service employees, and representatives of cultural and scientific groups. All seven *pedagogista* meet once a week with our director to discuss policy and problems related to the whole network of preprimary schools and infant-toddler centers. Each of us has certain specific responsibilities. For example, I work closely with several preprimary schools and infant-toddler centers and also have particular duties regarding communication with foreign visitors. But all of us must engage in a continuous exchange of information regarding what is happening within the schools, new advances in theory and practice, and political developments. We see ourselves as constantly transforming and growing professionally through exchange within the group. Our work in Reggio Emilia as *pedagogisti* requires constant striving for clarity and openness, one to another.

In my work at the schools I interact with all the adults to help sustain and implement the philosophy of our system. Many of the things I do involve issues of basic organization, the "backbone" of the system conceived as an organism. Just to give a few examples, I deal with issues of scheduling, staff assignments and responsibilities, workloads and shifts. I deal with issues about the physical environment, for example, reflecting on the needs and goals with parents and teachers and then sharing these reflections with an architect who designs building renovations or with parents and teachers who build new equipment.

**Gandini:** *As pedagogista, how do you support the work of teachers?*

**Filippini:** It is the responsibility of the *pedagogista* to work with teachers to identify new themes and experiences for continuous professional development and in-service training. This is a delicate task because of the insufficient basic preparation of many of our teachers. But we believe that the highest level of teaching is best achieved through work experience, supported by continuous reflection and enrichment. Teachers in our system each do about 190 hours a year of work outside the classroom, including 107 hours of in-service training, 43 hours of meetings with parents and committees (this is all part of

**Figure 6.1.** In-service training involves teachers of several schools working together, guided by the *pedagogista*.

our community-based management, see Spaggiari, Chapter 4), and about 40 hours for other seminars, workshops, school parties, and so on. The *pedagogista* works to promote within herself and among teachers an attitude of "learning to learn" (as John Dewey called it), an openness to change, and a willingness to discuss opposing points of view. Working with the other *pedagogisti*, I help organize in-service training meetings for teachers. For example—given the complexity of their roles—there must be a diversity of meetings that touch on issues of educational theory, teaching techniques, and sound social relations and communication. We help teachers improve their skills of observing and listening to children, documenting projects, and conducting their own research. During the course of the year there will be separate meetings for infant-toddler center versus preprimary school teachers— for instance, meetings dealing with issues of child development and guidance—and then also there will be joint meetings. There will be workshops devoted to the acquisition of technical skills, for example, the design and preparation of posters to document project work and explain the school to parents and visitors. Or an outside expert might be invited to give a lecture on some topic of new interest. Also, we make it possible for the adults to participate in open discussions or forums dealing with contemporary scientific and cultural debates; we always hold such a series every March and April, open to parents, teachers, and the citizens of the city.

Then, of course, I work closely with the teachers at my particular schools regarding all sorts of educational issues and problems concerning children, where my ultimate goal is always to promote teachers' autonomy rather than take on their problems and solve them for them. Particularly for the infant-toddler centers, we are convinced that an essential precondition for effective teaching is the creation of an especially close teacher–parent rapport. Here my work is not directly with the parents, but rather with the teachers. I help them think about problems with communication and interaction and how to organize fruitful exchanges with and among parents.

Certainly, the art of working and sharing with other adults—be they colleagues or teachers—demands a long apprenticeship. It is not easy, but it leads the way to full professional and personal development. My task, collaborating with teachers, is to analyze and interpret the rights and needs of each child and family, and then use this knowledge in our work with children. Equally important is to develop better relationships between parents and teachers and set up meetings so that everyone gets to know one another and the curriculum projects underway can be explored and created together. Educational continu-

**Figure 6.2.  Work session of the *pedagogista* with a pair of teachers from one classroom.**

ity between the school and home is a dialectic process, based on talking and listening. Naturally, problems arise. No single model or method can earn a permanent seal of approval, because things always change.

Finally, the *pedagogista* must be available to support teachers in their daily relationships with individual families. I must be receptive to everyone's expectations, needs, requests, suggestions, delicate concerns, and occasionally stressful relationships. For example, in one of my infant-toddler centers, there is this situation. A teacher has just called me to say that one little child, aged two-and-a-half, is suffering very much. She frequently cries to go home. I asked the teacher what they know about the family and learned that the parents work outside the city, so that during the week the child stays with her grandparents. So I wondered whether shortening the time that the child stays in the afternoon might not be beneficial. Consequently, I will go to the school and observe the little child. And I will, together with the teachers, meet with the parents to work out what might be the cause for the behavior and what might be a solution.

So you can see that the *pedagogista*, as a member of the team of pedagogical coordinators, has the complex and multifaceted task of promoting a cultural and social growth of systems for young children. This is accomplished in a variety of ways, always serving as a resource and reference point for all sorts of initiatives, and always acting as a

**Figure 6.3. Meeting of the pedagogical team.**

link between people and groups, creating a network of resources to build a citywide platform of early childhood education. It's a difficult but energizing role, because it must be constructed as we progress, and because of the way we work as a guiding team interfacing with other teams and groups. This is the way our entire educational experience builds itself inside a systemic outlook.

Vea Vecchi, *atelierista* of the Diana School.

# 7

# The Role of the *Atelierista*
## An Interview with Lella Gandini*

## Vea Vecchi

**Gandini:** *What are the reasons that made you abandon the work you were doing in the middle school and come to work in the atelier of the preprimary schools in Reggio Emilia?*

**Vecchi:** It is very easy to say negative things about the way art education is treated in middle schools in Italy. It is truly marginal there. What attracted me to the preprimary schools in Reggio was, first, the use of visual languages as a construction of thoughts and feelings within a holistic education, and second, the fact that the *atelier* becomes a cultural vehicle for teacher development. This was

---

* Translated by Lella Gandini.

declared to me by Loris Malaguzzi 20 years ago, at the very first meeting we had.

**Gandini:** *The role of atelierista was new and original in Reggio Emilia; it does not exist in other systems in Italy. Has it measured up to your expectations?*

**Vecchi:** Twenty years of work are a clear answer. They have shaped my identity as a person and a woman. The visual language, as interpreted—and constantly reinterpreted—within the wide philosophical perspective of the Reggio approach, provides the possibility to be involved in an ongoing process of communication and confrontation with people of different professional and social backgrounds. This has naturally affected my own personal and professional identity and offered me a way to examine and validate my daily work in an authentic way.

**Gandini:** *Do you think that your training in art school was too narrow—for example, with not enough broad background in the liberal arts, too much focus on technical skills—for such a specific job as being an atelierista with young children?*

**Vecchi:** The art school certainly had old-fashioned methods. But so had the school that formed the other teachers in the classrooms. The artistic training at least gave me an approach to teaching that wasn't overly structured—perhaps freer and with more potential for irony, humor, or pleasure. All in all, I think my artistic training produced a certain freedom of thought which has adapted itself very well to the different styles and attitudes of mind an *atelierista* must take on.

**Gandini:** *How could you define the place of the atelier in such a complex organization as the preprimary school?*

**Vecchi:** The *atelier* serves two functions. First, it provides a place for children to become masters of all kinds of techniques, such as painting, drawing, and working in clay—all the symbolic languages. Second, it assists the adults in understanding processes of how children learn. It helps teachers understand how children invent autonomous vehicles of expressive freedom, cognitive freedom, symbolic freedom, and paths to communication. The *atelier* has an important, provocative, and disturbing effect on old-fashioned teaching ideas. Certainly, Loris Malaguzzi (Chapter 3) has talked about this and expressed our views.

I'm not sure that we have always lived up to the expectations held for us, but I am at least convinced that having the *atelier* in every preprimary school has made a deep impact on the emerging educational identity of our system. Certainly, the *atelier* itself has changed with the passing of time, although the basic philosophy has remained the same. And, of course, the personality and style of each *atelierista* makes each *atelier* a different place.

**Figure 7.1.   Children working in the *atelier*.**

I will try to tell you about the place and significance of the *atelier* in the school where I have worked. In the beginning I read a great deal of literature on children's drawings, about which I then knew almost nothing. At the same time, I talked constantly with teachers, parents, and *pedogogisti*, trying to give them deeper appreciation of what they saw as purely aesthetic activities. At the same time I know that I had prejudgments about art, and I was still virtually blind and deaf when it came to understanding children's drawings and artwork. What I didn't realize was that gaining this understanding would be my ongoing quest from then on.

Working together, guiding the children in their projects, teachers and I have repeatedly found ourselves face-to-face—as if looking in a mirror—learning from one another, and together learning from the children. This way we were trying to create paths to a new educational approach, one certainly not tried before, where the visual language was interpreted and connected to other languages, all thereby gaining in meaning.

The other important function of the *atelier* was to provide a workshop for documentation. Documentation was seen then as a democratic possibility to inform the public of the contents of the schools. Already within six months after I began to work at the Diana School, we opened the school to the citizens with an exhibit of children's work. This work aroused much surprise and even some scandalized reaction, because among the themes displayed were a few usually censored for children, such as the nativity of Jesus and love.

I believe that few schools compare to the ones in Reggio Emilia in the amount of documentation prepared in the form of panels, slides, and now also videotapes—materials to use with the children and families, as well as with teachers in in-service training. For example, in recently reorganizing our Diana archives, we have realized that we have accumulated over 200 different sets of large panels (70 by 100 centimeters) presenting projects or experiences with children. Indeed, over time, our work in Reggio Emilia has tended to involve more and more research, visual education, and documentation. The educational work with children and the documentation have become more and more interconnected and mutually supportive.

Recently our interests have also shifted more and more toward analysis of the processes of learning and the interconnections between children's different ideas, activities, and representations. All of this documentation—the written descriptions, transcriptions of children's words, photographs, and now the videotapes—becomes an indispensable source of materials that we use everyday to be able to "read" and reflect critically, both individually and collectively, on the experience we are living, the project we are exploring. This allows us to construct theories and hypotheses which are not arbitrary and artificially imposed on the children.

Yet his method of work takes much time and is never easy. And we know that we still have much to learn. The camera, tape recorder, slide projector, typewriter, videocamera, computer, and photocopying machine are instruments absolutely indispensible for recording, understanding, debating among ourselves, and finally preparing appropriate documents of our experience.

The roles of the teacher and *atelierista* that emerge from the considerations above are certainly different from how they were conceived 20 years ago when I first came here. They require many competencies, including the capacity to reflect critically, different from what was emphasized before. Yet I am absolutely certain that the presence of the *atelierista* made possible many of the best projects in all of our schools. The environment of the *atelier* becomes a center of culture, where through the years the processes and tools have been modified. The relationship between the *atelierista* and teachers has grown and deepened, affecting in turn the professional relationship between teachers and children.

What has remained constant through time in my work is the way in which I work simultaneously with teachers and children, as well as the way in which I work directly with teachers. I am convinced that it is essential to construct with teachers a broad base of cultural knowledge, reflected in all of the details of our schools. This work requires immense time and effort.

**Gandini:** *I wonder whether through your experience of 20 years you have modified your views and theories or your relationship with the* *children and teachers. Have you discovered new visual and symbolic languages of children?*

**Vecchi:** Besides what I have said before, I can highlight a few things. I can say, first, that I have discovered how creativity is part of the makeup of every individual, and how the "reading" of reality is a subjective and cooperative production, and this is a creative act. Second, I have found it essential to have a high esteem for boys and girls, for men and women, in order to relate to them with genuine interest and curiosity. In the daily exchanges that I have with the children and adults, what has grown palpably is what I gain from them. I wish, although I am not sure, this will also increase what I give back to them. Third, I realize that we have widened a great deal our field of interpretations, both of the processes and the results of our work. Fourth, the field of visual languages used by the children has also widened. As a consequence, in our work we are following new paths, different from the usual and the traditional. For example, we are trying to understand the feminine and masculine ways of representing reality. Fifth, I realize more and more the importance of the work done among the peer groups of children. We spend a great deal of energy in thinking about, and providing, instruments and strategies to support this way of working as a vital act of learning and a path toward social competence and maturity. We do continuously combine educational theories and our empirical research, filtered through our own, never fully adequate, professional lenses. In the school in which I work we are all women. We are curious about the world that we are little by little discovering, the world of children constructing their theories. At times we think that the relationship with the children reawakens in us a sense of our own childhood, creating feelings of tenderness, curiosity, play, and true pleasure.

**Gandini:** *Much of what the children do in your schools is so beautiful. Is this art? Is there an art of children?*

**Vecchi:** The way one should examine what children do is very different from evaluating adult artwork. It happens very often that some of the children's products are so original that one wants to compare them to the work of famous artists. But that kind of comparison becomes dangerous and fraught with ambiguity, especially if one tries to consistently make comparisons. It leads to false conclusions, such as that the behavior of children unfolds innately, or that the product is more important than the process. To make comparisons that go beyond a simple and playful resemblance shows how little one understands either children or artists.

On the other hand, I think that artistic discoveries—conceptual breakthroughs made by artists—should circulate among the adults in

Figure 7.2.    "Little girl telling a story." Clay drawing.

our schools, because we can learn from them. For example, the way artists have solved problems of representing light, combining colors, and creating a sense of volume are all very interesting and help us explore new paths with children.

**Gandini:** *What advice could you give, after 20 years of work, to teachers who work with young children?*

**Vecchi:** I hesitate to give advice. Our research is really an adventure, often exciting and diverting, and how can I give advice about going on an adventure? This pleasure and amusement is taken up by the children in their self-directed process of learning; I wish this would happen more because it works so well. And it should be shared by the teachers.

**Figure 7.3.** "Rhinoceros." Clay sculpture.

**Gandini:** *Tell me more about how you work on a daily basis with teachers.*

**Vecchi:** We meet several times a day. Every morning I do a tour of each classroom. I am particularly interested in what is happening at the beginning of the day, both with regard to the larger ongoing projects and to the smaller, independent activities. Teachers and I briefly talk about how to introduce certain things to the children and what to anticipate, and then what to do about them. Sometimes I also suggest the use of particular materials. Often, in the middle of the morning, I do another circuit, being sure to go where something of particular interest might be happening. Or sometimes, a teacher comes to ask advice or to get me to come and visit. Then, at the end of every morning I find at least 15 minutes to consult with each teacher. And often, we gather as a group for discussion. An important part of my role is to ensure the circulation of ideas among teachers. I am really their constant consultant. Because my training is different from theirs, I can help them see the visual possibilities of themes and projects that are not apparent to them. I may even intervene directly with the children to create possibilities that have not occurred to others. For example, once I noticed that the sun, shining behind one of the trees outside the window, cast a shadow of the leaves onto the glass. I taped a sheet of translucent white paper onto the glass. As children came in that morning, they exclaimed with surprise and pleasure at the sight

Figure 7.4.   Exploring together the mystery of shadows.

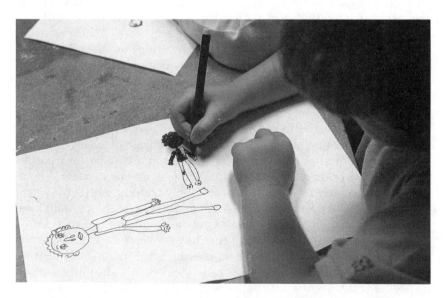

Figure 7.5.   And now she represents her ideas about the shadows.

of the shadow of leaves on the paper. Many things followed. The children even came to use the shadow as a clock. One said, "It's time to go to lunch. Look at the design on the paper!"

Certainly, I closely follow all of our major and longer-term projects. I always find most interesting and wonderful the project on which we are currently working, because it seems to me that with each project we advance and learn a little more, and thereby we work better with the children. For example, we have found that shadows offer extraordinary educational possibilities. This theme, described in our book, *Tutto Ha Un' Ombra Meno Le Formiche (Everything Has a Shadow Except Ants)*[1], involves an integration of acts of visual representation with scientific hypothesis testing. It goes far beyond the emphasis on aesthetic expression and perceptual exploration with which I began my work over 20 years ago.

---

[1] Published by the Comune di Reggio Emilia, 1990

## "THE INTELLIGENCE OF A PUDDLE"
## (DIANA SCHOOL)

When rain leaves a puddle, thanks to the good fortune of there being a hole in the ground and a little sunshine, children are full of joy. If the adults do not place limits and instead play the game, the puddle of water then can become for the children an entire universe to observe.

**Figure 1.** "The water is lazy, but when we walk in it it makes little waves. They get bigger and bigger." "Hey. I can see myself!" "Me too! But the colors are all dirty!" Children exclaim to one another as they explore the puddle.

**Figure 2.** "Help! Hey, guys, we are under water!" "I can touch the top of the tree because this is another world, a world of water."

Figure 3.   The teachers place a mirror on the ground. Children cry out, "Hey, now the colors are right!" "Help, I am falling into the hole of the world!"

All along the children discuss the reflections they see in the water, mirror, and shadows. Trying to make sense of these complex images, they exchange ideas.

Figure 4.   The teachers ask the children to draw trees and people and to place them around a mirror.

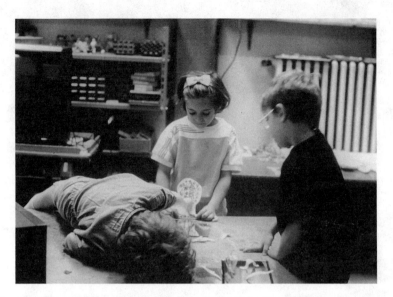

Figure 5. The children remark: "When you are close to a puddle, you see everything, but if you are far away, you see less and less." "But if I put my head down close, I see also the trees that are far away."

Figure 6. The children make more observations as they move the trees and people back and forth and then draw what they have noticed.

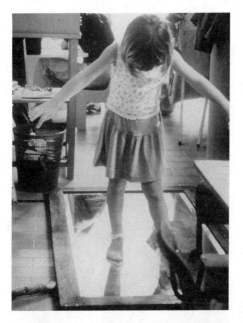

**Figure 7.   Now a child explores her image in the mirror.**

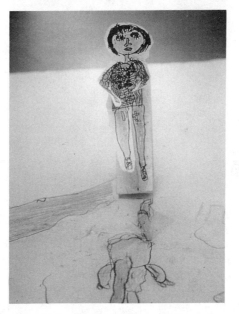

**Figure 8.   She represents how she saw herself, her reflection, and her shadow.**

The children comment: "The shadow is there when the sun is out. But can you see the reflection then also?" "When the sun is out, the reflection looks faded. The light fades everything." "No, you are wrong. The reflection is not close to you; it is deep and it has colors. Instead, it is the shadow that stays close and has no colors but is always dark."

# Part III

# From Theory to Practice

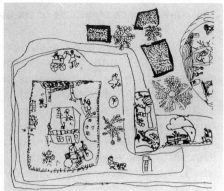

**"Plan of the Diana School,"**
**drawn by 5-year-old children as**
**part of an orientation booklet**
**for new, incoming 3-year-olds.**

# 8

# Educational and
# Caring Spaces

## Lella Gandini

In the entryway of the Diana School a poster compiled by some of that
school's 5-year-olds proclaims *the rights of children:*

> Children have the right to have friends, otherwise they do not grow up
> too well.
>
> Children have the right to live in peace.
>
> To live in peace means to be well, to live together, to live with things
> that interest us, to have friends, to think about flying, to dream.
>
> If a child does not know, she has the right to make mistakes. It works
> because after she sees the problem and the mistakes she made, then she
> knows. (Diana School, 1990)

This is an engaging way for a school to greet parents and teachers.
Next to the poster are photographs of each team of two teachers,
those who teach the 3-, 4-, and 5-year-old children, then photos of the

*atelierista*, the cook, and the auxiliary staff members, along with their names and welcoming smiles. On the same wall are posted schedules of events: teacher-training sessions, meetings with parents of each age group, meetings of the whole school, field trips, and celebrations.

All these messages are addressed to parents and visitors, but the children are also part of this welcome, for on the opposite wall are found photographs of small groups of boys and girls engaged in activities. And below, at the children's eye level, are self-portraits and small, square mirrors that open up like book covers. They reflect the image of the children as they enter, but they also allow for trying out a host of funny faces if one feels like it.

## SPACE AS AN ESSENTIAL ELEMENT OF THE EDUCATIONAL APPROACH

The visitor to any institution for young children tends to size up the messages that the space gives about the quality and care and about the educational choices that form the basis of the program. We all tend to notice the environment and "read" its messages or meanings on the basis of our own ideas. We can, though, improve our ability to analyze deeper layers of meaning if we observe the extent to which everyone involved is at ease and how everyone uses the space itself. We then can learn more about the relationships among children and adults who spend time there.

Educators in the United States are well aware of the importance of the environment. This is evident, for example, in their imaginative use of outdoor spaces, a marvelous American resource not so readily available to, or therefore so easily tapped by, Italian teachers who work in a highly urbanized environment. However, American teachers have always contended with funding limitations and thus been forced to make compromises with regard to indoor space. The unfortunate result, as seen in many day care centers and schools for young children, has been a set of discouraging physical conditions, especially a lack of natural light and uncluttered space.

Educators in Reggio Emilia have evolved through the years a philosophy based on partnership among children, teachers, parents, educational advisors, and the community. They succeeded, along with many teachers in other regions of Italy, after many years of effort and political action, in obtaining public funding for early education and local support for their program. Early in the development of their educational program, the participants in this collaboration appreciated the educational significance of space and invested a great deal of their energy into thinking and planning about it. To quote Carlina Rinaldi:

> Children must feel that the whole school, including the space, materials and projects, values and sustains their interaction and communication. (Rinaldi, 1990)

With these principles in mind, they have found many ways to make the space more than just a useful and safe place in which to spend active hours. Rather, they have created spaces in their infant-toddler centers and preprimary schools that reflect their culture in general and the histories of each center in particular. These spaces tend to be pleasant and welcoming, telling a great deal about the projects and activities, the daily routines, and the people large and small who make the complex interaction that takes place there significant and joyful.

This is a time in the history of education of young children in the United States when many educators are engaged in making their voices heard by the public, and by national and local governments, in favor of the rightful needs of children and of the people who care for them. It may be worthwhile at such time to see what choices were made and have been constantly renewed in this exemplary program with regard to space and physical environment.

## THE ARCHITECTURALLY PLANNED SPACE AND THE EXTENDED SPACE AROUND THE SCHOOL, THE CITY, AND BEYOND

Once the basic philosophy and choices of their educational program were in place, Reggio Emilia educators planned and worked out the structure and arrangement of space. According to the view that saw the education of young children as part of a community-based concern and responsibility, children's centers ideally had to be integral parts of the urban plan. Moreover, rather than occupy marginal space in a neighborhood, they had to be placed in full view of the public and become the focus of interaction among all people connected with the school.

For each building, whether built completely anew or modified from an existing one, pedagogical coordinators, teachers, and parents met to plan with the architects. The people who were going to work and live there for so many hours had to be participants in every decision: a wall too high or the lack of a partition could modify the possibility or the quality of interaction in an educational approach where partnership

**Figure 8.1.   The central space (*piazza*) of the Diana School.**

and interaction are paramount. In fact, as Tiziana Filippini points out, educators in Reggio Emilia speak of space as a "container" that favors social interaction, exploration, and learning, but they also see space as having educational "content," that is, as containing educational messages and being charged with stimuli toward interactive experience and constructive learning (Filippini, 1990). Therefore, the structure of interior spaces tends to evolve along with everything else about the educational program in Reggio Emilia.

The teachers also value what is special about the spaces that surround their schools, considering them to be extensions of classroom space. Part of their curriculum involves taking children to explore neighborhoods and landmarks in the city. One example of the extension of the school is a project undertaken for many months by the Villetta school, during which children went out to explore how the city is transformed during rainstorms. This project brought the children and teachers together to explore first the reality of the city without rain, taking photographs in both familiar and less familiar places, and then making hypotheses about how the rain would change them. Because that particular year, once the project got started, the rain took weeks and weeks to appear, the children had plenty of time to prepare the tools and equipment they thought would help them observe, collect, measure, photograph, and record everything about the rain  In the meanwhile the children's expectations grew tremendously. Everyday the teachers and children went up to the school roof-terrace to gaze hopefully at the sky, gaining much knowledge about cloud formations and wind direction.

When a good rainstorm finally arrived, the experience was feverish and exhilarating. The children noticed how people changed their speed and posture in walking, how the shining reflections and the splash from the puddles changed the streets, how the sound of the raindrops differed depending on whether it was falling on the pavement, the hood of cars, or the leaves of trees. Then, after experiencing the first rainstorm, and following the customary procedure in Reggio Emilia, the

Figure 8.2.    Children enjoy their city during a rainstorm.

children became engaged in representing many of its aspects. This, in turn, led to further questions, hypotheses, and explorations that the teacher and the *atelierista* thoroughly documented. The whole exploration eventually was recorded in "The City and the Rain" segment of the Hundred Languages of Children exhibit, and serves to tell us of the many ways in which the familiar space of the city can become the stage for and subject of activities and constructive explorations (Department of Education, City of Reggio Emilia, 1987).

## THE WELCOMING SPACE AS A REFLECTION OF LAYERS OF CULTURE

When one enters the schools for young children in Reggio Emilia, one senses immediately a welcoming feeling, an atmosphere of discovery and serenity. Moreover, one gains an overall impression of richness in the quality and types of activities of the children, as well as of high professional standards and care on the part of the adults. These impressions come from the way the environment is thoughtfully organized, and especially from seeing how children, teachers, and families move about in the schools. Yet, how does all of this come about? Loris Malaguzzi has said:

> To be sure our schools are the most visible object of our work; I believe they give multiple perceptions and messages. They have decades of experience behind them, and have known three generations of teachers. Each infant-toddler center and each preprimary school has its own past and evolution, its own layers of experience, and its own peculiar mix of styles and cultural levels. There has never been, on our part, any desire to make them all alike. (Malaguzzi, interview, June 1990)

The space reflects the culture of the people who create it in many ways and, upon careful examination, reveals even distinct layers of this cultural influence. First of all, there is in these schools a great deal of attention paid to the beauty and harmony of design. This is evident in the both functional and pleasing furnishings, often invented and built by teachers and parents together. It is also evident in the colors of the walls, the sunlight streaming through large windows, the healthy, green plants, and many other details such as the careful upkeep of the space. This special care for the appearance of the environment, along with the design of spaces that favor social interaction, are essential elements of Italian culture.

Built into the organization of the environment for activities and routines are features that favor cooperation, a concept with strong social and political value in the Emilia Romagna region, where a century-old organization of producers' and consumers' cooperatives is still thriving. Further regional touches can be seen in some of the materials and implements available, as well as in the typical food that the cooks prepare fresh each day, much to the children's delight. The culture of the city can also be detected in the documentation on the walls about outings and activities that involve city landmarks and people. One example is the famous visit to the stone lion, who sits forever waiting for the children in the market square of the city.

The next layer is the culture of the school: the particular school itself with its special beginning, its evolution, and the histories of children who have passed through it. Besides being beautiful, the environment is also highly particular. There are displays of pine cones, shells, or pebbles arranged by size, shape, or color. These displays record events in the children's lives. They contain treasures that the children have gathered on special outings or regular walks. Furthermore, children are encouraged to bring in tokens of their experiences at home connected with daily or special events.

For example, they bring traditional decorations when they return from their winter vacation. As a consequence, parents become involved in this flow of communication toward the school about life and happenings at home. The teachers collect these items and build displays where each child's contribution is respected and at the same time becomes part of a larger picture. When samples of the colorful fall leaves are brought in and pressed, each one's favorites can be placed in a small, transparent pocket with other colored treasures. All these packets are put together and placed on the glass wall to make a large display that catches the light and creates arresting shadows. This is one very simple example of the many ways in which the importance of the individual's contribution, and the significance and strength it brings to the group contribution, is manifested. This message becomes part of the space and makes the children aware that what they have done is valued.

## SOCIAL SPACE, INDIVIDUAL SPACE
## AND APPARENTLY MARGINAL SPACE

For the educators in Reggio Emilia, social exchange is seen as essential in learning. Through shared activity, communication, cooperation, and even conflict, children co-construct their knowledge of the world, using one child's ideas to develop another's or to explore a path yet unexplored. Because social development is seen as an intrinsic part of cognitive development, the space is planned and set up to facilitate encounters, interactions, and exchanges among children. The space has to guarantee the well-being of each child and of the group as a whole. At the same time the space is set up to favor relationships and interactions of teachers, staff, and parents among themselves and with children. For example, adults can meet, work in small or large groups, discuss problems, and eat together inside the school. The well-being of the adults who work in the schools and the trust of parents, who confide their children to the school before going about their activities, are essential for the educational project to work. As stated by Loris Malaguzzi,

> We have tried always to help and maintain strong ties between work and research, a healthy cooperation with the school staff and with the families, an unfailing faith in the potential and capacities of children, and lastly, a ready willingness to think about and discuss what we do. (Malaguzzi, interview, June 1990)

In the Diana School (see plan), as in others, there is a main common space designated by the same term used for a city square (*piazza*). Here is a clear instance of the school as a reflection of the society around it. In this case the concept and name of the central, common space come from the key element in Italian urban structures. The other interior

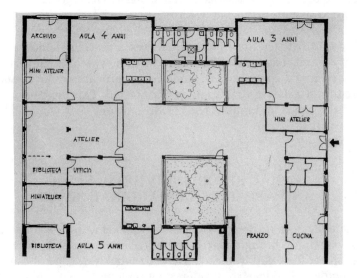

Figure 8.3.  Plan of the Diana School.

spaces can open toward this *piazza*, or common space. There is the large *atelier*, a library with space for computers, an archive, and a storage room. The *atelier*—a workshop, or studio, used by all children and adults in the school—is described by Loris Malaguzzi in this way:

> The *atelier*, in our approach, is an additional space within the school where to explore with our hands and our minds, where to refine our sight through the practice of the visual arts, where to work on projects connected with the activities planned in the classroom, where to explore and combine new and well-known tools, techniques, and materials. (Malaguzzi, 1988)

The teacher in charge of the *atelier*, the *atelierista*, has a training in art education, is co-organizer of the children's and teacher's experience, and serves as editor and designer of the documentation of the work done in the school (see Vecchi, chapter 7, this volume).

Each age group has a classroom (a large room) and next to it a *mini-atelier*. Again, Loris Malaguzzi comments about this decentralized workshop:

> Years ago the space had exploded with the growth of ideas. Technology had brought into the *atelier* the camera, the tape-recorder, the videotape, the photocopy machine, the computer, and more. Our tool-box had become larger. We had to decentralize the *atelier* into smaller spaces. We had to build archives in the schools and in the Municipal administration; furthermore we instituted a Documentation Center. (Malaguzzi, 1988)

Continuing our visit to a school we would see that kitchen, dining room, a room with sinks for washing or water play, and bathrooms are all laid out in an efficient and pleasant way. None is considered marginal space; for example, the mirrors in the washrooms and bathrooms are cut in different shapes to inspire the children to look in a playful way at their image. The ceilings are used as host to many different types of aerial sculptures or beautiful mobiles all made with transparent, colored, and unusual material, built by children and set up by teachers. There are glass walls to create a continuity between interior gardens and outside gardens; they contribute much natural light and give an occasion for playing with transparencies and reflections. Glass walls also separate working spaces to create a communal feeling. However, if one desires to be alone or to work alone or to chat with one friend, there are various options, such as the space of the *mini-ateliers* or other comfortable small enclosures to which one can retire and spend time.

## SPACE APPROPRIATE FOR DIFFERENT AGES
## AND LEVELS OF DEVELOPMENT

In the infant-toddler centers the attention given to the physical environment has a particular quality that reminds one of the need for
closeness and nurturing exchanges that the youngest children have.
Right at the entrance, comfortable wicker chairs invite parents to take
time to pause with their infants, meet with one another, or converse
with the teachers. There are rooms covered with carpets and pillows
where children can crawl safely or else snuggle up with a teacher to
look at a picture book or listen to a story. There is a large space with
equipment appropriate for movement. But there is also an *atelier*
where the children explore with paint, markers, flour, clay, and much
more. The glass partitions are used especially in the infant-toddler
centers, where children tend to feel a greater sense of separation.
There, glass walls are used to allow one to see into the kitchen and into
the room where the children's clothes are changed, or to look back and
forth between the rooms where children of different age groups play.

Similarly, in the preprimary schools, in the classroom of the youngest group, more space is left in the classroom of the youngest group for
play with unstructured materials such as blocks, legos, toy animals,
and recycled materials. The area covered with rugs is larger to allow
the children to play on the floor; furthermore, the housekeeping space

**Figure 8.4. Communication between two rooms, in the Infant-Toddler Center
Arcobaleno.**

is wide and rich with small replicas of pottery and glassware commonly found in the homes and jars of pasta of different sizes and beans of
different colors. Entering the *mini-atelier*, one might notice, in late
autumn, that the children explore the potential and properties of clay,
paper, and wire. They spend several weeks on each of these materials.
In later months, teachers and children will return to them in order to
develop higher level of skills and understanding. Throughout the year,
then, as they acquire more self-assurance, these children carry out
many explorations and projects also in the main *atelier*.

## ORGANIZED SPACE, ACTIVE SPACE,
## AND PARTICULAR SPACE

Every morning around 9:00, when all the children have arrived at
school, each classroom has a meeting. In some schools the meeting
space is on a sort of bleachers. Then, once the children have opted for
one of the activities available or to continue with one of the projects in
progress, they will find the necessary supplies and tools set up on
tables, light tables, and easels, or placed in convenient spaces. They
will be able to find everything else they need on well-organized open
shelves, stocked with recycled and nonrecycled materials. Those materials have been previously selected and neatly placed in transparent
containers with the help of teachers. All these aspects of daily organization stem directly from the basic educational choices. Materials and
objects, which are in the space where children spend many hours, have
to be chosen or built according to the context in which they will be
used, with consideration of how the children will react to them. Careful
note must then be taken of how children act upon them and eventually
reinvent them.

The arrangement and use of space for activities, for constructive
exploration of materials, or for work on projects and themes is critical.
Loris Malaguzzi says:

> What actually goes on in the schools is a basic test for all of us. The
> continuous activity is the most important thing for us and represents
> that which can contribute the most to keeping fresh (a term dear to
> Dewey) our interest and the continuous mobility of our thought and
> action. I believe that our schools show the attempt that has been made to
> integrate the educational project with the plan for the organization of
> work and the architectural and functional setting, so as to allow for
> maximum movement, interdependence and interaction. (Malaguzzi, in-
> terview, June 1990)

One of the images that Malaguzzi uses to make a point about setting up the space for stimulating and meaningful centers of activity is that of "market stalls" where customers look for the wares that interest them, make selections, and engage in lively interactions.

## SPACE THAT DOCUMENTS

According to Loris Malaguzzi:

> The walls of our preprimary schools speak and document. The walls are used as spaces for temporary and permanent exhibits of what the children and the adults make come to life. (Malaguzzi, Chapter 3, this volume)

One of the aspects of space that strikes visitors is indeed the quantity of the children's own work exhibited all around the schools. In fact, this is one of the children's main contributions to shaping the space of their school. They do it through the mediation of the teachers and especially of the *atelierista* who selects and prepares the displays with great care. Most of the time these displays include, next to the children's work, photographs that tell about the process, plus a description of the various steps and evolution of the activity or project. These descriptions are meaningfully completed with the transcription of the children's own remarks and conversation that went along with their particular experience (which is often tape-recorded). Therefore, the displays, besides being well designed and contributing to the general pleasantness of the space, provide documentation about specific activities, the educational approach, and the steps of its process. Above all it is a way to make parents, colleagues, and visitors aware of the children's potential, their developing capacities, and what goes on in the school. Of course, it also makes the children aware of the regard adults have for their work. Finally, it helps teachers assess the results of their activities and contribute to their own professional advancement.

## SPACE AND TIME

> An environment is a living, changing system. More than the physical space, it includes the way time is structured and the roles we are expected to play. It conditions how we feel, think, and behave; and it dramatically affects the quality of our lives. The environment either works for us or against us as we conduct our lives. (Greenman, 1988, p. 5)

When one observes children and adults in the schools of Reggio Emilia one perceives that there is a particular connection between time and space and that the environment truly works. The consideration of the children's own needs and rhythms shapes the arrangement of space and the physical environment, while in turn, the time at disposal allows for the use and enjoyment, at a child's pace, of such carefully thought-out space. In fact, the way time is thought of in the Reggio Emilia approach is influenced by at least three major factors. First of all, their experience has extended over 30 years since the first municipal school was established, and that in turn was based on the parent-run schools established immediately after World War Two. Therefore, what we see in the arrangement of spaces is based on many changes and much learning through a long experience, and as a consequence educators do not push to obtain immediate results.

Secondly, parents and their children establish a long-standing rapport with the program, since many start sending their sons and daughters to the infant-toddler center before age one. When they are three years old the children transfer to the municipal preprimary schools, which takes them on through the ages of three and six years. The system provides for teachers to be with the same children from the beginning to the end of each school cycle. The relationships that become established during this long stay with the same groups of children, parents, and teachers shape the space, which in turn becomes a familiar niche for them. Since there is no separation at the end of each year, and thus no period of adjustment to new relations, there is less pressure to reach certain goals, to finish the year's work with a clean break, or to start each year with a clean slate.

Thirdly, the public programs for young children in Italy are not divided between education and day care. These programs do differ, but only because they cater to children of different ages; they are all supposed to provide both care and education. The programs are considered social services, with flexible schedules. While most of the children stay in the municipal centers between 9 a.m. and 4 p.m., there are parents who need to leave their children from as early as 7:30 a.m. to as late as 6 p.m., and still others prefer to pick up the children right after lunch, at 12:30 or 1 p.m. Most of the children, in fact, spend many hours in group living. Accordingly the educators provide a leisurely social setting for their meals; a quiet, protected environment, for their naps; and for their activities, several areas with a great deal of interesting and engaging proposals that are carried out at a generally unhurried pace that creates a sense of security, self-esteem, and the opportunity to work problems through. Loris Malaguzzi comments:

One has to respect the time of maturation, of development, of the tools of doing and understanding, of the full, slow, extravagant, lucid and ever-changing emergence of children's capacities; it is a measure of cultural and biological wisdom. (Malaguzzi, Chapter 3, this volume)

## A SPACE THAT TEACHES

The environment is seen here as educating the child; in fact, it is considered as "the third educator" along with the team of two teachers.

In order to act as an educator for the child, the environment has to be flexible: It must undergo frequent modification by the children and the teachers in order to remain up to date and responsive to their needs to be protagonists in constructing their knowledge. All the things that surround the people in the school and which they use—the objects, the materials, and the structures—are not seen as passive elements, but on the contrary are seen as elements that condition and are conditioned by the actions of children and adults who are active in it. In the words of Loris Malaguzzi:

> We value space because of its power to organize, promote pleasant relationships between people of different ages, create a handsome envi-

**Figure 8.5.   The 4-year-olds' classroom at the Villetta School.**

ronment, provide changes, promote choices and activity, and its potential for sparking all kinds of social, affective and cognitive learning. All of this contributes to a sense of well-being and security in children. We also think that the space has to be a sort of aquarium that mirrors the ideas, values, attitudes, and cultures of the people who live within it. (Malaguzzi, 1984)

The schools in Reggio Emilia could not be just anywhere, and no one of them could serve as an exact model to be copied literally elsewhere. Yet, they have common features that merit consideration in schools everywhere. Each school's particular configuration of the garden, walls, tall windows, and handsome furniture declares: This is a place where adults have thought about the quality of environment. Each school is full of light, variety, and a certain kind of joy. In addition, each school shows how teachers, parents, and children, working and playing together, have created a unique space, a space that reflects their personal lives, the history of their schools, the many layers of culture and a nexus of well thought out choices.

## REFERENCES

Department of Education, City of Reggio Emilia. (1984). *L'Occhio se Salta il Muro* (If the Eye Jumps Over the Wall). Catalogue of exhibit of the same name published by the Comune di Reggio Emilia, Assessorato all' Istruzione, Regione di Emilia Romagna.

Department of Education, City of Reggio Emilia. (1987). The City and the Rain. In *The hundred languages of children: Narrative of the possible*. Catalogue of the Exhibit, "The Hundred Languages of Children," published by the Comune di Reggio Emilia, Assessorato all' Istruzione, Regione di Emilia Romagna.

Diana School. (1990). In *Viaggio coi Diritti dei Bambini* (*A Journey with Children's Rights*). Booklet published by the school.

Fillipini, T. (1990, November). Introduction to the Reggio approach. In R. New (Chair), *The hundred languages of children: More contributions from Reggio Emilia, Italy*. Symposium at the annual conference of the National Association for the Education of Young Children, Washington DC.

Greenman, J. (1988). *Caring spaces, learning spaces: Children's environments that work*. Redmond VA: Exchange Press.

Malaguzzi, L. (1988, December). Se l'Atelier è Dentro una Storia Lunga e ad un Progetto Educativo (If the *Atelier* is Part of a Long History and an Educational Program). *Bambini*, pp. 26–31.

Rinaldi, C. (1990, October). *Social constructivism in Reggio Emilia, Italy*. Keynote Address, annual conference of the Association of Constructivist Teachers, Northampton, MA. Translated by Baji Rankin and Lella Gandini.

"Portrait of a teacher," by 5-year-old
child from the Pablo Neruda School.

# 9

# Partner, Nurturer, and Guide: The Roles of the Reggio Teacher in Action

## Carolyn Edwards

In Reggio Emilia, the teacher's role in assisting learning is a subject of central and abiding interest and concern. Over the past 30 years, teachers and administrators have discussed and considered much about the responsibilities, goals, difficulties, pleasures, and opportunities faced by the teachers in their public child care system. They have evolved together a coherent way of thinking and talking about the role of the teacher inside and outside the classroom, based on—as are all aspects of their organization, environmental design, pedagogy, and curriculum—an explicit philosophy about the nature of the child as learner. This chapter describes the view in Reggio Emilia of the teacher's role. The chapter draws from videotaped observations in one preprimary school, the Diana School, and recorded discussions and interviews with teachers and administrators conducted since 1983 as

**151**

part of a forthcoming study, *Collaboration and Community in the Preschool Classroom: Amherts, Pistoia, and Reggio Emilia,* by Carolyn Edwards, Lella Gandini, and John Nimmo. Quotations from formal interviews, group discussions, and observations (collected, transcribed, and translated by members of the project team) are used throughout this chapter to illustrate the concepts and convey the distinctive meanings, the particular ways of packaging ideas and communicating with others, that we encountered in Reggio Emilia.

## DEFINITIONS OF THE TEACHER'S ROLE IN REGGIO EMILIA

In the United States, when defining the role of the early childhood teacher, we usually begin by laying out its essential dimensions, for example: (a) promoting children's learning in cognitive, social, physical, and affective domains; (b) managing the classroom; (c) preparing the environment; (d) providing nurturance and guidance; (e) communicating with important constituencies (parents, colleagues, administrators, the public); and (f) seeking professional growth. The work of Reggio Emilia's teachers covers these same aspects, and in addition they would stress two other roles that they see as essential: (g) engaging in political activism to defend the cause of public early education; and (h) conducting systematic research on daily classroom work for purposes of professional dissemination, curriculum planning, and teacher development.

Yet, although Reggio educators take on these many roles, they invariably begin, in defining the teacher's role, by discussing the essence of what teachers do to promote intellectual growth by children in groups. They begin by noting that it is impossible for a culture to exist without an image of children. Children, as understood in Reggio, are active and competent *protagonists* who seek completion through dialogue and interaction with others, in a collective life of the classroom, community, and culture, with teachers serving as guides.

This intrinsically social view of the child—a communicator with a unique personal, historical, and cultural identity—leads to their particular view of the teacher's work. Tiziana Filippini, speaking to a large audience of Americans in 1990, defined this role clearly. The teacher, Filippini said, sometimes works "inside" the group of children and sometimes "just around" them. The teacher studies the children, provides occasions, intervenes at critical moments, and shares the children's heightened emotions:

The role of the adult is above all one of listening, observing, and understanding the strategy that children use in a learning situation. The teacher has, for us, a role as dispenser of occasions; and it is very important for us that the child feel the teacher to be not a judge but a resource to whom he can go when he needs to borrow a gesture, a word. According to something Vygotsky [the Russian psychologist] said, if the children have gone from [point] A to B and are getting very close to C, sometimes to reach C, the child needs to borrow assistance from the adult at that very special moment. We feel that the teacher must be involved within the child's exploration, if the teacher wants to understand how to be the organizer and provoker of occasions. . . . And our expectations of the child must be very flexible and varied. We must be able to be amazed and to enjoy—like the children often do. We must be able to catch the ball that the children throw us, and toss it back to them in a way that makes the children want to continue the game with us, developing, perhaps, other games as we go along. (Filippini, Lecture, National Association for the Education of Young Children, Washington, DC, November 16, 1990).

This concluding metaphor of catching the children's ball and tossing it back, was earlier put forward by Loris Malaguzzi in a formal discussion with our research team and the professional staff of the Diana School (June 15, 1990). It was an important metaphor, useful for others, because it was used later in that discussion by Vea Vecchi, the *atelierista* of this school, and then it resurfaced in other interviews held in subsequent months, as well as during the NAEYC lecture of Filippini, the *pedagogista*. In originally formulating this idea, Malaguzzi was stressing the importance of taking note of exactly what children say in dialogue so that the teacher can pick up an idea and throw it back—and thereby make their play more significant. Vecchi then elaborated on the reasons why she saw this task as vital: because often children express a new insight tentatively and partially, in a way that is not clear to either the self or others. The teacher, noticing the idea's potential to stimulate intellectual work and growth by the group as a whole, steps in to restate the idea in clearer and more emphatic language, and thereby makes the insight operative for the children, a kind of intellectual spark for further talk and action by the group:

In this way the play of participation and the play of communication really take place. Of course, communication may take place without your assistance, but it would be important not to miss such a situation. (Vecchi, Group Discussion, June 15, 1990)

# THE VARIOUS DIMENSIONS
# OF THE TEACHER'S ROLE

Thus, the teacher's role centers on provoking occasions of discovery through a kind of alert, inspired facilitation and stimulation of children's dialogue, co-action, and co-construction of knowledge. Because intellectual discovery is believed to be an essentially social process, the teacher assists even the youngest children to learn to listen to others, take account of their goals and ideas, and communicate successfully. As in the United States, such optimal teaching is understood to be a complex, delicate, multifaceted task, involving many levels and calling for much expertise and continuous self-examination.

## Different Aspects of the Teacher's Role

Carlina Rinaldi, *pedagogista*, likewise has sought to explain the most critical things teachers must do in Reggio Emilia. Speaking in a 1988 interview with Lella Gandini, Rinaldi offers a description complementary to Filippini's. Although it first seems a simple list, in fact, she presents us a spiraling perspective as she speaks over and again about teachers, children, *atelierista*, and parents. Moreover, her list is also spiral in its temporal dimension, as opposed to a strict sequence. That is, Rinaldi describes a set of events that are visited and revisited, according to the teacher's judgment, as a project proceeds. Such a spiraling rather than linear way of thinking is, in fact, very characteristic of Reggio educators, whether they are describing the process of learning and development, planning a project, or as here, talking about pedagogy.

Another key element of Rinaldi's perspective is her social progressivism and idealism. She is proud of the long tradition of cooperative enterprise and progressive politics in the Emilia Romagna Region of Italy, and she strongly believes that adults should invest public resources in children's welfare and enter into a continuous and permanent process of knowledge construction alongside children, "in order for Reggio Emilia to progress, and hopefully all of society, too."

Thus, according to Rinaldi, the teacher leads the learning of a group of children by searching for individuals' ideas to use to frame group action. Sometimes this involves leading group meetings and seeking to stimulate a "spark"—writing down what the children say, then reading back their comments, searching with them for insights that will motivate further questions and group activity. At other times, it involves the teacher sitting and listening, noticing provocative or insightful comments, then repeating or clarifying them to help the chil-

**Figure 9.1.  Teacher working as partner of a child.**

dren sustain their talk or activity. And as yet other times, especially at the end of a morning's activity, it involves searching for an idea—especially one that emerges in an intellectual dispute between chilidren—and shaping it into a hypothesis that should be tested, an empirical comparison that should be made, or a representation that should be attempted, as the basis for future activity by the group.

Examining the question, hypothesis, or argument of one child thus becomes part of an ongoing process of raising and answering questions for all. With the help of the teacher, the question or observation of one child leads others to explore territory never encountered, perhaps never even suspected. This is what Reggio Emilia educators mean by "co-action" of children.

As a project gets underway, teachers reflect, explore, study, research, and plan together possible ways to elaborate and extend the theme by means of materials, activities, visits, use of tools, and so on. These ideas are then taken back to the classroom and investigated. In Reggio Emilia municipal preprimary schools, teachers have for years worked in co-teaching pairs in each classroom. The co-teaching organization is considered difficult, because the two adults must adapt and accommodate constantly in order to work together, but nevertheless it is best because it allows each adult to become used to cooperating with a peer, acquire a value for the social nature of intellectual growth, and thereby become more helpful to children (and parents) as they engage in social process.

Teachers communicate with parents about the project theme and encourage them to become involved in the activities of their child through finding necessary materials, working with teachers on the physical environment, offering supplementary books, and so on. In this way, parents are provoked to revise their image of their child and understand childhood in a more rich and complex way.

The teaching team works closely with other adults (at times the *atelierista*, at times the *pedagogista*) to plan and document the project. This happens in different ways in different schools, but in general, documentation includes tape-recordings and transcriptions of children's dialogue and group discussions, print and slide photographs of key moments and activities, and collection of products and constructions made by children.

Throughout the project, the teachers act as the group's "memory" and discuss with children the results of the documentation. This systematically allows children to revisit their own and others' feelings, perceptions, observations, reflections, and then reconstruct and reinterpret them in deeper ways. In reliving earlier moments via photography and tape-recording, children are deeply reinforced and validated for their efforts and provided with a boost to their memory that is critical at their young age.

The teachers constantly pay close attention to the children's activity. They believe that when children work on a project of interest to them, they will naturally encounter problems and questions they will want to investigate. The teachers' role is to help children discover their own problems and questions. At that point, moreover, they will not offer ready solutions, but instead help children focus on a problem or difficulty and formulate hypotheses. Their goal is not so much to "facilitate" learning in the sense of "making smooth or easy," but rather to "stimulate" it by making problems more complex, involving, and arousing. They ask the children what they need in order to do experiments—even when they realize that a particular approach or hypothesis is not "correct." They serve as the children's partners, sustaining the children and offering assistance, resources, and strategies to get unstuck when encountering difficulties. Often teachers encourage children to continue with something, or ask them to complete or add to something that they are doing. They prefer not to leave children always working on their own, but try instead to cooperate with the children's goals.

While working with a group of children, each teacher takes written notes to discuss later with her co-teacher, *atelierista*, *pedagogista*, and other colleagues, concerning the course of the project. She will then, when possible, work with an even larger peer group of teachers (including those from outside her own school) to redirect or extend a project and enrich the children's experience. Such analytic and critical activities are vital to the development of the individual teacher and, ultimately, the educational system as a whole. Systematic documentation allows each teacher to become a producer of research, that is, someone who generates new ideas about curriculum and learning, rather than being merely a "consumer of certainty and tradition."

## THE DIFFICULTIES OF THE TEACHER'S ROLE

Educators in Reggio Emilia do not consider the teacher's role to be an easy one, with black and white answers guiding what teachers should do. They do possess, however, the confidence and sense of security that their approach to teaching, developed collectively over the past 30 years in Reggio, is the way they *should* be working. As teacher Laura Rubizzi put it, "It is a way of working not only valid but also right" (Interview, November 11, 1989). Her colleague at the Diana School, Paula Strozzi, said:

> We are part of a project that is based on the co-action of children, and on the sureness that this is a good way of learning. (Interview, June 14, 1990)

This day-to-day work, nonetheless, involves constant challenge and decision making because of the use of emergent curriculum. One difficult task for the teachers is to help children find problems that are big enough and hard enough to engage their best energies and thinking over time. It is clear from Baji Rankin's description of the Dinosaur Project at the Anna Frank School (chapter 11) that teachers sometimes back away from a project that doesn't seem to be going anywhere.

Not only must the larger project contain meaty problems, but even a daily work session should ideally contain sticking points, or "knots." These "knots" are more than just moments of confusion or disagreement, rather, they are moments of cognitive disequilibrium, containing possibilities for hypothesis testing and intellectual comparison of ideas. The teachers' task is to notice those knots and help bring them to center stage for further attention—launching points for tomorrow's activities.

A second aspect of the teacher's role that Reggio teachers experience as difficult is knowing how and when to intervene, because this depends on a moment-by-moment analysis of the children's thinking. Teachers Magda Bondavalli and Marina Mori stated:

> With regard to difficulties [in teaching], we see them continuously. The way we offer possibilities and suggestions to children leaves things always open. This is a way to be with them through readjusting continuously. There is nothing that is definite or absolute. We try all the time to interpret, through their gestures, words, and actions, how they are living through an experience; and then we go on from there. It's really difficult! (Interview, June 14, 1990)

Also in the United States, teachers worry about how much and when to intervene, how to support problem solving without providing the solution (Edwards, 1986). As Malaguzzi (1987) has written, children are "dangerously on the brink between presence that they want and repression that they don't want" (p. 17). Thus, the teacher should not intervene too much, and yet he or she does not want to let a valuable teaching moment go by. Vea Vecchi expressed this eloquently:

> But you are always afraid that you are going to miss that hot moment. It's really a balancing act. I believe in intervention, yet personally I tend to wait because I have noticed that children often resolve the problem on their own, and not always in the way that I would have told them to! Children often find solutions that I would never have seen. But sometimes waiting means missing the moment. So it's a decision that you have to make very quickly. (Group discussion, October 18, 1990)

What they are describing here is a genuine commitment to emergent curriculum, not a subtle manipulation of the project theme so that it will end up in a certain place. The teachers honestly do not know where the group will end up. Although this openness adds a dimension of difficulty to their work, it also makes it more exciting. As Laura Rubizzi put it:

> I work in a state of uncertainty because I do not know where the children will arrive to, but it is a fabulous experience! (Interview, November 11, 1989)

> [I]t is as if we are starting off together on a voyage. It could be short; it could be long. But there is an eagerness in doing it together. (Group discussion, October 18, 1990)

Moreover, beyond being exciting, their way of working has the added advantage of the built-in support structures. The teacher is not expected to figure out all by herself what she should be doing. Always she works in collaboration with other adults, as Bondavalli and Mori attest:

> It's really the way to be in this school, where we compare notes continuously, and we talk to one another all the time. (Interview, June 14, 1990)

Such conferring takes place on an almost daily basis, in short meetings between teacher and co-teacher, teacher and *atelierista*, and informal discussions between teachers of different classrooms at lunchtime. Teachers believe that by discussing openly they offer models of cooperation and participation to the children and parents and promote an atmosphere of open and frank communication. More formal and extended analysis occurs during staff meetings of one's own school or some larger group meeting involving administrators, teachers from other schools, and perhaps even outside visitors or lecturers.

It is important to note that analysis and feedback in Reggio Emilia involves both support and criticism. In contrast to a system where concern for hurt feelings or ownership of ideas prevents extended examination and argumentation, in Reggio Emilia intellectual conflict is considered pleasurable for both adults and children. As Paola Strozzi said, "I am convinced that there is some kind of pleasure in trying to agree about how to do things" (Interview, June 14, 1990). The point of a discussion is not just to air diverse points of view, but instead to go on until it is clear that everyone has learned something and moved somewhere in his or her thinking. A discussion should go on until a solution or next step becomes apparent; then, tension dissipates and a new, shared understanding provides the basis for future joint activity or effort. The discussion can require a certain toughness and perseverance.

Certainly, teachers and staff offer one another emotional support and encouragement as well as concrete suggestions and advice. In addition, however, a method of extended mutual criticism and self-examination is very much accepted. Our research team participated in three such meetings at the Diana School, each several hours long and involving teachers, auxiliary staff, cooks, *atelierista, pedagogista,* and Loris Malaguzzi. For example, at one of them, teacher Marina Castagnetti presented an edited videotape and behavioral analysis of a session involving two five-year-old boys trying to create a castle on a large piece of paper using a Logo turtle activated by computer. Her presentation was followed by lengthy discussion addressing the pedagogical choices and decisions. Had the children been adequately prepared to solve their problem? Could they handle the computer commands? Did they need a set of rulers nearby on hand to stimulate ideas of measurement? Were they left too long to flounder on their own without the teacher's assistance? Did the teacher let a "hot moment" go by or "abandon" the children too long? Did the children's frequent language of joining ("Let's do this," "Let's try this," "Let's see," "We must," and so on) indicate productive collaboration or desperation? At one point in this discussion Castagnetti asked, "At this point, as a teacher, what am I supposed to do that I didn't do?" The members of our research team were impressed by the depth of these discussions and lack of defensiveness by teachers. We commented on their method of critical

Figure 9.2. Teachers' meeting.

reflection, and Malaguzzi, with an affectionate smile for Castagnetti, said, "We always have to have two pockets: one for satisfaction and one for dissatisfaction" (Group Discussion, October 16, 1991).

Intellectual conflict is understood as the engine of all growth in Reggio. Therefore, teachers seek to bring out, rather than suppress, conflicts of viewpoints between children. Similarly, among themselves they readily accept disagreement and expect extended discussion and constructive criticism; this is seen as the best way to advance. The teachers' pleasure in teamwork and acceptance of disagreement provides a model for children and parents.

## EXAMPLES OF TEACHER BEHAVIOR

To give a fuller picture and provide concrete examples of the abstract principles presented above, we offer four short observation records drawn from videotapes taken at the Diana School in 1988 and 1990. They illustrate different kinds of teacher behavior commonly seen in the Reggio Emilia preschools.

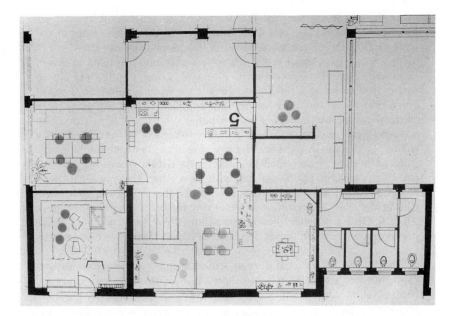

**Figure 9.3.    Plan of the 5-year-olds room at the Diana School. Dots indicate typical distribution of children during morning activities.**

## The Teacher Gets Children Started

In this episode (May 24, 1988, videotape taken by research team), teacher Giulia Notari acts as "dispenser of occasions" in helping children make the transition from morning group meeting to their first activity. Notice her flexibility and nurturance in meeting the needs of one little girl who is not ready to enter into a focused activity.

It is 9:23 a.m. in the 3-year-old classroom, and morning meeting has just ended. During this meeting, teacher Giulia Notari has told the whole class about the morning's activities, all of which concern the theme of Springtime that they are currently pursuing. Then her co-teacher, Paola Strozzi, departs with eight children to work with clay in the school's central *piazza*. Giulia supervises the remaining 12 or so children. She moves around the classroom encouraging children to settle into an activity, and she spends a few moments with each small group in turn getting them started.

For instance, at one table she introduces a group of four children to the materials set there, "Feel it, this paper is different from other paper."

"It is cold," a child says.

"It is cold," she agrees. "It is cold. And here is another paper that is still different. And look, here are markers, chalks, and craypas, all yellow."

As she moves from one table to the next, Giulia sees children not yet involved and asks, "Do you want to work with the green colors in the little *atelier?* Or do you want to cut with scissors and use glue?"

She comes to a small table, where two children sit facing sheets of white paper and little baskets full of leaves, grass, and flowers picked earlier that morning. Giulia says, "Do you see what is here? Little bits of green that you found. And flowers that you picked. You can place them on the paper as you like. If one piece of paper is not enough, you can place a second right next to it. Okay?" (Giulia explains later that the activity communicates the importance and pleasure of exploration and helps the children become accustomed to collage.) As Giulia moves off, the two children proceed happily, chatting with each other. "Do you want this?" "I've taken that kind, too." "Look how pretty this is." "Take your time" (this is obviously an imitation of something the teacher sometimes says). At 9:26, Giulia returns to look and admire their work, saying, "I like it very much. You can use extra sheets of paper. If you want something, tell me."

At 9:28 she enters a small room which is an annex to the classroom. Two girls are seated at a table there. One is drawing with markers. Giulia Notari gives this first girl more drawing materials, then goes to the second one.

"Well, them, shall we look for the work you have already started? Let's see where it is." She takes a folder out of a drawer and begins leafing slowly through it, saying, "Which one is yours? Which one? Which one? Which one?" The child looks despondent and does not answer. They eventually locate the child's drawing, then Giulia says, "What does this need? Do you need some more black marker to continue? . . . Do you want to work on another drawing? Do you want another paper to go work with the glue? Would you like to go and play? Love, what do you want to do?" The despondent child does not answer any of her questions. Finally, the teacher simply crouches down, kisses her, and talks with her gently. Then she takes down some picture books from a high shelf and puts away the drawing. Another child appears in the doorway looking for help, and Giulia says, "I'm coming, sweetheart." She leaves the little girl wiping away her tears and looking through a book. As she goes by, she stops to praise the drawing of the first little girl.

## The Teacher Provides Instruction in Tool-Use and Technique

It is now 9:34 on the same morning (May 24, 1988), in the large shared space (*piazza*) where co-teacher Paola Notari is working with eight 3-year-olds and large mounds of artists' modeling clay. She provides the children instruction in the correct use of the materials and tools as part of the process of facilitating, supporting, and encouraging. When asked about this, she says she tries to provide the help and advice that is needed for children to accomplish their own artistic and representational goals and not be defeated by the materials. For example, she knows that if children roll out the clay too thin, then it breaks during firing and children are upset.

> The children are seated around a long rectangular table, while Paola stands and moves among them. In front of each is a large wooden tablet on which to work the clay. Paola is preparing each child a flat slab of clay: she tears off a hunk of clay, rolls it out thin with a rolling pin, cuts off the sides to make a neat square, then gives it out. She is using a knife to cut the clay and says, "This tool we can use to cut the clay when it is nice and thick."
>
> The children have many cutting and rolling tools nearby. They are working on the problem of "representing movement, on a surface." With a knife, they can cut out a piece of the clay, then fold it up and over to give a sense of motion on the surface of the slab. (She explains later that some of the children don't actually succeed in getting any sense of movement into theirs. But Paola doesn't interfere and insist on her idea of movement. Since all are very involved in what they are doing she does not impose her ideas on them. However, she does instruct them on matters of technique—showing them how to roll and cut the clay and use the tools.)

**Figure 9.4.   Children and teachers discussing a project.**

At 9:34 Paola Notari is seen using a spatula to give a newly rolled slab of clay to a child. "Do you need this?" she asks. She tells another, "'You are pressing too much. If you press too much, we will not be able to pick it up, and then we will not be able to fire it in the kiln. Don't press too hard." Then another child turns to her, "Is this all right?"

"Yes, yes," Paola replies, "That's fine. If you want another slab of clay, I can prepare one for you."

She observes a little disagreement between two children. One wants the pastry cutter that the other has been using. That child protests, "This is mine. I had it before."

"But they are all the same," says Paola, pointing out more cutters. "They really are all the same." She moves closer and the first child shows her that in fact the desired cutter makes a different kind of track in the clay than the others. So she revises her opinion, "Oh, I see. Well, if you look in the tool box, there you will find another, precisely like this one." The child goes off happily to look.

She begins to prepare a slab of clay for one of the girls, and while doing so, looks up at the child opposite her. "What are you doing?" she asks. The boy shows, and Paola says, "That's nice."

Finishing the new slab, she takes it over to the girl needing it. Seeing her first piece, Paola comments, "Look at that marvel! Now you have to think about what else you want to do. You could put the same marks in it [the new slab] you did before. Or you could place these pieces folded, or standing up." She demonstrates, using little strips of clay. The little girl has in her hand a pastry cutter, which she moves over the slab without saying anything. Paola continues, "You only want to cut with this little wheel, don't you? It does make very beautiful marks."

Paola goes to the opposite side of the table where a very small child seems to be having difficulties. She asks him, "May I clean it up for you?" Her hand smoothes down his slab, using slip. She explains to him, "This is sort of like an eraser. And now I will show you how to use this tool [a cutter]. You can make a thin strip, like this, and fold it or pick it up." She shows him to lift one end of the strip. Then she puts the cutter into his hand and standing behind him, guides him in the use of both his hands. "With this hand, hold the clay. Now with this other hand, push very hard. More. This way. Okay? Now you can do it."

At 9:41 she asks all the children at large, "Do you want more clay? I can go get it."

"Also I!" "Also I!" shout all the children.

"Okay," Paola says, "I'm going to get some more." She goes out of the room for a few minutes, leaving the children alone for a few moments. The observation continues in the same way when she returns.

## The Teacher Turns a Dispute into a Hypothesis to Test

In is 9:12 on a morning late in May (1990, videotape taken by research team), and teacher Laura Rubizzi sits with six 5-year-old children at a table in a small room off the *atelier*. Her group is involved in a project to prepare an "instruction booklet" about their school to send to the homes of those small children who will be entering the Diana School next fall. The group of three boys and three girls has decided, among other things, to include in the welcome booklet some directions for how to find the way to the *atelier*.

But how to communicate those directions? In a discussion that had taken place on the previous day, one girl, Giulia, had proposed that since little children can't read, the group should instead draw them a picture. But Silvio then asserted that little children speak differently than big ones do, so they should write their instructions in "scribbles" to speak the language of 3-year-olds. The others strongly disagreed! A scribble picture would be no good!

Laura had made a constructive suggestion, that the children draw both kinds of pictures to see which one works better. So at the end of their time yesterday, the children had prepared two pictures. Silvio drew his scribble diagram, while Giulia drew a picture of a child playing on the video machine in this small room next to the *atelier*. To test which picture communicates better, the group of six proposes to enter the classroom of the smallest children in the Diana School and asks them, "Which picture do you prefer? Which do you understand?" Cristina, another of the girls, notes that they should show the picture to a group of children containing an equal number of boys and girls, because the girls will understand Giulia's picture better, while the boys will understand Silvio's.

Thus, at 9:18 we see the six 5-year-olds standing with Laura Rubizzi at the head of the circle where all of the children in the 3-year-old classroom are seated, along with their teachers, Paola Strozzi, and Giulia Notari. Notice how the teachers cooperate to highlight the interesting problem to resolve through a comparison of ideas, and how Laura, without heightening or calling attention to possibilities of hurt feelings, nevertheless offers Silvio nurturance at a potentially sensitive moment.

Laura tells the expectant 3-year-olds, "We have a big, big problem." The child, Giulia, begins to explain how they need to find out what pictures work best with 3-year-olds; Laura takes over and standing close to Giulia, looking at her, echoes and inserts points to make the explanation clearer. Then teacher, Giulia Notari, looking around at the faces of her 3-year-old group, speaks as if for them, again repeating the main points. As she finishes, voices are heard all around the circle as the 3-year-olds chime in their initial opinions.

Teacher Laura takes her six 5-year-olds into a huddle to work out a game plan for how to proceed next. Then, with her help, they get ready: Silvio and Giulia stand at the head of the children's circle, excitedly holding their pictures. Laura says that the 3-year-olds will come up, study the two pictures, decide which communicates best, then stand behind the boy or girl holding that picture. To the side of Silvio and Giulia, at right angles to the circle, stand the remaining 5-year-olds; their job will be to decide which line of children turns out to be the longest.

Giulia Notari selects, one by one, individual 3-year-olds to go up. One boy goes forward, studies the pictures, points to Silvio's, then with the teacher's help takes his place behind Silvio. Another boy comes up, points to Giulia's picture, then returns to his seat, although his teacher tells him to go stand behind her. The next child to go up also points to Giulia's picture and then correctly goes to stand behind Giulia. Now the system is working. Another boy goes to stand behind Silvio; then the next four children select Giulia's picture and take their places behind her.

At this point, teacher Laura decides the case has been made and she should intervene. "Very good," she states, then looking at her little group of judges, "Children of the group! This is the line of those who select the scribble drawing. According to you, which line is longer?" The group points decisively to Giulia's line. "This one!" they say.

It is now 9:26. Laura bends over and speaks directly to Silvio alone. Then she straightens up and says, "Okay! Thank you very much! We'll return to our room," and off they go.

As the 5-year-olds take their seats and begin to discuss drawing a map of their school for the booklet, everyone, including Silvio, seems equally cheerful and involved.

## The Teacher Encourages Children to Solve Their Own Disputes

It is just before lunchtime (Spring, 1990, videotape taken by the staff of the Diana School), and two 5-year-olds boys, Daniele and Christian, are setting the tables for their class. In this school, children of each succeeding age are given more responsibility in preparing the table for lunch. The 5-year-olds take turns at deciding who is to sit where. The teachers at this school believe that their system of letting a few children each day set the table and decide upon the seating arrangement works better and is more in line with their philosophy than either having a fixed seating order (controlled by the teachers) or allowing free choice for everyone at the moment of seating themselves.

Daniele and Christian lay out the tablecloths, plates, and silverware, and decide where everyone is to sit by placing their individual napkins (each in a little envelope with the name sewn on). As they work, another boy comes in and asks to be seated near a certain boy. The tablesetters agree, and he leaves. Then a girl, Elisa, comes in and asks, "With whom did you put me?" Daniele answers, "Look for yourself." She says, "Well, Daniele, don't you want to tell me where you put me?"

In the meanwhile other children have come in. It is difficult to follow exactly what they say, as they are struggling with the caps on the mineral water bottles. This distracts Daniele and Christian from Elisa's request. Eventually Daniele says, showing her one of the napkin envelopes, "Is this yours?" She replies yes. Christian comments, "Near Michele." This obviously displeases Elisa, who protests, "And I don't like it."

The teacher, Giulia, enters, and observes the dispute. Daniele asks Elisa, "You don't want to stay near Michele?" She says, "NO! Finally, you do understand!"

Giulia glances toward the second teacher, who is silently videotaping the scene, and makes a decision not to intervene. "Find an agreement among yourselves," she tells the children, "Elisa, find an agreement with them." She returns to the next room. Christian seeks to find out with whom Elisa wants to sit, then explains to her that she must sit where they placed her. She cries out, "All right!" and leaves, mad, stamping her feet and slamming the door. Christian runs after her, calling her name, and bringing her back into the classroom. He asks twice, "Do you want to sit near Maria Giulia?" She remains angry. "Do what you like!" she shouts. (Later, in discussing this situation, teacher Giulia Notari stated that she thought it appropriate to minimize this situation and let the children take care of it themselves. Elisa often has such reactions, she noted, and it was not really a very painful situation for her.)

## CONCLUSIONS

The role of the preprimary teacher in Reggio Emilia shows many similarities to the role as commonly conceived in the United States. In both settings, goals are set high—as ideals that are expected to be difficult to attain and sustain in practice. In both, early childhood education involves complex interaction with multiple constituencies (children, parents, colleagues, government, the public) and stimulating children's learning and development through the design of optimal school organization, physical environments, curriculum, and pedagogy.

In Reggio Emilia, however, the preprimary teacher always stays with the same group of children and parents for three years, and always works with a co-teacher. As a pair, these two relate to the other teachers, auxilliary staff, and the *atelierista* in their school, and moreover, receive support from a *pedagogista*, who works with several schools, as well as the central city administration. In their interaction with children, Reggio Emilia teachers seek to promote children's well-being and encourage learning in all domains (cognitive, physical-motor, social, and affective), at the same time taking advantage of key moments to instruct children in ever more sophisticated use of tools and materials needed to express themselves in the multiple symbolic

**Figure 9.5.    A pair of teachers meeting with the *atelierista*.**

and artistic media. From their own point of view, the teachers' classroom work centers on "provoking occasions" of genuine intellectual growth by one or more children: especially, by listening to the words of children and then offering them back to the group to restimulate and extend their discussion and joint activity. Such a method of teaching they consider important, complex and delicate, constantly evolving and changing, and a matter of collective effort and concern.

Their tendency to engage with colleagues in extended mutual criticism and self-examination of their teaching behavior seems to notably distinguish the educators of Reggio Emilia. Just as they see children as learning best through communication, conflict, and co-action, so they see themselves as learning in this way. They see the work and development of teachers as a public activity taking place within the shared life of the school, community, and culture; they place a strong value on themselves communicating and interacting within and outside the school. Striving to fulfill these ideals is demanding, they well know, but rewarding and sustaining as well, and vital to the progress of society and human well-being.

## REFERENCES

Edwards, C.P. (1986). *Promoting social and moral development in young children: Creative approaches for the classroom.* New York: Teachers College Press.

Malaguzzi, L. (1987). *The hundred languages of children: Narrative of the possible.* Catalog of the Exhibit, "The Hundred Languages of Children," published by the Comune di Reggio Emilia, Assessorato all' Istruzione, Regione di Emilia Romagna.

**The symbol of the long jump.**

# 10

# Multiple Symbolization in the Long Jump Project*

## George Forman

The Long Jump Project has become a well-documented case study of the pedagogy of the preschools in Reggio Emilia.[1] This project, which lasted about eight weeks, occurred at the School Diana, a school for 3- to 6-year olds, nestled in the heart of the city park of Reggio Emilia. Four children volunteered to coordinate a schoolwide competition to be held on the school grounds. Many examples of quality education are

---

* I wish to thank Mary Scott, director of the Cushman Hill Children's Center, for commenting on early versions of this chapter and to my co-editors for helping me to say less than I wanted, but no less than I should.

[1] This project was led by Laura Rubizzi and her co-teacher Paola Cagliari, and Vea Vecchi, the *atelierista*, who also documented the project. Loris Malaguzzi was a frequent consultant.

exhibited in this project: the use of children's own ideas, the integrative power of projects, the constructive use of debate among children, the involvement of parents and community, practical applications of science and math, and the use of multiple forms of representation. All of these factors will be briefly mentioned as context, but this chapter will focus primarily on the last factor, the multisymbolic approach.[2]

## THE PROJECT

### Planning the Project

In the Reggio schools, small group projects begin with a series of teacher meetings. There teachers review established principles about what makes a good project. A good project both allows for individual contribution from each child, while it also allows the children to interact around common goals. It allows children not only to pursue clearly defined goals, but also to discuss and decide on their own subgoals, rules, and incentives. There should be dialogue and conflict leading to the coordination of different views. Not only does a good project use verbal discussions, but it should use other modes of representation, such as graphics and mimicry and gestures. The graphics and gestures will help the children communicate their divergent ideas, and the verbal dialogue will help them reach a consensus.

After the meeting, teachers then return to their classrooms and do some pilot work to check out their expectations. In the case of the Long Jump event, teachers felt this project would present many opportunities to explore concepts of fairness, concepts of measurement, and concepts of time and distance. The teachers particularly liked the Long Jump event because it was not well practiced at the school. The children would need to invent their own meanings and methods of assuring fairness in the competition. The teachers then reconvened to make the final commitment to do the project at the School Diana, but for the educational benefit of all 22 schools in the system. This chapter is based on the documentation compiled by Vea Vecchi, Laura Rubizzi, and Paola Cagliari at the Diana School in Spring 1985 with consultation from Loris Malaguzzi.

---

[2] All of these factors are presented in a two-hour videotape entitled "The Long Jump: Using Small Group Projects in Early Education—Reggio Emilia, Italy" produced by George Forman and Lella Gandini. Available from Performanetics Press, 19 The Hollow, Amherst, MA 01003.

Four children volunteered to plan and design this athletic event, but at various times the committee called for the assistance of their entire class, and toward the end, the whole school and community were involved, particularly during the six days for the qualifying meet and the championship meet. The activities during this project emerged in an organic way and were documented daily (mostly in audiotapes and observational records). The teachers and *pedagogista* (see Chapter 6, this volume) would study the documentation and plan the means for facilitating the direction of learning they discerned in these documents.

## Sequence of Activities

This chapter will abstract principles from the many activities throughout the eight-week project. General principles, common across many projects, will be highlighted in bordered paragraphs. To reduce confusion we need to place these activities in time. The chapter sometimes will refer to the index number to facilitate the discussion. These activities are listed in chronological order without comment as follows:

*1.0*  Looking at and Acting Out Photographs of Olympic Long Jumpers
*2.0*  Verbal Outpouring of Initial Knowledge of Long Jump
*3.0*  Making an Initial Sketch of Track, Jumpers, and How to Score
*4.0*  Drawing the Track Layout: Run-up and Landing Area
*5.0*  Experimenting with Running Speed × Jumping Distance
*6.0*  Laying out the Track in the Courtyard using White Chalk
*7.0*  Debating about Handicap for Girls using Small Replica Objects
*8.0*  Designing Six Posters for Rules of the Long Jump
    *8.1*  Place to start
    *8.2*  Three false starts allowed
    *8.3*  Three days allowed before starting
    *8.4*  Speed and place of the run-up
    *8.5*  The touch of the foot
    *8.6*  Measurement of the footprint
*9.0*  Presenting the Rules to Whole Class
*10.0*  Designing Training, Clothes, and Diet
*11.0*  Making Posters Calling for the Registration of Each Participant
*12.0*  Making Posters for Designating Ability Flights
*13.0*  Making Posters for Calendar of Competition by Ability Flights
*14.0*  Writing a Letter of Invitation to All Children of the School
*15.0*  Designing Posters of Citywide Advertising
*16.0*  Writing the Rules for Prizes

*17.0*   Writing the Closing Speech for After the Competition
*18.0*   Making a Poster of Rules for Measuring Three Jumps per Person
*19.0*   Learning to Measure Distance—Six Phases
    *19.1*   One: Using string to record the distance jumped
    *19.2*   Two: Trying to use the tape measure
    *19.3*   Three: Correcting the tape measure
    *19.4*   Four: Transcribing tape measure symbols to paper
    *19.5*   Five: Comparing tape measure to carpenter's ruler
    *19.6*   Six: Reinventing conventional place value notation
*20.0*   Preparing Insignia for Each Jumper to Wear at the Meet
*21.0*   Writing Rules for the Referee and Assistants
*22.0*   Implementing the Plans: The Day of the Final Competition
    *22.1*   The run and the long jump
    *22.2*   Measuring each jump with string
    *22.3*   Posting the strings on the wall
    *22.4*   Using the tape to measure the longest strings
    *22.5*   Awarding the trophies
    *22.6*   The kisses from the misters and misses

First the four children, Lorenzo, Augusto, Stephania, and Silvia, ages 5½ to 6 years old, sought to understand the cultural form of the Long Jump. They looked at photographs [*1.0*] and reminisced about their own rather meager experiences. The children also observed each other jump near the table, and returned many times to discuss the photographs. (Photographs elicit a type of *verbal outpouring* of initial knowledge and assumptions [*2.0*].) The photographs and the teacher stimulate this verbal outpouring but the details are missing. There is much to be understood.

---

The teachers often provide the children with complex events as a catalyst for group discussion. The associated cultural artifacts (in this case, photographs of the Olympics) are presented full blown rather than presented in a cartoon or simplified form. This technique is common across many of the projects. For example, in other projects children study a set of blueprints for a table, and a scaled drawing of a dinosaur, and later in this project, a real tape measure and carpenter's ruler.

---

## CYCLES OF SYMBOLIZATION

We can grant that children live an experience in a linear manner, from day to day. But learning and the construction of knowledge has a mental course of its own, full of mental replays, reflections, and re-

representations. The remaining sections map this mental course of how children learn to verbally review and debate their facts, act out or draw their present understanding, make graphic representations of their discoveries and inventions, and develop notations and scripts to communicate this knowledge to others. These cycles repeat many times within any one project. It follows that cycles of symbolization is an apt descriptor of this process.

Accordingly, the next sections depart from a straight chronological order so that we might trace the evolution of specific cycles of symbolization. The cycles occur within and throughout the entire project. A single cycle is defined by a common problem, such as the relation between running space and landing space. Within a single cycle the children confront and discuss a problem using a variety of symbol systems, some invented, some conventional. Their motivation for using and inventing symbols is (a) to gain better purchase on their own understanding of something, and (b) to present that understanding clearly to others.

## Run-Up and Landing Space

After looking at the photographs the children were encouraged to make a pencil sketch of the long jump event [3.0]. The drawings help the children look at each other's thinking. All children can see and comment on a drawing. A drawing is a commitment to specifics. The teachers want the children to make these commitments explicit so that specific agreements or disagreements can occur.

Both Augusto and Lorenzo laid out a rather short run-up space and proportionately much longer landing space (above the dashed line in Figure 10.1). This relation will be reconstructed when children actu-

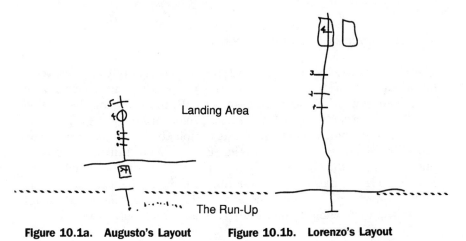

Landing Area

The Run-Up

**Figure 10.1a.  Augusto's Layout**          **Figure 10.1b.  Lorenzo's Layout**

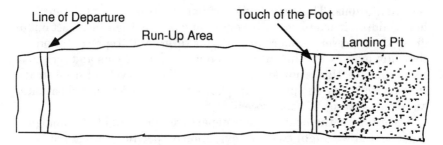

Line of Departure        Touch of the Foot

Run-Up Area              Landing Pit

**Figure 10.2. The layout of the track on the posters.**

ally go outdoors to run (5.0) and to lay out the track (6.0). But the initial drawings bring relative distance to consciousness and increase the probability that children are testing ideas when they make the track outdoors. This is how a cycle of symbolization works to support deeper learning.

Gradually the children come to understand that the run-up distance will be much longer than a long jump itself could ever be. This new understanding first takes the form of a rule stated in a large poster the four children make for their classmates [8.0]. The rule states that the run must begin at a certain point. But by the day of the competition [22.0], the children understand that this distance need not be prescribed because once a child hits her top speed, more run-up distance is superfluous. So by cycling first through an initial sketch [3.0], which raises questions that are then tried out with the body [5.0 and 6.0], then by redrawing this learning [8.0] the children bring their practical knowledge into formal consciousness to the point that they question, during the final practical application of the rule [22.0], the necessity to prescribe a starting point.

### The Sequence of the Long Jump Itself

The children used at least seven types of symbols to construct their knowledge about the sequence of the jump. They used drawing of *figures*, drawings of *footprints*, gestures with their *fingers*, the printed *word*, practical actions with their *body*, reference to *photographs*, and movement of small wooden *dolls*. The complexity of the long jump may have first been raised as an issue during their initial viewing of photographs [1.0]. They saw photographs that virtually animated the long jump from the start-up to landing in the pit. The issue of the long jump sequence gained more details in the heated debate [7.0] about where the girls should start their run, as compared to the boys.

In this debate [7.0] the boys insisted that the girls would have difficulty competing in the long jump. Perhaps they should be given an advantage. The teacher prepared a scaled-down version of the running track and gave the children two dolls, one to be the boy jumper, the other to be the girl jumper. The cycle of symbolizations of speed, distance run, and distance jumped began [5.0] indoors while making a drawing, experimented with empirically outside with some runs and jumps [6.0], and then reconsidered in the context of making formal rules [7.0]. These multiple forms of symbolizing the question facilitated the clarity with which the children were able to debate these relations [8.0] using the little dolls on the miniature track (about three-feet long on a narrow table).

Augusto says that the faster the runner the farther the jump. He also speculates that if children had more run-up space they could run faster, and therefore jump further. So he offers that they make a rule that girls be allowed to start further back from the touch of the foot (jumping line). He places the girl doll back behind the starting line (Figure 10.3a).

Sephania, perhaps because she sees "herself" being placed farther back, empathizes with the girl participants and says, "No, if they start farther back they will get tired, and they cannot make it, they cannot jump." She is about to move the girl doll when Lorenzo intervenes.

Lorenzo, "Maybe I have misunderstood. She has to start farther up, because she has very little strength and this way she doesn't get tired." With these words he moves the girl doll forward of the original line of departure, closer to the jumping line than the boy doll (Figure 10.3b).

Neither Sephania nor Silvia like this idea. Stephania takes a definite stand. "Hey no, come on. We have already decided the rule. The girls should start from the same line of departure as the boys." She then moves the girl doll back to the original line of departure adjacent to the boy doll (Figure 10.3c).

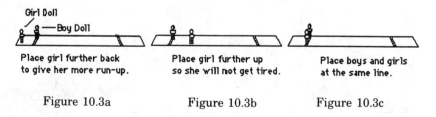

Girl Doll

Boy Doll

Place girl further back to give her more run-up.

Place girl further up so she will not get tired.

Place boys and girls at the same line.

Figure 10.3a                     Figure 10.3b                     Figure 10.3c

**Figure 10.3.   Three placements of replica objects during a debate about a handicap for the girls.**

The impressive aspect in this group discussion rests on the quickness of both Lorenzo and Stephania to relate their ideas to the current state of the debate. The replica objects help children keep the complex relations in mind so that they can perform mental transformations on these relations. The replica objects also serve as presentation tools of each child's idea. Thus the replica symbols are quite useful for keeping track of relations, presenting relations, and transforming those relations for review by the other members of the committee. Had these children relied exclusively on verbal symbols they would have surely become sidetracked by the cognitive demands of verbal expressions. The replica objects help children disambiguate their meanings and get on with the substance of the subject matter.

> The teachers found many ways to help children externalize their thoughts for others, ways to make it possible for all children to share a common meaning. The teachers often provided the children with replica objects as props to explain complex relations, as in a project to explain the rules of Drop the Handkerchief or in explaining the direction of shadows or a reflection in a water puddle.

The end of this portion of the cycle lead directly to [8.0] the drawing of posters for the rules of the long jump sequence. At that point they "commissioned" a child outside the committee, a child known for his drawing skills, to render six figures for different moments in the long jump (Figure 10.4).

These four children realized that if the competition was to be fair, the rules had to be clear and made permanent through some sort of poster [8.0]. They decided to make six posters, one for each component of the running long jump.

**Figure 10.4. The six figures of the long jump sequence.**

Earlier they thought they would make one big poster that contained all the rules. They changed their mind. One poster, they reasoned, would be too confusing. This is another instance of how the children thought about the communication value of their symbols. As a general technique across projects, the teachers often stage the project as one of communicating with less-informed children.

Looking across all six posters the children draw where all runners should begin. The footprints in Figure 10.5a show the legal moves and illegal moves, the crossed out footprints indicate the runner had started ahead of the line of departure. In Figure 10.5b the children explain that each participant gets three chances to start at the correct line. But if the participant makes a third false start, indicated by the arrow, the participant is out of the competition.

In Figure 10.5c the children state that young children have up to three days to decide when to begin their run. The hand with the watch indicates that, ordinarily, participants have five minutes to start their jump. But if a child is young and shy, the child has three days. The sun and moon cycle through three full days. If they do not begin their run after this time, the child must stay out of the competition for one year, which would be sad (see icon of crying eye).

Symbols are used and reused, such as the crying eye in Figures 10.5b and 10.5c, the background for all of these posters, and the layout of the track itself. Figure 10.5d states that children can run at whatever speed they can, but they must run within the sidelines of the track. In Figure 10.5e, titled *the touch of the foot*, the rules state that the jump must be made always with the right foot and that you can not begin the jump with a step into the sand pit (see the crossed out footprints to indicate illegal jumps). Figure 10.5f combines rules about the flight of the jump ("one must jump as if one were seated, with arms forward as if at the steering wheel of a car.") and rules about how to measure the jump. The text and the pictures show that the footprints are measured, never with a diagonal placement of the measuring tape, but always straight. Elsewise the measure "can be sometimes longer and sometimes shorter."

The six figures of the jumper were photocopied and then used by the committee to make the posters. Each time a given figure was used it symbolized some core meaning that was invariant across the different posters. Thus, these icons became a type of picture morpheme, a small unit of meaning. Look at the jumper at the start, the picture of the jumper standing up straight. This icon appears in Figures 10.5a, 10.5b, and 10.5c. The rules stated in the text of these posters (not shown, but printed on the original posters) all deal with conditions prior to the actual run.

Yet, the context for the standing figure icon changes slightly as the children place it in different locations. In Figure 10.5a and 10.5b the figure is outside the running track. In these two posters this icon has a slightly different meaning than in Figure 10.5c, where the icon is within the running track. In Figure 10.5c the icon is a portrayal of the

Figure 5a: Point of Departure

Figure 5b: Three False Starts

Figure 5c: Three Days to Wait

Figure 5d: The Run-Up

Figure 5e: Touch of the Foot

Figure 5f: Measuring the Jump

**Figure 10.5.   Six posters for rules of the long jump.**

action under discussion, much as are the footprints. But in Figures 10.5a and 10.5b the figure has a more declarative status, rather than a procedural status. That is, the icon in these two posters say: This is a poster about rules of the start. But the icon itself, in Figure 10.5a and 10.5b, give no instruction about the procedure, as the icon does in Figure 10.5c. The icon in Figure 10.5c actually shows where the runner should begin, that is, the icon is placed in a replica space and some of its meaning is drawn from this spatial location. These variations of meaning are carried by a protosyntax, the relation of one symbol to other symbols.

Note that the children appreciate the age appropriateness of different symbol types. This understanding is made clear by a discussion the children had about the cluster of three symbols in the upper left hand corner. Since the posters will be seen by all the children in the Diana School, children from 3 to 6 years old, our committee of four decided to use pictures for the little children, arrows and footprint schematics for the middle children, and words and letters for the children over five (see Figure 10.6).

Thus, the communication context gives the children a reason to cycle a given concept through a variety of symbol types that in turn increases the depth of knowledge constructed by the four child authors of these posters.

Figure 10.6.   Three symbols for a multiage audience.

The teachers often encourage the children to individually invent symbols and then choose from these "nominees." They vote on which set of symbols capture the intended meaning the best. This practice of choosing some and eliminating other symbols cause the children to talk at the metasymbolic level. For example, in the case of invented footprints, the children chose those with arrows as less ambiguous and the one drawn on bent paper to show both forward motion and upward leaping (Figure 5e, the touch of the foot as it leaps). Critiques of each other's work are common to other projects, such as in a map-making project where a 5-year-old group debated one member's use of scribbles for a 3-year-old audience versus another member's insistence that pictorial icons would be better even for the 3-year-olds (see Chapter 9, this volume).

In summary, the sequence of the long jump itself was worked out by cycling through photographs (*1.0*), actual running and jumping outdoors (*5.0*), debating handicap issues using small wooden dolls (*7.0*), making large graphics on posters for classmates to study (*8.0*), culminating in verbal explanations of these rules (*9.0*) and the actual contest at the end of the project (*22.1*). Thus, we see how a common project can lend integrity to the various symbolic activities and deepen world knowledge as well as symbolic skills per se. Each portion of the cycle relates to each other and deepens detail and finesse as the cycle proceeds.

## Measuring the Distance Jumped

The cycles are interwoven. Any one cycle can alternate with another as the children leave and return to a given problem. The problem of inventing a reliable means to measure everyone's jump was one of the most interesting cycles in this project. This cycle of symbolization has many turns and loops too complex for this chapter. (See the Forman-Gandini videotape for an in-depth analysis of this interesting part of the Long Jump project.) The highlights are as follows.

The children knew that they wanted something more than the footprint in the sandpit as a record of the jump. They wanted a record that was both portable and accurate. Their first idea was to use a piece of string. Each jump would be "measured" by cutting a string the linear distance from the landing footprint to the jumping line. The strings would then be stretched out with their starting ends matched. The longest string, thereby, would be an analog to the longest of any set of jumps.

But analog records are cumbersome and are in a sense local. They are local in that they yield a winner only when a contesting jump is physically compared to the current winner. Furthermore, analog records are only ordinal in nature. That is, one cannot say by what amount one jump exceeded another. With the strings one can only say Augusto's jump was the longest, Silvia's the next longest, and so forth. These are the issues with which the children were dealing in their initial sketches [3.0] and then more specifically in a special poster [18.0], and using the string to measure [19.1].

The children realize [19.2] that strings are not the preferred cultural representation of distance. It is not clear why they decided on using a tape measure, but we can speculate that they at least recalled from recounts, photos, and other experiences that tape measures are what you use. So what begins in [19.2], learning to use the tape measure continues for many days to follow, for learning to use the tape measure was no less than learning to deal with standard place-value notation of our number system.

By [19.3] they have noticed that the black numerals, written every 10 centimeters on the tape measure, repeat themselves. This, of course, is true because, say, the black numeral 20 would reoccur every meter. The red numerals, which stood for the meters, did not reoccur. The children decided that something was wrong with the tape measure and wanted to cut it off at the first red numeral because this first meter was o.k. (it had no repeating black numerals). Instead of ruining the tape measure they set about to copy on strips of paper the first meter of the cloth tape measure. While doing this they lay out the one meter strips side by side to confirm that they were the same length. But then they reasoned that these strips, individually, would be no help if anyone jumped more than a meter. These longer jumps often happened in practice.

The children then lay out the strips end to end so they could measure longer jumps. And in so doing they made the important discovery that the strips of paper were no different from the tape measure. That

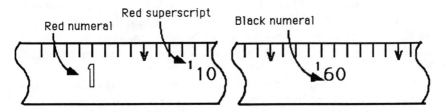

**Figure 10.7.    The cloth tape measure—large red numerals are meters.**

meant, conversely, that the tape measure was, in effect, a series of one meter strips laid end to end. Therefore, the repeating black numerals were accounted for the same way that the "repeating" black numerals occurred on the three strips of paper measures they had copied. Voila!

Copying the cloth measuring tape, somewhat of a symbol for a symbol, was not a trivial event. For one, the children, in copying the symbols, sometimes too literally, began to process the regularities of the cultural artifact. For another, by having transformed the one object (cloth tape) into three objects (paper strip tapes), the children began to concentrate on each meter being an ending. That is, the physical separateness of a one-meter strip, laid end to end, made it easier to consider that one meter's ending is the next meter's beginning. This is the key concept they were missing when they were first concerned about the repeating black numerals on the cloth tape. By making a symbol of a symbol they were better able to understand the original symbol system: the cloth tape.

In this example of making a paper replica of the tape measure we see another general teaching technique used in these schools. Children are encouraged to make symbols of symbols. This encourages the children to take a metasymbolic stance toward the symbol. In one project children reinvented highway symbols, but in the context of giving a shining knight directions to the castle of the wicked witch. In another project, children made pictures of the changing *piazza* by looking at photographs of the *piazza* changing from morning to evening. In the act of making symbols of symbols, children become more aware of just how the symbol carries its message.

They changed their focus from copying the whole tape to copying just the numerals [*19.4*]. At this point they were thinking more about making a record of the distance jumped rather than trying to understand the tape measure per se. The cycle of symbolization shifts from making objects (the tape measure) to making a record (the numerals). This is an important shift and will eventually lead them to reconstruct standard place-value notation. Once they embark on this new objective we find that they are trapped midway between making pictures and making notations. These transitional symbols occur during activities *19.4* to *19.6*.

The children invented a set of tally marks to help them merge the black numbers on the tape measure with the little hash marks that represented, on the tape measure, unnumbered centimeters. The jump that was being measured was actually one meter and 65 centimeters.

$$^{1}\text{6}0 \,|\,|\,|\,\downarrow \implies 34$$

**Figure 10.8.  Transitional notations from tally marks to place value.**

On the tape measure the numeral 60 was printed in black and to the left was placed, in a red superscript, the numeral 1. Children would literally copy the mark immediately adjacent to the masking tape on the floor. *(See previous inset on the importance of copying symbols.)* The masking tape itself marked the place where the jumper's feet first hit. The children understood that making a single hash mark on the paper would carry no meaning, even though the masking tape was actually adjacent to just such a mark. To be more exact, this tape measure had a small arrowhead at every fifth hash mark as an additional aid for keeping track of the unnumbered hash marks. Children copied this arrowhead too.

The numeral 60 plus the hash marks made sense to the children. (Note, they were rather casual about the exact number of hash marks, perhaps because, as one child said, these marks were "not important enough to be numbered.") The numeral 60 told one where the tally marks were on the tape, sort of like the nearest important neighbor. So their invented system was perfectly reliable if one only wants to locate the spot on the measuring tape that corresponds to marks made on the floor.

This invention obviated the need for the children to deal with place-value notation. In this transitional notation, the zero stands for units as do the several tally marks thereafter. The symbol system uses both the numeral system in part and a tally iteration system in part, an analog/digital hybrid of great intuitive appeal.

Two children, Stephania and Lorenzo, become dissatisfied with this hybrid system upon seeing a carpenter's ruler (*19.5*), a tool where all the centimeter hash marks have numerals printed above them. By using a pair of scissors, opened and held constant, they determine that 10 units on the cloth measuring tape is always the same gap as 10 units on the wooden carpenter's ruler. So, by a type of transductive reasoning they conclude that these little black hash marks on the cloth tape can be represented as numerals. At that point Stephania and Lorenzo become determined to use only numerals, no hash marks, to represent the place where the masking tape touches the measuring tape.

The teacher gives them the distance "34 centimeters" and asked them to find this number on the tape. This number is less than one meter, so they need to find the first set of 34 centimeters. And this number does not fall on either a printed black numeral nor on one of the arrow heads. The following statements come directly from an observational record of how they solved this problem.

The children look for the first black number that has 3. When they find it they notice that it has a zero next to it, that is 30. To eliminate this zero they pretend to remove the zero, sort of get it out of the way for the moment. Now they feel comfortable calling the 30 "three." Then they count the black lines beyond 30 saying: "one, two, three, four equals thirty four." So the three and four together can refer to both tens and units. Three for the centimeters and four for the black marks.

Herein the children have made their first attempt to use a notation system that collapses symbols for tens and units into one multidigit numeral. Units as the tenants of the first column may not quite be understood, as seen in their felt need to evict the zero. But with this depth of processing, complete understanding can be far behind.

This construction of place-value notation actually came later than the rules for using the red and black numerals on the measuring tape. Read this with due respect, but appreciate that these rules do not yet mean the children understood the place-value notation itself. What the following rules do indicate, however, is the understanding of a conditional logic: Ignore black when one jump has a higher red, attend to black when both reds are the same. Figure 9 presents a printed list of the rules as the children dictated them to the teacher.

The cleverness of this set of rules rests on the use of color. By designating the "hundreds" place as red (i.e., 2 is really 200 centimeters) and by designating black as the centimeters, they can copy the tape literally without having to deal with a monochromatic place-value notation. In other words, 135 is one hundred and thirty-five centimeters. But the rules would yield a reading of 1 red and 35 blacks. This color coding could indicate a more qualitative form of numbering, something like, 1 giant and 35 dwarfs. We are not sure how many dwarfs make a single giant. That is, we are not sure the children understand that the difference between 100 and 101 is the same as the difference between 10 and 11. Furthermore, the rules do not help when a jump falls on 34 or any other place without a black numeral printed on the tape. This is why Stephania and Lorenzo continued their quest for understanding when confronted with the carpenter's ruler.

To summarize this cycle of symbolization, children first make marks on the floor. To compare marks they make strings the same length as the jump. Strings are spatial analogs to the jump, but present problems

In order to write the measure we write with the red colored

marker the red number (these are the meters) and with

the black colored marker the black numbers (these are

the centimeters)

We write all the measures on a large piece of paper.

Then we look at the red numbers, which are the most

important.

Then the black numbers.

The winner is the one who has the largest red number or

the largest black number or if two have the same red

number, the winner is the one who has the largest

black number.

**Figure 10.9.  The written rules for using the cloth tape measure.**

when one wants to determine how long a single jump is or how much longer one jump is to the other. The tape measure, another symbol system, seems relevant, but presents a problem: how to translate the marks on the tape into a reliable record. The children create a hybrid symbol of hash marks and numerals, but are dissatisfied with the combination of numerals and hash marks. This dissatisfaction comes from a comparison of two cultural artifacts, the tape measure and the carpenter's ruler. It may also come from the awareness that a length can be stated precisely, rather than approximately. So two children continue their quest for the conventional notation system, and in large measure succeed. The different symbol systems are marvelously inter-related and create the type of constructive conflict we deem to be the power of this multisymbolic approach to education.

## SYMBOLS AND SYMBOL SYSTEMS

So ends this particular set of passes through the complexities of the Long Jump project at the School Diana. From this documentation we can learn much about how symbol systems can support each other or generate constructive conflict. As these children sought to gain a more

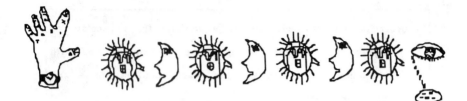

**Figure 10.10.  Symbols to represent specific temporal intervals.**

generate constructive conflict. As these children sought to gain a more coherent understanding of time, distance, and rules of equity, they externalized their nascent theories as icons, gestures, speech, text, pictograms, diagrams, and notations. These symbols were embedded in the coherence of a real-world event which in turn helped to convert a random list of symbols into a symbol system.

A list of symbols can be judged for the readability of each symbol. When these individual symbols are used and reused into one of the cycles discussed above, the symbols develop something new, a syntax of sorts. So when the wrist watch is combined with the sun-moon symbols (Figure 10.10), the watch refers to the initiation of an event. But when the wrist watch symbol is placed between each row of jumpers in a later poster [18.0], the watch symbol refers to the lag between each attempt. The core meaning, brief interval, is preserved, but the syntactical relations gives the symbol nuance. We saw this same use of syntactical relations with the arrowheads, the footprints, and the transition from red and black numerals to monochromatic numerals. Place value is essentially a syntactic system.

The "Hundred Languages of Children" is the title chosen by the educators in Reggio Emilia to refer to their traveling exhibit. The appropriateness of this title has been interpreted differently by American educators. . To some this title refers to Reggio's use of the multi-arts in their curriculum. To others the title refers to their appreciation of diversity in how children learn. For this chapter, the title has been interpreted to mean that all children learn best when they can use multiple symbol systems to understand complex relations, particularly when these complex relations are part of a real-world project that gives these relations a holistic gestalt. This holism assures that the symbol systems will ultimately converge to deepen knowledge rather than increase facts.

**"A long neck dinosaur."** Drawing by Valentina, Anna Frank School.

# 11

# Curriculum Development in Reggio Emilia: A Long-Term Curriculum Project About Dinosaurs

### Baji Rankin

*Paolo (5.8):*     "Dinosaurs are enormous. . . ."
*Federico (6.0):*  "It's almost as if we would crush an ant."
*Paolo:*           "And dinosaurs would crush us!"

This exchange between Paolo and Federico is one fragment of many conversations that took place during a project about dinosaurs in a Reggio Emilia preschool. This chapter describes the unfolding of this project, which took place over four months (44 separate sessions) from mid-February through June 1990. A group of 5- and 6-year-old children in the Anna Frank School for 3–6 year olds took part in the project, guided by their *atelierista*, Roberta Badodi. My own role evolved gradually from observer to participant, as I documented the experience for Roberta and myself on audiotape, slides, and videotape. Roberta would use the documentation in her work with children, teachers, parents, and the community. I would use it for better understanding the Reggio approach and then communicating to United States audiences (Rankin, forthcoming).

I lived in Reggio Emilia for most of one school year, a nine-month period from October 1989 through June 1990. Living in Reggio for such an extended period of time allowed me to observe and participate in the project as well as in the surrounding system of social relationships in the Anna Frank School, the municipal early childhood system, and the city.

## HOW IT BEGAN

I first heard of Reggio Emilia in 1982 while conducting my CAGS (Certificate of Advanced Graduate Studies) thesis in Italy on policy concerning early childhood education (Rankin, 1985). Struck by the profound philosophy, aesthetical environments, spirit of reciprocity, tolerance of conflict, and integration of theory and practice, I carried my interest forward over the next seven years of work and study in the United States, leading finally to a decision in 1989 to return to Reggio and do my doctoral dissertation on emergent curriculum development.

My first several months of exploratory investigation led to a decision to study the course of one single project. Supported by the Reggio administration, I began work with Roberta Badodi in mid-February. She was just about to begin a new project with children and graciously accepted my presence, along with all of my questions, comments, cameras, and tape and videorecorders, and even invited my active participation. She received my questions and comments as a welcome stimulus to her own professional growth.

A similar openness was apparent in all of the educators with whom I worked in Reggio Emilia, an example of their guiding philosophy of reciprocity, or circularity, put into action. Carlina Rinaldi, *pedagogista* at Anna Frank, was a particularly strong model of this attitude. And in varied ways, all of the teachers and staff demonstrated interest in learning from me—someone with a cultural background and a set of experiences different from their own—just as they seek to learn from all visitors to their schools.

What, then, can educators in the United States learn from my report on the unfolding of a project in Reggio Emilia, when our cultures, systems of education, and political realities are so different? Many people in the United States, first learning of the Reggio Emilia approach, ask both large and small questions. How does the Reggio approach differ from progressive education and open education, two movements that have been a prominent part of our experience in the United States? How does the Reggio approach compare to the concepts behind "developmentally appropriate practice," as defined by standards of the National Association for the Education of Young Children? How does emergent curriculum in Reggio compare to what U.S. educators seek to implement in "the project approach?" More specifically, what is the role of the teacher in guiding children's learning; how much does she lead them and structure their activity? All of these questions are considered in depth in this book. This chapter, however, is the only one to provide empirical observations of the actual unfolding over time of a particular project. My goal is to provide the kind of information that readers can use to better come to their own conclusions regarding these important questions cited above.

The dinosaur project, like any other in Reggio, had its own unique momentum and sequence of events. It could never be exactly duplicated in Reggio Emilia or any other place. Roberta made numerous decisions based on the particular group of children with whom she was working, their preferences and capabilities, and the daily features of the situation. Therefore, this report should not be thought of as providing a model to copy, but rather a description of a process that illustrates principles that can be applied in other situations. A central principle is that of *reciprocity* which involves mutual guidance of the educational process by teacher and learner and responsiveness in circular paths of communication, caring, and control (see Malaguzzi, Chapter 3, this volume). A metaphor used by educators in Reggio Emilia to describe this sense of reciprocity is that of a ball being tossed (see Edwards, Chapter 9, this volume). As Tiziana Filippini said in her 1990 speech to the National Association for the Education of Young Children:

> Our expectations of the child must be very flexible and varied. We must be able to be amazed and to enjoy—like the children often do. We must be able to catch the ball that the children throw us, and toss it back to them in a way that makes the children want to continue the game with us, developing, perhaps, other games as we go along.

The adults involved in the dinosaur project sought to toss the ball in just such a way.

## THE UNFOLDING OF THE PROJECT

### The Initiating Context

In Italy, just as in the United States, images of dinosaurs abound. Children participate in a culture of dinosaurs through books, movies, television, and toys. Often they are fascinated and excited, as well as worried or frightened, by the images they see of those dinosaurs most immense, powerful, and aggressive.

Children in Reggio Emilia, just as in other places, like to bring things from home to school. At the Anna Frank school, beginning in Fall 1989, teachers of the 5–6-year-olds noticed that many children were bringing dinosaur toys to school. The children's play sometimes spontaneously turned to dinosaurs. The teachers took note, valuing the interest in dinosaurs as an opportunity to understand more about the children. In keeping with the principle of reciprocity, teachers decided to begin a journey together with the children and study dinosaurs in depth.

As is the customary practice in Reggio Emilia, a group of children, rather than the whole classroom, conducted this project. Educators in Reggio (see Malaguzzi, Chapter 3, and Rinaldi, Chapter 5, this volume) believe that small group work activates the most intense learning and exchange of ideas. Everyone benefits when small group work is coupled with systematic rotation (so that every child participates in at least one such experience a year), interaction between the project group and the whole class at key points (so that knowledge and insights are shared), and collaboration among adults—parents, teachers, and *atelierista*, and *pedagogista* (to deal with the complexities and problems that arise and jointly grow from all that is learned). In the case of the dinosaur project, the adults decided to work with the children who were most interested in dinosaurs. These children represented the spectrum of the class in terms of cognitive and linguistic maturity; and they were about equally divided between boys and girls.

Another customary practice in Reggio Emilia is that before the children actually gather to begin the project, the adults involved meet to discuss various possibilities, hypotheses, and potential directions that the project might take. This is important, Carlina Rinaldi pointed out in a meeting with Roberta and myself on April 20, 1990.

> If adults have thought of 1,000 hypotheses, then it is easy to accept the fact that there can be 1,001 or 2,000 hypotheses. The unknown is easier to accept and adults are more open to new ideas when they have generated many potentialities themselves. The problem comes from having only one hypothesis which then draws all the attention of the adult.

Accordingly, before opening the project with the children, Roberta and Carlina brainstormed many possibilities and potential directions. They also formulated some "provocatory" questions for Roberta to use in a first discussion with the children, to open the project and assess their initial level of knowledge about dinosaurs. The adults had caught the idea of dinosaur study from the children, and now they wanted to return it to them in a way that would generate observations, questions, suggestions, hypotheses, and set the initial direction of the project work.

Continual collaboration among adults throughout this project is critical to its progress. In this case the primary adults involved were the *atelierista*, who works exclusively in the Anna Frank School, the *pedagogista*, Carlina, who works with adults in several preschools and infant/toddler centers, and myself. (In many other projects, classroom teachers take leading roles as well, for example, see The Long Jump Project, described by Forman in Chapter 10, this volume.) Accordingly, we three met to talk and plan together through a variety of means. We held formal scheduled meetings together. We made frequent phone calls to Carlina during many phases of the project. We held informal conversations whenever Carlina came to the school for other purposes. Roberta and I conferred continually—before, during, and after activity times. Roberta held frequent discussions with the two lead teachers of the 5–6 year-old classroom to inform and involve them in events.

### The Beginning

The initial phase is an essential part of any project: the aim is to open up and to assess the children's knowledge and interests concerning the subject. The adults want to help children set up a context in which the children can find their own questions and problems to explore. The goal is to help each individual and the group as a whole advance the construction and co-construction of knowledge. Thus, instead of only responding to those questions that adults think they will find interesting, the children are involved right from the start in defining questions to be explored.

The initial phase also involves establishing the community of the small group. Emphasis is placed on learning as a group and developing a sense of "we." Reggio Emilia educators use the phrase, "*Io chi siamo*" ("The I who we are") to express the idea that it is within this shared space of "we" that each child can offer his or her best thinking, leading to a rich and fertile group exchange and stimulating something new and unexpected, impossible for any one person to create alone. The teacher's role in this process is to galvanize each child to participate and to grow, as much as he or she can, within the context of the group investigation. This is done within a framework of seeing that the project belongs to the group: each child is a part, an essential part, but only a part. The reality of "we," which the Reggio educators believe is inside each child from birth, is valued and encouraged in all of the activities of school life. In this sense the actual theme or content of the project is not as important as the process of children thinking, feeling, working, and progressing together with others.

At the beginning of the dinosaur project, then, about half the 5–6-year-old class gathered in the *atelier* of the Anna Frank School for the first time. Roberta, establishing the sense of "Io chi siamo," explained to the children that they would be working on dinosaurs for awhile. She encouraged all of them to do their best and pointed out that they had a special opportunity to work together. She initiated first a graphic (pictorial) and then a verbal investigation. The children began to draw dinosaurs, anyway they liked, around a large square table. They talked together as they drew and asked each other questions about their drawings and about other things. Good ideas spread contagiously around the table. Several times a child changed his or her drawing because of comments or questions from a friend. "Oh, that's not a dinosaur. Dinosaurs have four legs!"

After the children finished their drawings, Roberta spoke individually with each child about his or her drawings. Then she gathered the children together for a group discussion and asked a series of open-ended questions, encouraging discussion among the children. Where did dinosaurs live? What did they eat? How did they take care of their babies? How were the babies born? Are dinosaurs living now? What are the differences between male and female dinosaurs? These questions, growing in part out of the children's earlier play and comments, and in part of the questions compiled by the adults, evoked a great deal of interest and response.

The ideas discussed by the children became the catalysts for later activities and conversations which adults gave back to the children on later occasions. The game was expanding. This critical process was facilitated (as is typical in Reggio Emilia) by tape-recording all of the major conversations related to the project. The tapes were transcribed by Roberta at home and typed up by myself and parent volunteers, so that the adults could study and reflect on what the children had said and not said, what issues aroused the greatest interest, how children interacted, and so on. (But note, in different schools and on different occasions, the process of transcription and typing will be done by various people.)

The boys in the dinosaur group—three in particular—started with a great deal of knowledge that informed the others. Here is an excerpt from the discussion:

| | |
|---|---|
| *Federico:* | "There aren't any more dinosaurs . . . because among all the animals that were already born, the dinosaurs already existed; therefore the dinosaurs were already of two species. . . ." |
| *Francesca:* | "But all the dinosaurs are dead. They killed and buried them." |
| *Michele:* | "No! They didn't bury them! They died themselves." |
| *Fabio:* | "In fact, it's not true [they were killed] because who could have killed the dinosaurs? Primitive people were there after the dinosaurs, not at all when there were dinosaurs. Cartoons show that when there were dinosaurs there were primitive people, but really there weren't primitive people when there were dinosaurs. The primitive people existed after the dinosaurs." |
| *Federico:* | "Men came when dinosaurs were dead." |
| *Fabio:* | "When there were dinosaurs, there were all the little animals that were all small insects when the dinosaurs disappeared. They became big and they became the monkeys and all the other animals . . . but not at all the elephants that there are now." |

Francesca's statement that "they buried dinosaurs" was resoundly defeated by the three boys, who had more information and confidence than she did on this topic. They also had agreement among themselves. This is an example of cognitive conflict where one position dominates.

The pictorial investigation revealed intriguing differences in ways of thinking between boys and girls. The educators in Reggio have noticed that boys and girls often approach situations differently. They are interested to learn more about those differences. Here the boys' knowledge was more accurate. Several boys indicated which dinosaurs were female by drawing baby dinosaurs inside the mother's belly. The girls, on the other hand, represented female dinosaurs by using decorations such as long hair, and by drawing baby dinosaurs close to the mother.

The next day, a Thursday, the second day of the investigation, neither the discussions nor the drawings were as rich or as extensive as the first day. Afterwards, the adults decided to wait a few days before continuing, to assess whether the children were genuinely interested enough to go ahead with a long-term project. Such a project requires a deep sense of inquiry on the children's part to sustain the effort.

However, another possible cause of the second day's lowered energy could have been the approach of the adults. Reactivating a group, maintaining the inquiry between one day and the next, is a very important and delicate manner. We had chosen to introduce the topic the second day in much the same way as we had on the first. But perhaps it would have been more effective to focus on one or two of the themes that had been of greatest interest to children on the first day, for example, the time period in which dinosaurs lived, their size, their origin and disappearance, or the differences between females and males. In any case, when we met with the children the following Monday, their interest was high once more when we offered them clay to use in constructing dinosaurs.

These initial investigations revealed the children's many interests in the dinosaur topic. In part these reflected the questions that Roberta had raised with them; however, the attention children showed to certain questions and the exchanges that ensued demonstrated their genuine curiosity as well as their capacities to construct knowledge collaboratively.

The adults used the children's tape-recorded conversations throughout the project in many ways. They referred to specific conversations as they spoke with children. They used quotations in speaking with the parents. They enlarged written quotes as parts of displays for the school as a whole. The thoughts of the children were highly valued, and everyone knew it—children, teachers, and parents. As Roberta put it (in a formal presentation to a Swedish delegation on May 9, 1991):

> A determining contribution to children's construction of knowledge, we believe, is the involvement of the adult, not only because the adult legitimizes children's knowledge and curiosity, but also because the adult values and addresses children's investigations with supports and suggestions.

## The Need for More Information

It was clear that the group needed more information. Roberta the following day initiated a discussion asking them where they could get more information about dinosaurs. This set off an explosion of excitement as children remembered possible sources: television, movies, stores, magazines, newspapers, books from home and library, older brothers, sisters, and other relatives: "My grandfather knows about dinosaurs!" "My sister!" "My brother!" "My uncle!" "My cousin, because he goes to school."

The children went to the local library the next day and found many books. They studied the books at the library and brought many back to the school. These became long-term residents of the *atelier* (the work site for the project), enabling the children to browse or to refer to the books for specific information. Children enjoyed books both in small groups and individually. They compared their own drawings to the drawings in the books. When they formulated a question, they often retrieved a book to help them clarify what they were asking about.

The children invited friends and relatives to school to share information. The task of writing a letter of invitation to friends and relatives generated much enthusiasm. The letter was composed by the whole dinosaur group, each child offering ideas while Roberta acted as scribe, reiterating, every once in a while, the purpose of the letter. Then, taking turns, two children at a time wrote out the final draft, copying Roberta's model, while others addressed envelopes, drew accompanying drawings, and made posters about the coming events. The visitors, arriving over the next few weeks, were enthusiastically received. They included two older siblings, graduates of the Anna Frank School, bearing impressive notebooks and full of zeal from their third-grade study of dinosaurs; a father, a grandmother, and an expert from a local nature society. The children prepared questions ahead of each visitor so that each child had specific questions to ask. These discussions were very rich for all participants, especially for the particular children whose relatives came.

During this period, children were also constructing dinosaurs out of clay, painting them with tempera and water color, and drawing with chalk. Differences reemerged in how girls and boys used clay. Just as in the earlier case with the drawings, the girls used more decorations, embellishments, tiny details, than did the boys. A group of four boys built a large clay dinosaur, and this collective activity produced talk about making a really big dinosaur. Children then engaged in shadow play before images of dinosaurs projected onto the wall. In this way they had the opportunity to directly experience the large dimensions of dinosaurs.

## How to Make a Big Dinosaur

At this point, many topics were of interest to the group, including the size and physical dimensions of dinosaurs, their origin and disappearance, their daily habits, differences between male and female dinosaurs, and how baby dinosaurs were raised. However, one theme kept recurring—that of size and dimension.

To follow up on this theme, Roberta asked the children what they could do to build a really big dinosaur. The discussion was lively; there were many ideas and many different suggestions about materials and techniques to use. In the midst of this discussion, an important point emerged: the necessity of deciding what kind of dinosaur to build.

*Francesco:*  Well, the thing to think about is what dinosaur to make . . . which dinosaur!
*Roberta:*  It's true. We know many dinosaurs and maybe the first thing to do is to understand which one we want to make. Why is that important to you, Francesco?
*Francesco:*  Because if not, we'll make all different things of each different dinosaur!
*Giulia:*  First we need to decide about what dinosaur to make. We need to say, 'Let's do this dinosaur! Let's do this dinosaur.'

After much debate, the children eventually decided to take a vote. *Tyrannosaurus Rex* won in a close victory over *Stegosaurus*. With more discussion the next day about what kinds of materials to use and how to use them, the children set themselves to work, spontaneously dividing themselves into smaller groups to do the work. Four girls came together to form one group, and four boys formed another. Once more, different patterns were seen in how boys and girls proceeded.

**Girls.** The girls quickly chose one book to look through, easily selected one *Tyrannosaurus Rex* to make together, and soon began looking for construction materials. They headed first towards small materials that they could use for decorating the dinosaur. It was only after Roberta talked with them that they began to think about and seek larger material for the structure of the body, Roberta brought in a ladder and encouraged them to use it to search for bigger materials higher up on the shelves of the *atelier*.

The girls chose styrofoam as their medium. This material turned out to be rather easy to work with as it was easy to handle and the shape and size of the styrofoam pieces often suggested to them different parts of the dinosaur. They had to ask for Roberta's help only at specific times; she did some things they were unable to do, such as attaching pieces of foam in a stable way with a piece of wire. A satisfying, three-dimensional, approximately four-foot high, highly decorated *Tyrannosaurus Rex* resulted, along with a stronger friendship among these particular girls.

**Boys.** The four boys, in contrast, had a more difficult time. To start with, each chose a different book and it took them a much longer time than the girls to choose which image to use as a model. Then they chose wire and metal as their construction material. Perhaps the hardness of the wire suggested to them the roughness and sharpness of *Tyrannosaurus Rex*. In any case, it is was a very difficult material to use. They had to ask for Roberta's help during most of the stages of construction, and their work went quite slowly. While the girls had seemed oblivious to other people in the room, the boys were highly distracted and at times discouraged by seeing the girls' dinosaur tak-

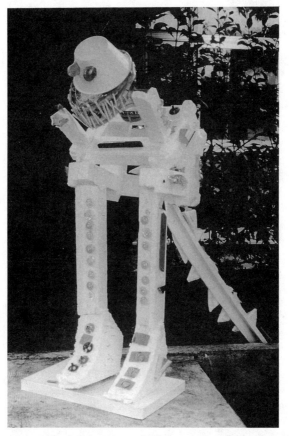

**Figure 11.1.   Four girls collaborate on building and stylishly decorating a *Tyrannosaurus Rex* out of styrofoam.**

ing rapid form. The boys had to return over the next several days to finish their work. However, in the end, their dinosaur was also very satisfying to them.

## Measuring and Drawing a Life-Size Dinosaur

As the adults read and reread the texts of the children's conversations and searched for a next direction in which to move, they noticed how the theme of size and dimension kept recurring. They decided to challenge the children to draw a life-size dinosaur and find some way to hang it, so it actually could be seen standing upright on its feet. I must admit, as a participant in these discussions, that I found this proposal

**Figure 11.2.  Four boys choose wire and metal for their dinosaur. The toughness of
the material makes the construction process difficult—but satisfying in the long run.**

preposterous. How could the children do such a difficult thing? But
then I gradually became more and more excited. Would the children
want to do it? Could they do it? I knew that they would have to be
highly motivated to get through the difficulties.

Roberta and I marked the transcribed texts so that she would be
able to remind the children of what they had said in previous sessions
about the size of dinosaurs. Roberta gathered six children, those who
remained the most curious and active in their participation up to this
point. We decided that six children—three girls and three boys—would
make a good group to confront the challenge of making a life-size
dinosaur. Although educators in Reggio Emilia have found that five or
fewer is ideal in order to maximize the cognitive learning processes in
the group, we wanted a fairly large group and a balance of girls and
boys.

Roberta's suggestion was met with great enthusiasm; it stimulated
a productive and multifaceted discussion and led naturally to the

proposal to make a life-size drawing. Notice her active role in guiding and shaping, but not controlling, the discussion:

*Roberta:*   Rereading all the things that you said, there's one thing that came to our minds that you could understand better. It has to do with the real measurements of dinosaurs, the real measurements. We've talked many times and you've said many things, but, in fact, no one has talked exactly about the real measurements of dinosaurs, no one's talked about that really."

*Federico:*   In fact, we have it in there, the 'thing-a-ma-jig' of dinosaurs. (Federico is referring to a poster of dinosaurs in the classroom that a child brought to school. It shows the height of a dinosaur in relation to the height of a man.) Only that if there is a dinosaur as high as that, then, yeah, he could be high! (Federico shakes his head; his eyes open wide; and he smiles as if in amazement, imagining how high that would be.)

Roberta listens carefully and then asks: What are you talking about? What's over there?

*Federico:*   That is, we have a big poster of dinosaurs. There is a big *Tyrannosaurus Rex* behind and a small man in front.

*Roberta:*   Oh.

*Giulia:*   We can also look in the books and take a meter and make it as big as it really was.

*Roberta:*   Certainly, in fact, it's true what Giulia said.

*Federico:*   I think the legs are as high as the ceiling.

*Roberta:*   Of all dinosaurs or of some?

*Tommi:*   No, of the *Tyrannosaurus Rex*, maybe. (He looks up to the ceiling.)

*Federico:*   Of some. (Tommi and Federico continue talking between themselves.)

*Roberta:*   Well, Giulia has already mentioned something important. If we look for a drawing of a dinosaur as big as . . . (Roberta pauses.)

*Giulia:*   As this picture.

*Roberta:*   As a real one, eh?

(The three boys talk among themselves, very quickly.)

*Federico:*   Maybe we'll need a piece of paper as big as this table.

*Roberta:*   Or maybe much larger.

*Federico:*   It has to be big and long.

*Fabio:*   Or you could copy a dinosaur that we made ourselves, that we built.

This animated conversation continued in many directions, concerning the probable size of the drawing, where they could work, what kind of dinosaur to draw. There turned out to be no need to reread texts from previous conversations. The children exploded with interest and amazement at the proposal. The difficulties faced seemed to be the most fascinating aspects to the children.

They went to the books and started looking for an image of a dinosaur to use. They gravitated to a simple line drawing of a *Diplodacus* placed in a rectangle clearly blocked off into 3-meter units of height. The represented animal was 27 by 9 meters in size (about 81 by 27 feet). Next to it there was the figure of a standing man (2 meters tall), drawn to provide a sense of the dinosaur's gigantic size.

The first problem the children wanted to tackle was to see how big 27 meters was. They were familiar with meter sticks and took the two of them from the *atelier* out into the courtyard. But their first problem was that they only had two meter sticks, when they wanted 27. The idea of using one meter stick 27 times did not occur to them. Instead, they went in search for 25 more sticks, but were only able to discover one more in another classroom.

At this point the children were stuck. What could they do? Roberta suggested going back into the *atelier* to look for other measuring material. There on the shelves the children found a bunch of long plastic rods for hanging posters! The children and Roberta verified that they were each one meter long. The children counted the rods and found more than 27, more than enough. The investigation could con-

**Figure 11.3.** After finding too few meter sticks to measure the length of 27 meters, the children return to the *atelier* to find other objects they might use. They discover several plastic roads which Roberta measures: They are one meter long!

tinue! By suggesting that the children return to search for other materials, Roberta enabled the investigation to go on. Her intervention—not the only one she could have made—supported the children in the quest for a solution but did not impose upon them an adult one.

Trying to lay out 27 of these rods in the courtyard made it evident that the courtyard was too small. An idea, suggested earlier by one child, came up now again: use the sports field in front of the school. There was clearly enough space there. The next problem became that of laying the rods in straight lines and forming the huge rectangle.

After trials, errors, and corrections, three sides of the rectangle were measured out: 27 rods by 9 rods by 9 rods. On the fourth side, however, another problem arose: there were not, after all, enough plastic rods to complete the rectangle. Two of the children went back to the school in search of other objects and arrived several minutes later, victoriously, with a roll of toilet paper! The rectangle could now be completed.

Sitting down on the grass, looking at what they had done, was satisfying to the children. However, it was also clear to them that there was a long way to go. Elena said, "Let's try it on a small piece of paper, how it should be done. Then we'll make it bigger." Every one agreed the next step should be on smaller paper.

*The Girls.* Before starting to work the following day, Roberta telephoned Carlina. Because two of the boys were sick, it made sense to Roberta and me to go ahead with the three girls first and then work

**Figure 11.4. Running out of plastic rods, two children return to the school in search of other objects they can use to close the rectangle. They return victoriously with a roll of toilet paper.**

with the boys another day. Carlina agreed, and suggested offering the girls a choice of papers to use—unlined, lined, and blocked. This choice of papers was a key element for them because, without them realizing, it forced them to render their hypothesis more concrete and therefore more public and accessible. Roberta's role was then to permit the children's problem-solving abilities to flourish in whatever ways the children chose.

Given the choice of three kinds of paper, two girls chose graph paper and one chose the unlined paper. The two using graph paper began to draw, while the third focused on telling stories. After much trial and error, and through interaction with Roberta, the girls got the idea to search the shelves of the *atelier* for objects that came in amounts of at least 27. By placing these objects on the paper, they would be able to recreate the rectangle they had made outside, but this time on paper in a smaller scale. At this point, all three girls started to use graph paper. They experimented with various materials. After several attempts, one girl succeeded with 27 small rectangular blocks that she placed along one edge of her paper. Then she made the other three sides with the same blocks. The other two girls ended up collaborating by counting out the 27 squares on the graph paper, then 9, 9, and 27 to make the rectangle.

The girls then became interested in the horizontal lines seen in the reference book to indicate 3-meter units of height. Using the squares on their graph paper, in one case, and the small rectangular blocks in the other, they counted off 3 and then 6 measures and were able to draw on their papers the two horizontal lines that marked the height. This was a tremendous accomplishment this particular morning for these three girls.

**The Boys.** When the boys had their turn, the importance of the choice of paper was dramatic. Federico immediately chose graph paper and began to count off 27 squares. He obviously had some kind of understanding that graph paper would be most suitable. Tommi, on the other hand, chose blank paper and began making dots, 27 of them in a rough row. He then made 27 more dots, in a row parallel to this first row but higher up on his paper, and when he finished he was very surprised to see that the bottom line was longer than the top one.

At this point, Tommi was curious, eager, and a little upset. Something was not working right.

The role of the teacher in this kind of moment is important. Roberta could have made some comment or asked a question, but instead she chose to pause. Federico stepped in:

*Federico:*    It's because, I think, here you made them closer together. Try and
count them. . . .
(Tommi recounts his dots.)
*Federico:*    Yeah, here you made them too close because look here, they are all
messed up here, and look how they are here (He compares the top
and bottom lines.) Maybe you were in too much of a hurry.

While this incident has similarities to a traditional Piagetian
conservation-of-length task, it arose spontaneously out of the children's ongoing work. As a result, the two children were very motivated
to solve this problem. Tommi was clearly a boy in the process of
establishing conservation of length. While he was counting the 27 dots,
he demonstrated that he knew counting was a way to establish equiva-
lence of length. However, upon completing the counting, the obvious
discrepancy between the length of the two lines confused him. He did
not yet understand how the counted number of units only applies when
the units are of equal length. Federico, whose concept of conservation
of length was clearly established, was able to articulate the relationship of distance between dots and overall length. He was easily able to
coordinate two relationships and explain it to Tommi.

After Federico's comments, Tommi appeared indecisive and stuck.
Roberta suggested he could change paper if he wanted to, and he
jumped at the chance: His enthusiasm was evident as he stood up to get
a new piece of paper. He selected a piece of unlined paper. While
Federico ad Roberta went back to their respective works, Tommi pon-
dered. He looked at Federico working on his graph paper; he looked at
the three choices of paper in front of him; slowly he put the blank paper
back, chose graph paper, and began counting the squares.

Roberta's intervention, a quiet suggestion, was just enough to get
Tommi started again on his exploration. In the words of Loris Malaguzzi (founding director of the Reggio Emilia municipal preschool
system):

> The teacher must intervene as little as possible but in a way that's
> sufficient to start the exchange again or to reassure the children. There-
> fore interventions must be measured, not overbearing, not subverting
> what the children are doing. Rather it is a kind of taking the child by the
> hand, always letting the children stand on their own two feet. (Mal-
> aguzzi, interview, June 21, 1990)

It was not so much Federico's intellectual capacity that made the
difference in this situation, but rather the reciprocity between Tommi

**Figure 11.5.**  The children choose this figure to draw their life-size dinosaur. By creating a grid on graph paper, the children are able to calculate the length of various body parts.

and Federico in grappling together over what they knew and didn't know. Tommi came to appreciate the benefit of the evenly spaced marks provided by the graph paper, and Federico developed his capacity to express himself about these ideas.

The two boys then glued in a cut-out shape of the dinosaur, 27 × 9 centimeters long that fit into the 27 × 9-square rectangle on the graph paper. They were interested in how long the body parts of the dinosaur were, and by counting squares they could figure it out. "Let's pretend that one square stands for one meter," said Federico. They counted squares to find out how long each body part was and then made vertical lines on their drawing, marking out how long the tail was, the body, the neck, and the head.

*The Group of Six Back Together.* The next day, the boys and girls presented to each other and to Fabio, who had been out of school for a few days, what they had done. They asked questions about what the others had done. It was not at all a smooth discussion; there was excitement, disbelief, and incomplete understanding. Giulia summed it up quite well with her comment, "I think the drawings of both the girls and the boys are needed!"

Each child made his or her own plan, using photocopies of 27 × 9 centimeter dinosaurs. The drawings were then taken outside to use

**Figure 11.6.** The grid previously done on paper is now reconstructed outside: The outline of the back of the dinosaur begins to appear.

while redrawing the rectangle in the sports field—much easier this time although still difficult—and while beginning to think about how to draw the dinosaur inside of it. Tommi and Federico suggested laying out the vertical lines so they could mark out the length of the body parts as they had done on their papers.

Giulia suggested putting on the horizontal lines that the girls had drawn on their papers, confirming what she had said earlier that the drawings of both the girls and the boys were necessary. With this grid of horizontal and vertical lines now in place, it was possible to mark the outline of the back of the dinosaur, connecting crucial points on the grid with a rope. The back of the dinosaur was visible; the dinosaur was taking shape.

An interesting point about this morning is the timing of the activities. The discussion among the six children had started at around 9:30 that morning, and when lunch time arrived, at noon, the children were still in the midst of working in the field. Roberta told the children to go in for lunch and said that they could come back right afterwards if they wanted to. Everyone did. Working after lunch represented a departure from the usual schedule, but this is done from time to time. It was seen as acceptable because the children were in the midst of a problem. In fact, several times during the project, children even worked through nap time.

## Completion of the Life-Size Dinosaur

The group of six children went through several other transitions before the actual drawing of the life-size *Diplodacus*, including having to change the dinosaur's dimensions when it was discovered that they

**Figure 11.7.** How many children do you think can fit in the tail of the dinosaur?

could no longer use the sports field. Instead, the children had to draw a 13 × 6 meter Diplodacus to fit into the courtyard behind the school. The problem changed from one of defining the space based on the dimensions of the dinosaur to that of fitting the dinosaur into the defined space (see Rankin, 1992).

A few days later, the children went out in the courtyard with new drawings. The group was now able to construct a 13 × 6 meter rectangle, the grid of horizontal and vertical lines, the top line of the dinosaur's body, and finally the rest of the body.

The hardest work was now done. Over the next few days, painting the dinosaur on a huge piece of plastic drew the participation of most of the children in the 5-year-old class. It attracted the attention of all the children and teachers in the school who came to watch the progress of this dinosaur in their back yard.

## CONCLUDING PHASE

The children in the dinosaur group were interested in sharing what they had learned and done with the rest of the children in the school. Roberta, like other educators in Reggio, values this kind of exchange and had, indeed, talked about it with children right from the beginning. As she explained later (in her May 1991 lecture):

> The rereading of the experience was important: Children identified the steps that they decided were most meaningful. They were able to transfer knowledge that they just acquired.

Organizing the information to present to classmates clarifies and consolidates the knowledge the children gain from their work. Moreover, it allows adults to evaluate that work and the children's progress.

The children in the dinosaur group prepared an exhibit for the rest of the school, laying out the activities they had done and the steps they had gone through. The preparation of the exhibit was significant. They chose drawings and sculptures, they made invitations and posters, they thought of ways to present their experience to their classmates. The other children were excited to come to the exhibit and seemed to enjoy it; however, I judged the children of the dinosaur group to enjoy it the most, as they explained with animation the course of their adventures.

An inaugural festival was also planned for one Friday afternoon at pick-up time. The adults had arranged for the dinosaur to be raised to its feet by a set of pulleys attached to the high fence around one part of the sports field. This generated much excitement and represented a culminating moment for the project—especially for the children among the dinosaur group—as they beheld their creation rising to its feet.

A final meeting of the dinosaur group came as a result of a letter they had written to the city mayor, asking for a permanent place to hang the dinosaur (it was too big to stay in the school). The children met with the mayor, who commended them on their work and said he would do his best to find a place to hang the dinosaur.

Figure 11.8.    At its inauguration, the dinosaur stands on its own feet!

## SUMMARY

We have seen one example of a project unfold in a preprimary school in Reggio Emilia. Like any other experience, its development was unpredictable and emergent. It unfolded as a particular group of adults and children interacted, setting in motion a unique dynamic.

Even though there is not, and cannot be, one right way a project should go, nevertheless, there are some general guidelines and principles that are worthwhile to review. First, establish and maintain reciprocity as a central operating principle, with emphasis on developing a sense of "we," both among the adults and children. Second, start the project with a graphic and verbal exploration. Third, base the development of the project on the questions, comments, and interests of the children involved. Collaboration among the adults provides the necessary space for adults to think together about this. Fourth, provide ample time for children to come up with their own questions and their own solutions. Finally, bring the knowledge and experience of the children back to other children in the school. Share the experience of the project with other adults.

How many of these guidelines are relevant here in the United States? While every reader will have to answer that for himself or herself, here are my thoughts. It seems that in the United States, many teachers value such things as observing and listening to children as a basis for planning, having children work in small groups, emphasizing both cognitive and social growth of children, and encouraging children's active involvement in meaningful activities where they have power to make decisions. Thus, there are many similarities between the Reggio Emilia approach and developmentally appropriate practice as understood in the United States (see New, Chapter 12, this volume). What seems most different from early education in the United States is the fact that in Reggio Emilia there exists an operative network of 35 public schools for 0–6-year-olds. The leaders of this public system work together with teachers and parents to promote and stimulate growth and enact their shared principles of reciprocity, communication, and interaction. The network of relationships validates and supports development in a cohesive direction.

How can we learn from this in the United States? We can build on what we are doing right now in a more collaborative way. Interested people can find one another and share what is happening in their classrooms. We can observe, tape-record, analyze, and document the work of children and then exchange our documentation of projects and experiences with others. Besides providing delight and sustaining enthusiasm, this sharing will help us take our work to a higher level.

With a greater sense of "we," we can begin to construct a better world together, a world where the needs and rights of children are placed where they properly belong, center stage.

## REFERENCES

Rankin, B. (forthcoming). *Collaboration as the basis for curriculum development for young children in Reggio Emilia, Italy: An in-depth look at a long-term project related to dinosaurs.* Unpublished doctoral dissertation, Boston University, Boston, MA.

Rankin, B. (1992, May/June). Inviting children's creativity—A story of Reggio Emilia, Italy. *Child Care Information Exchange.* Redmond, WA: Exchange Press.

Rankin, B. (1985). *An analysis of some aspects of schools and services for 0–6 year olds in Italy with particular attention to Lombardy and Emilia Romagna.* Unpublished CAGS thesis, Wheelock College, Boston, MA.

# Part IV

# The Extension of the Reggio Emilia Approach into American Classrooms

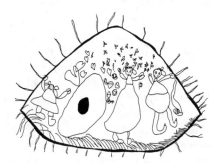

"The eye of a ballerina." Drawing by
Carlotta, 5 years old.

# 12

# Cultural Variations on Developmentally Appropriate Practice: Challenges to Theory and Practice

## Rebecca New

As previous chapters have attested, there is much about Reggio Emilia that is inspiring. The degree of collaboration and continuity evidenced through community support, ongoing staff development, parent involvement, classroom organization, and curriculum planning and implementation has created an early childhood environment that appears optimal for adults and children alike (New, 1990). Yet even as we ponder the means by which such a setting might be implemented in the U.S., we are challenged to reflect upon our own values and beliefs as they influence our interpretation of our roles as educators.

The purpose of this chapter is to examine certain aspects of Reggio Emilia's espoused theory and observable practice that appear contrary to contemporary American beliefs about child development and developmentally appropriate educational practice. A secondary aim is to consider the extent to which child development norms and processes are culturally determined, thereby leading to a broader discussion of what is particularly American about our notions of childhood and sound early childhood pedagogy.

Current interest in Reggio Emilia is supported by a growing body of literature on child development and early education practices in diverse societies around the world. Cross-cultural research on patterns of early child care and education has the potential of making important contributions to our knowledge about children and their development. Knowledge about other countries' beliefs, goals, and practices with respect to child care and development can:

- enhance our understanding of the characteristics of normal child development and expand our conceptions of the range of normal behavior in young children;
- refute currently held beliefs regarding the processes of child development; and
- increase our understanding of the influence of the developmental context—particularly those features associated with culture—on child development outcomes (Harkness, 1980; LeVine, 1980; Lewis, 1986; Rogoff & Morelli, 1989).

Cumulatively, cross-cultural studies contribute to a better understanding of developmental processes, thereby providing a powerful impetus for a closer examination of theoretical principles guiding current educational interpretations of developmentally appropriate practice. For example, several decades' worth of Japanese studies challenge American ideas about direct instruction, class size and ratio (Stigler & Perry, 1988), and classroom management strategies (Tobin, Wu, & Davidson, 1989), as well as the overall aims of education (Stevenson, Azuma, & Hakuta, 1986). Such studies, by way of exposing divergent belief systems, lead to a better understanding of the relationship between cultural values, parental and teacher goals and expectations, educational practices, and the child. As such, one of the primary values of becoming acquainted with Reggio Emilia—as with all comparative research in early childhood—is to force us to reflect upon our own beliefs and practices.

# THE REGGIO EMILIA APPROACH

Features of the Reggio Emilia approach which challenge beliefs and practices typically espoused by American educators fall into three roughly defined categories: (a) organizational and structural characteristics of the classroom environment; (b) general interpretations of the teacher's role in relation to children, other teachers, and parents; and (c) specific strategies developed to promote the symbolic languages among children of varying ages and competencies.

## Classroom Environment

American visitors to Reggio Emilia classrooms are spellbound by the remarkable appeal of the physical surroundings. The sense of aesthetic appreciation and attention to details, not to mention the abundant display of children's work, far surpass expectations of what a good quality child-care facility should look like (Gandini, 1984). There is no simplistic interpretation of children's aesthetic preferences such as typically appears in children's cartoons, nor is there a reliance on primary colors to brighten up a classroom. Instead, there is a concerted effort to respond to aspects of the environment which give children aesthetic pleasure—for example, the frequent use of mirrors, light, and translucent spaces to highlight images. Other aspects of the physical space are arranged in such a fashion as to draw attention to otherwise mundane aspects of daily living—even the toothbrushes are colorfully arranged in the bathroom. Children are not only drawn to closer inspection and appreciation of their physical world, but the environment supports their efforts and interests as well. Children's work (drawings, verbal transcripts, symbol making) is incorporated into the classrooms and school hallways by means of large and dramatic displays, and reflects the *serious* attention adults pay to children's ideas and activities (Katz, 1990).

Other features of the classroom environment challenge American notions of an appropriate setting for young children. The class size and child–teacher ratio (2 teachers in a class of 12 infants, 18 toddlers, or 28 preschoolers) are higher than that suggested by research (Phillips, 1987) or recommended by United States early childhood educators (Bredekemp, 1987). Yet, when Reggio Emilia teachers are asked if they would like more staff, the typical response is "we'd rather have more space!" There is a strongly held belief that too many adults preclude opportunities for children to utilize and learn from each other—a judgment not dissimilar to that expressed by Japanese teachers (Tobin, Wu, & Davidson, 1989); and incidentally, one that finds

**Figure 12.1.   Bathroom in the Diana School.**

some support in current day care research noting increased social competence among children in large classes as well as those in classes with more children per teacher (Clarke-Stewart, 1987).

A second aspect of the classroom incompatible with American ways of thinking is the organization of the group. Teachers stay together with the same children for three years, coming to know one another almost as members of an extended family. While the benefits of such an arrangement seem obvious within Reggio Emilia (and, in fact, this strategy is common throughout Italian preprimary school and elementary schools), American teachers and parents are less likely to see such an arrangement as either practical or desirable. U.S. early childhood professionals are advised to acquire age-related expertise [i.e., "specifically related to infant development," "specific to the toddler group," "qualified to work with 4- and 5-year-olds through college-level preparation . . . and supervised experience with this age group" (Bredekamp, 1987)] within the broader period of early childhood. It has also been my experience that American parents express reservations about their child spending too much time with any one teacher. Thus, even though it is acknowledged that changing teachers, peers, and classrooms from year to year is often a highly stressful experience for young children, recommendations to American teachers and parents are usually aimed at reducing the stress rather than providing children with a more continuous experience (Glicksman & Hills, 1981).

Not only do children in Reggio Emilia get to know one another quite well over the course of three years together, but they gain a strong sense of group membership. In fact, much of the activity of children in Reggio Emilia is within the context of a group, and is often measured by what might be described as group standards. The Reggio Emilia explanation for the strong group orientation is straightforward: A child can't develop a good sense of self isolated from other people; children acquire an identity in the context of their group (Sergio Spaggiari, personal communication, June 1986). Thus, children spend a great deal of time moving back and forth between small groups (usually four to a group) and the larger class. As they share and debate their ideas, they are encouraged to listen to and critically evaluate one another's thinking rather than to "be nice and mind your own business." This "social education"—in which they have frequent opportunities to hear multiple points of views, as well as to express and clarify their own—is not seen as cancelling individual differences, but as a means of identifying them. Thus, the unique aspects of a child's interests and abilities are identified within the context of the group, and it is also within that setting that they are most likely to be expressed.

Children in Reggio Emilia are encouraged to disagree, debate, and resolve their problems among themselves. Children commonly criticize and then attempt to remedy one another's efforts by drawing directly on one another's papers. While much of this type of activity reflects the value placed on children's communicative intentions, and a belief in the group exchange as facilitative of concept development, such authorized dissent challenges American standards of appropriate social behavior.

Certainly, American preschool teachers acknowledge the high priority given to children's social relations and each child's social development. As such, teachers in this country strive to assist children in gaining entry into play groups, encourage their efforts at conveying complex feelings ("tell him how it makes you feel when he takes your truck"), and highlight children's pro-social behaviors such as being friendly, cooperative, or helpful (Edwards, 1986). Yet, most such strategies are designed to foster the child's social competencies in ways that promote the individual rather than the group. Thus, there is little tolerance for arbitration once "please" and "thank-you" have been said. Multiple copies of favored toys and materials are seen as preferable to allowing children to negotiate over the use of valued and limited objects. And certainly the strong orientation to the opinions and needs of others as demonstrated in Reggio Emilia classrooms is contrary to American values of independence and individuality, and inconsistent with our notions of self-esteem and respect for others. When cooperative work efforts extend into areas approximating academic investigation, American teachers have additional concerns. Research in this country has noted that many classroom teachers are unwilling to "sacrifice" academic skills or content in order to teach children the social skills considered necessary to be productive group members (Slavin, 1985; Whitworth, 1988).

The cumulative effect of these cultural values and beliefs is to make American teachers somewhat ambivalent about the role the group plays in an individual child's development. Thus, practitioners are advised that "3-year-olds are not comfortable with much group participation" and expectations for them to participate in whole group activities are considered inappropriate (Bredekamp, 1987, p. 48); it is "appropriate" for 4- and 5-year-old children to "work individually or in small, informal groups most of the time" (p. 54).

The notion of *time* as interpreted in the Reggio Emilia classrooms challenges the American classroom teacher's sense of structure as well as interpretations of appropriate curriculum planning. On the surface, classroom routines in Reggio Emilia appear similar in many respects to that typical of preschool programs in the United States. There is a morning group meeting time, followed by a lengthy activity time (which includes free play as well as project work); there is outdoor time, lunch, snack, and quiet times as well as time for book sharing and other group experiences. Yet, within this fairly predictable routine is a degree of flexibility and slowness of pace that would frustrate many American educators. Even the aspect of waiting is viewed differently. Whereas situations in which young children must wait, for example, to be served a meal, are seen as developmentally *in*appropriate in the U.S. (Bredekamp, 1987), teachers in Reggio Emilia consider the experience to be a valuable lesson in socialization.

Other differences in the interpretation of time include the multiple opportunities given to children in Reggio Emilia to repeat activities in order to reflect *and improve* upon their previous levels of skill and understanding (for example, drawing a self-portrait three times in so many weeks). Perhaps the most extreme difference in interpretations of a well-planned schedule is with respect to the long-term projects that characterize the Reggio Emilia curriculum. With a firm conviction in young children's abilities to concentrate on and remain involved with topics of interest for extended periods, there is no anticipated time of closure for a project once it has begun. Instead, teachers and children work together as long as interest can be maintained, suggesting that the short attention span often attributed to young children might more aptly be attributed to American teachers.

Other aspects of Reggio Emilia's approach to early education which are in conflict with American views of early education center around interpretations of the teacher's role.

## The Role(s) of the Teacher

Teachers in Reggio Emilia have multiple relationships—with parents, children, and one another—and previous chapters have described the multifaceted nature of the teacher's role. The beliefs that surround these interpretations deserve further elaboration here.

*Teacher–child relationship.* Teachers' conceptions of children as competent is a basic assumption upon which the Reggio Emilia program is built. The resulting curriculum might be described as both child-centered *and* (often) teacher-directed. These terms are not seen as dichotomous, but as part of a natural reciprocal relationship that has much to offer in contrast to an approach which views child-initiated activity as paramount. Thus, Reggio teachers work alongside the children on their projects, ever ready to veer the course of investigation in the direction suggested as children discover their own sources of puzzlement. While clearly acknowledging the potential content as well as concepts that may be acquired—for example, teachers may well introduce a situation requiring measurement in order to promote numerical concepts—the interest in how children go about the business of learning is equally high.

This open-ended relationship between the teacher and the children is risky business to American eyes. Perhaps the most obvious challenge to our way of thinking about the teacher–child relationship is the manner in which curriculum decisions are made. In Reggio Emilia, there is no predetermined set of knowledge to dispense nor concepts to be acquired other than an ongoing acquisition of problem-solving strategies and the ability to convey concepts through a variety of symbol systems. Because teachers often follow children's leads in pursuing avenues of inquiry, they are willing to take cues from children for curriculum development that would be unwelcome in many U.S. classrooms. Thus, Barbie dolls, video games, and cartoon heroic figures may play prominently in the design and direction of Reggio Emilia projects, which focus on the mundane (shadows and puzzles), the taboo (gender roles, war play), and the profound (death, love).

American classroom teachers, in contrast, struggle to compete with Teenage Mutant Ninja Turtles, going so far as to ban not only the toys and the associated play but even, in some cases, children's efforts to talk about or draw the cartoon figures. While early childhood educators are beginning to acknowledge the futility of such actions and the importance of facilitating more creative interpretations of media-based dramas (Carlsson-Paige & Levine, 1990), U.S. teachers continue to feel uncomfortable in responding to what they consider to be controversial children's interests. Instead, American early childhood educators employ a highly selective filter through which children's cues are viewed, even as they enthusiastically describe their programs as "child-centered." Thus, curriculum "units" or themes of study focus on innocuous topics often far removed from the actual pursuits and passions of the children.

*Teacher–teacher relations.* The Reggio Emilia conception of adults as lifelong learners has vast implications for the ways in which adults in the school setting work together. Originally instituted to compensate for the meager preservice teacher training required in Italy, extensive in-service training is seen as integral to the nature and success of the Reggio Emilia approach to early education. Through the use of a constructivist framework to guide staff development goals and activities, teachers in Reggio Emilia actively seek out multiple perspectives, exchanging points of view with each other and with parents as well. While such collaboration sounds similar to teacher-development activities in the U.S., some aspects of such exchanges might be seen as threatening and/or nonprofessional to many American classroom teachers. The view, in Reggio Emilia, of adults as learners enables teachers to acknowledge their uncertainties as they construct for themselves an understanding of children's development. Furthermore, this attitude includes a tolerance for debate that far exceeds American notions of productive conversation. When commenting on the satisfaction of working together for more than 17 years in the same school, two Reggio Emilia teachers begrudgingly acknowledged that such familiarity brought its own set of problems: "We don't argue as much anymore." This priority on continuous on-the-job training infers a greater value on limited preservice education than most early childhood teacher-educators would care to admit and challenges American conceptions of competence as well as criteria for quality early childhood programs (Phillips, 1987).

*Teacher–parent relationships.* The home-school partnership is facilitated and reinforced by a shared understanding of the role of the teacher. The adults readily identify their respective areas of expertise; parents acknowledge the teachers' ability to focus observations around specific cognitive and social issues, particularly the child's position within the group. The parental role, on the other hand, focuses on the privitization aspects of children, relying on their sociocultural awareness of the place the children hold in the family as well as the larger society.

**Figure 12.2.   Teachers meeting as usual at lunchtime in the school.**

Such a partnership would likely be appreciated in the U.S. as well. Yet Reggio teachers want more than a mutual *understanding* between themselves and the children's parents; they advocate for active and extended participation. As noted by one educator, "We don't want them to be involved for two years—we want six years!" Reggio Emilia teachers do not see themselves in the role of parent educators; instead, they learn together with the families. Thus, they share in the care and education of the children, with an expectation that such relationships are "and *should be* complicated" (Malaguzzi, 1989, p. 11; emphasis mine).

The benefits of a multiplicity of roles for adults have been observed in a number of cultures. Children, too, benefit as their education and living experiences in their "extended" family reinforce one another (Snow, Barnes, Chandler, Goodman, & Hemphill, 1991) and sometimes become one and the same thing (Greenfield, 1981). Yet there is no equivalent to the *gestione sociale* in the American culture. Without such supporting structures for engaging in extended discussions of serious and controversial issues, American classroom teachers bemoan the overly curious parent, or the one who has too many good ideas, or most especially the one who questions the appropriateness of classroom practice.

## Teaching Strategies

Perhaps the most exciting and challenging aspect of the Reggio Emilia approach to the care and education of young children is the emphasis on children's symbolic languages as a means of making sense of their world. Yet, many teaching strategies which accompany this emphasis are counter to American expectations of developmentally appropriate practice.

There is a concerted emphasis, among Reggio Emilia teachers, on what might be called the *product* of a child's efforts as representative of the child's current understanding of a concept or experience. Teacher conversations with children concern the intent as well as the outcome of activities, and children are frequently encouraged to continue their efforts until they are satisfied that they have adequately expressed themselves. This satisfaction is often obtained after incorporating feedback from others into a revision of the product. Such a strategy is dramatically different from the recommended U.S. practice of emphasizing the *process* of the child's efforts (Schirrmacher, 1986), with adults often brushing aside a child's complaints that the finished product "doesn't look right."

Not only are children encouraged to rework their images if they fail to convey the intended purpose, but—as noted previously—various representational activities (such as drawing a self-portrait) are repeated throughout the year, thereby providing the opportunity to reflect on earlier interpretations and perceptions, to modify previously held beliefs, and to increase observational and representational skills. Yet, the development of what might be called artistic talent is seen, in most U.S. classrooms, as the prerogative of a select few; the belief that all children have such creative potential is not commonly shared.

Reggio Emilia teachers not only provide opportunities for repetition and reflection with respect to children's symbolic representations, but they utilize praise, encouragement, and comparisons to encourage children to refine their skills. I observed one educator lavish praise on a child's representation of a three-dimensional space; later, she was asked about the effects of ignoring a second child working at the same table. Her response was that the one-sided praise was intentional; she hoped to draw attention to the perspective-making strategies the child was using in his drawing as a means of provoking the less-skilled child to model and learn from his more competent peer.

These goals and strategies for reinforcing excellence in children's representational skills are in dramatic contrast to American teachers' reticence to foster skill development in the arts as well as the current recommendations to avoid praise in favor of less judgmental (and more generalized) encouragement for children's creative efforts (Hitz & Driscoll, 1988). Thus, in spite of recent research and theoretical interpretations of the value of supporting and enhancing children's efforts at symbolic representation (Forman & Landry, 1992; Gardner, 1982), American teachers rarely consider the development of children's graphic representational skills to be an area of concern, much less responsibility. Indeed, classic texts warn them that direct efforts to

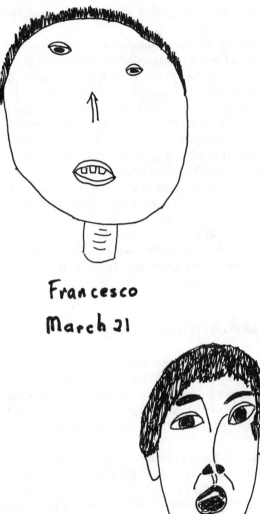

Francesco
March 21

Francesco
March 30

Francesco
April 12

**Figure 12.3.    Three self-portraits by Francesco, drawn on March 21, March 30, and April 12.**

improve children's representations are both futile and discouraging (Lowenfeld, 1968).

A final dimension of the Reggio Emilia teachers' belief in the importance of children's many ways of self-expression and exploration is the tolerance for, and elicitation of, emotional displays. Not only are children allowed to escalate—in terms of both noise and activity level—within the confines of their own dramatic play, but teachers actually plan activities and experiences knowing that they may worry or frighten some children. For example, teachers will arrange, with the town puppeteer, for a puppet show utilizing a frightfully exaggerated creature such as the wolf in the Red Riding Hood tale, anticipating that some children will be frightened to the point of tears. When asked why they would purposefully provide such an experience, the explanation, simply enough, was that children need opportunities, within the safety of the group setting, to understand and learn how to cope with their own and others' feelings. The American preoccupation with protecting young children from experiencing negative emotions is in marked contrast to this practice.

## CONCLUSION

There is much to ponder about the beliefs and practices of Reggio Emilia, not the least of which is that some of what we are attracted to is in direct competition with what we espouse in American classrooms. As a result, we are challenged to reconsider the relationship between (and consequences of) our values and beliefs and our teaching goals and strategies.

Certainly, the classrooms of Reggio Emilia have revealed *what children can do* when they work together on projects of interest, utilizing their multiple symbolic languages to convey ideas and understandings to themselves and each other. Reggio Emilia practices have also *challenged some strongly held beliefs* (e.g., the role of the teacher in the development of children's art skills, the significance of low pupil–teacher ratios, the importance of preservice teacher training), some more easily shed than others. As we are moved by the Reggio Emilia example to examine the developmental outcomes of such features within the context of high rather than poor quality programs, we will surely increase our understanding of the *contributions of the environment* to early child development and education.

In spite of the prevailing cultural differences described in this chapter, there are a number of trends in contemporary U.S. education that suggest an affinity to Reggio Emilia. Implications of constructivist

**Figure 12.4. Children exploring their shadows.**

theory for early education are being seriously explored at a number of levels (DeVries & Kohlberg, 1990), with a growing recognition of the importance of childrens' interactive processes to their cognitive and social development (Corsaro & Eder, 1990; Hickmann, 1988) and the rights of children to meaningful feedback (Beane, 1991). Whether as a result of self-consciousness fostered by Japanese references to our roles as "marriage counselors" (Tobin, Wu, & Davidson, 1989) or a more theoretical interpretation of the child as social constructivist (Forman & Cazden, 1988; Rogoff, 1990), U.S. teachers are also beginning to observe more and intrude less in children's ongoing social interactions (Paley, 1990).

Even as educators continue to be cautious about usurping the parental role, especially in social and health care areas, a vast majority of parents and teachers now see the need for schools to be involved in teaching children about such previously taboo topics as sexuality ("Teaching children about sex," 1988). There are also numerous and eloquent advocates for parents and teachers to work together to determine the curriculum, particularly in settings characterized by culturally diverse populations (Delpitt, 1988; Greenberg, 1990; Hauser-Cram, Pierson, Walker, & Tivnan, 1991).

Most encouraging is the recent body of work advocating for the treatment of teachers as epistemologists, benefiting from the same opportunities for exploration, discovery, and the construction of knowledge as are recommended for young children (Fosnot, 1989). As others advocate for building a professional culture in schools (Lieberman, 1988) that acknowledges the importance of teachers who are empowered as thinkers (Murray, 1986), research on teacher collaboration points to its usefulness as a strategy for bringing about educational improvement as well as reform (Ellis, 1990).

The question that is implied by the title of this chapter remains. What *is* developmentally appropriate practice? The material presented in this volume suggests that such an interpretation is highly dependent on teachers' and other adults' views of development; and that variations in practices may reflect cultural differences in both beliefs about, and expectations for, their children (Edwards & Gandini, 1989). As we continue our love affair with Reggio Emilia, then, we might begin an exploration of what's American about our own notions of sound educational practices. There are many seemingly sacred rituals, routines, and responsibilities associated with early childhood settings in the U.S., ranging from the ubiquitous circle-time calendar and clean-up times to the imperatives of lesson plans, curriculum guides, and low child–teacher ratios. Through our attempt to understand the values and beliefs associated with these and related practices, we may discover that we are working towards different sets of competencies than those valued by teachers in Reggio Emilia. Then and only then will we be in a position to thoughtfully evaluate and selectively take advantage of what Reggio Emilia has to offer us.

David Hawkins (1990) proposes the term *evolution* to describe the "long-term commitment of effort and inquiry" necessary to improve American schooling (p. 3). Such a concept goes beyond traditional conceptions of reform and captures the essence of the Reggio Emilia approach to early education. We would do well to begin our emulation at that point.

## REFERENCES

Beane, J.A. (1991). Enhancing children's self-esteem: Illusion and possibility. *Early Education and Development, 2*(2), 153–160.

Bredekamp, S. (Ed.). (1987). *Developmentally appropriate practice in early childhood programs serving children from birth through age 8.* Washington, DC: National Association for the Education of Young Children.

Carlsson-Paige, N., & Levin, D.E. (1990). *Who's calling the shots: How to respond effectively to children's fascination with war play and war toys.* Philadelphia, PA: New Society Publishers.

Clarke-Stewart, A.K. (1987). Predicting child development from child care forms and features: The Chicago study. In D.A. Phillips (Ed.), *Quality in child care: What does research tell us?* Washington, DC: National Association for the Education of Young Children.

Corsaro, W.A., & Eder, D. (1990). Children's peer cultures. *Annual Review of Sociology, 16,* 197–220.

Delpitt, L. (1988). The silenced dialogue: Power and pedagogy in educating other people's children. *Harvard Educational Review, 58*(3), 280–298.

DeVries, R., & Kohlberg, L. (1990). *Constructivist early education: Overview and comparison with other programs.* Washington, DC: National Association for the Education of Young Children.

Edwards, C.P. (1986). *Promoting social and moral development in young children.* New York: Teachers College Press, Columbia University.

Edwards, C.P., & Gandini, L. (1989). Teachers' expectations about the timing of developmental skills: A cross-cultural study. *Young Children, 44,* 15–19.

Ellis, N.E. (1990). Collaborative interaction for improvement of teaching. *Teaching and Teacher Education, 6*(3), 267–277.

Forman, E.A., & Cazden, C.B. (1988). Exploring Vygotskian perspectives in education: The cognitive value of peer interaction. In J.V. Wertsch (Ed.), *Culture, communication and cognition: Vygotskian perspectives.* New York: Cambridge University Press.

Forman, G., & Landry, C. (1992). Research on early science education. In C. Seefeldt (Ed.), *The early childhood curriculum: A review of current research.* New York: Teachers College Press, Columbia University.

Fosnot, C.T. (1989). *Enquiring teachers, enquiring learners: A constructivist approach for teaching.* New York: Teachers College, Columbia University.

Gandini, L. (1984, Summer). Not just anywhere: Making child care centers into "particular" places. *Beginnings,* pp. 17–20.

Gardner, H. (1982). *Art, mind, & brain: A cognitive approach to creativity.* New York: Basic Books.

Glicksman, K., & Hill, T. (1981). *Easing the child's transition between home, child care center and school: A guide for early childhood educators.* Trenton: New Jersey Department of Education.

Greenberg, P. (1990). *The devil has slippery shoes: A biased biography of the Child Development Group of Mississippi.* Washington, DC: Youth Policy Institute.

Greenfield, P.M. (1981). Child care in cross-cultural perspectives: Implications for the future organization of child care in the United States. *Psychology of Women Quarterly, 6*(1), 41–54.

Harkness, S. (1980). The cultural context of child development. In C.M. Super & S. Harkness (Eds.), *Anthropological perspectives on child development. New Directions in Child Development.* San Francisco: Jossey-Bass.

Hawkins, D. (1990). The roots of literacy. *Daedalus, 119*(2), 1–14.

Hauser-Cram, P., Pierson, D.E., Walker, D.K., & Tivnan, T. (1991). *Early education in the public schools: Lessons from a comprehensive birth-to-kindergarten program.* San Francisco: Jossey-Bass.

Hickmann, M.E. (1988). The implications of discourse skills in Vygotsky's developmental theory. In J.V. Wertsch (Ed.), *Culture, communication and cognition: Vygotskian perspectives.* New York: Cambridge University Press.

Hitz, R., & Driscoll, A. (1988). Praise or encouragement? New insights into praise: Implications for early childhood teachers. *Young Children, 43*(5), 6–11.

Katz, L. (1990). Impressions of Reggio Emilia preschools. *Young Children, 45*(6), 4–10.

LeVine, R. A. (1980). Anthropology and child development. In C.M. Super & S. Harkness (Eds.), *Anthropological perspectives on child development. New directions in child development.* San Francisco: Jossey-Bass.

Lewis, C. (1986). Children's social development in Japan: Research directions. In H. Stevenson, H. Azuma, & K. Hakuta (Eds.), *Child development and education in Japan.* New York: W.H. Freeman and Co.

Lieberman, A. (Ed.). (1988). *Building a professional culture in schools.* New York: Teachers College Press, Columbia University.

Lowenfeld, V. (1968). On the importance of early art expression. In W.L. Brittain (Ed.), *Viktor Lowenfeld speaks on art and creativity.* Washington, DC: National Association for the Education of Young Children.

Malaguzzi, L., & Department of Education. (1989). *A historical outline, data, and information.* Reggio Emilia, Italy: Center for Educational Research.

Murray, F. (1986). Goals for the reform of teacher education: An executive summary of the Holmes Group report. *Phi Delta Kappan, 68*(1), 28–32.

New, R. (1990). Excellent early education: A city in Italy has it. *Young Children, 45,* 4–10.

Paley, V.G. (1990). *The boy who would be a helicopter.* Cambridge: Harvard University Press.

Phillips, D.A. (Ed.). (1987). *Quality in child care: What does research tell us?* Washington, DC: National Association for the Education of Young Children.

Rogoff, B. (1990). *Apprenticeship in thinking.* New York: Oxford University Press.

Rogoff, B., & Morelli, G. (1989). Perspectives on children's development from cultural psychology. *American Psychologist, 44*(2), 343–348.

Schirrmacher, R. (1986). Talking with young children about their art. *Young Children, 41*(5), 3–7.

Slavin, R. (Ed.). (1985). *Learning to cooperate, cooperating to learn.* New York: Plenum Press.

Snow, C., Barnes, W., Chandler, J., Goodman, I., & Hemphill, L. (1991). *Families and schools: Effects on literacy.* Cambridge, MA: Harvard University Press.

Stevenson, H., Azuma, H., & Hakuta, K. (Eds.). (1986). *Child development and education in Japan.* New York: W.H. Freeman and Co.

Stigler, J.W., & Perry, M. (1988). Mathematics learning in Japanese, Chinese, and American classrooms. In G. Saxe & M. Gearhart (Eds.), *Children's mathematics. New directions for child development* (vol. 41, pp. 27–54). San Francisco: Jossey-Bass.

Teaching children about sex. (1988). *The Harvard Education Letter, 5*(5), 1–6.

Tobin, J., Wu, D.Y.H., & Davidson, D.H. (1989). *Preschool in three cultures.* New Haven, CT: Yale University Press.

Whitworth, R. (1988). Cooperative learning and other disasters. In J. Golub (Ed.), *Focus on collaborative learning.* Urbana, IL: National Council of Teachers of English.

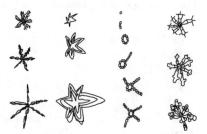

"Snow flakes."

# 13

# The City in the Snow: Applying the Multisymbolic Approach in Massachusetts

## George Forman, Moonja Lee, Lynda Wrisley, and Joan Langley

### ORIGINS OF THE PROJECT

**Ties with Reggio Emilia**

In Fall 1988, four classroom teachers at the Marks Meadow Elementary School, a public school in Amherst, decided to initiate a long-term project based on our understanding of the multisymbolic approach used in Reggio Emilia. Several of the education faculty at the University of Massachusetts visited the Reggio preschools and we were shortly to host a visit from three of the Reggio educators. Marks Meadow became a type of sister school during this period, with several exchange visits.

This first of two projects completed at Marks Meadow was based closely on a project completed in Reggio Emilia called, The City in the Rain. This project is well documented in the traveling exhibit, The Hundred Languages of Children. Basically, the City in the Rain was a study of how the city and the people in the city changes when it rains. The project began in a manner that has become standard in Reggio Emilia, a type of verbal outpouring of children's ideas: from where does the rain come; how does the rain sound as it hits different surfaces; what in the city is built because of the rain; how is rain harnessed for good uses; and so on.

Then, as the children waited for the first rain, they drew their ideas on large poster paper. Some drew their theories of the rain's source: "The devil makes it rain," said one 5-year-old. Another insisted that "the rain is made by big machines in the sky, and the rain goes into the clouds, and when the clouds are too full the rain falls out." These drawings were the children's initial theories about the rain cycle and served as a platform from which to discuss and expand the children's understanding (see Forman, 1989).

The project in Reggio Emilia continued for many weeks, including such activities as making audiotapes of the rain sounds on different surfaces and then making a graphic rendering of these sounds, going into the city filled with questions that had been raised from the classroom discussions and drawings, drawing machines that could make rain, drawing a system of water works that brings the rain water from the sky to the ground to pipes to homes, using a sequence of photographs that show a changing sky and then drawing these changes on paper, drawing a city before and during a rainfall, and drawing many more examples of multisymbolic learning.

## Adaptation of the Project for Amherst

The teachers at Marks Meadow Elementary School were quite attracted to the basic idea of using nature as a theme. Our New England version was The City in the Snow. The snow season was near and we discussed how to modify the Reggio project on rain into a project on snow for children from 5 to 7 years old. The four classes involved were as follows: the young fives, Lynda Wrisley's kindergarten class; another kindergarten class taught by Cindy Weinberg; a group of 6-year-olds taught by Sharon Edwards; and a class of 7-year-olds taught by Joan Langley. Collectively these four classes occupied what at Marks

Meadow is called the Early Learning Center. The classes had between 19 and 22 students per class. The head teacher typically had an aide or intern. The documentation team consisted of George Forman and Moonja Lee. We six met for several hours each Wednesday to plan the project and to study the documentations. The project lasted several months all told.

Note that the age range extends to 7 and even some 8-year-olds by the project's end. At no time did we feel that the instructional activities were too elementary for these children. In fact, this chapter will make comments on how the multisymbolic approach is suitable for all ages. Furthermore, unlike the small group of four used in the Long Jump project (Chapter 10, this volume), the City in the Snow project more typically was carried out as a series of full class activities.

## SEQUENCE OF ACTIVITIES

Consistent with the method of running projects in Reggio Emilia, this City in the Snow project blended planned objectives with emergent objectives, the latter derived from discoveries the teachers made during the course of the project. For the sake of discussion, the actual sequence as it evolved is laid out here in advance. These segments are indexed, as done in the chapter on The Long Jump, so the reader will have an easy guide for the actual chronological order of events.

1.0  *Verbal Outpouring*: Children discuss the recollections of snow fall, how it changes the playground, how it effects walking, what you can do in the snow, and how the city handles huge quantities of snow. These class discussions occurred for several weeks before an appreciable snowfall.

2.0  *Initial Drawings of Snow Scenes*: Children drew scenes of skiers, houses covered with snow, even children falling through ice into a pond. These pictures were also included in further discussions.

3.0  *Simulated Snowfall*: We realized that a major concept of this project was the relation between form and function, for example, whether the form of a particular roof functions as an efficient shelter from snow. Therefore, we decided to use a symbolic version of falling snow by sifting baking flour onto a miniature city of wooden blocks. This medium simulates rather closely what would happen in a real snowfall, the upper edges coated with "snow," the covered areas shielded. We also were using our time well as we waited for the first snowfall, which was, not surprisingly, later than usual.

4.0 *Mural of the City*: During this snowless period, Cindy Wein-berg's class made a wall-size cityscape without painting in the snow. The cityscape, filled with office buildings, pet shops, fire trucks, school buses, mostly cut out from construction paper and pasted to the wall-length bulletin board, remained without snow for several weeks. The children thought about how they would add the thick white paint to represent the results of a snow storm. This they did. Other classes did this same activity on a smaller scale.

5.0 *Field Experience of First Snow*: It snowed in early January 1989. The children went into the snow filled with questions raised from the earlier activities.

6.0 *Second Drawing of the Snowfall*: After the simulated snowfall and actual field experience, the children once again made draw-ings of snow on the city. These new drawings showed more concern with the exact placement of the snow on edges and pro-truding surfaces.

7.0 *Drawing Sounds of the Snow*: The children became interested in the silence of the snow and also the special sounds of walking, running, and shoveling the snow. These sounds were audio-recorded and the children tried their hand at making graphic representations of these three sounds.

8.0 *Drawing Individual Snowflakes*. From observations with micro-scopes [5.01], and by looking at enlarged photographs of snow-flakes at the beginning of this segment [8,0], the children be-came interested in the beauty of the snowflake. So the children set about drawing individual snowflakes. They used a variety of media, including white chalk on black paper, bits of colored paper, beans, macaroni, and parquetry blocks.

9.0 *Watching a Video on the Growth of a Snowflake*: As coincidence happens, we had a three-minute videotape available that showed the growth of a snowflake in time-lapsed photography. The children watched this video clip several times knowing that they would then draw what they were watching.

10.0 *Drawing the Growth of a Snowflake*: The children were given long pieces of paper and asked to divide the paper into four panels. Then the children set about drawing their understand-ing of how a snowflake grows from time 1 to time 4.

11.0 *Drawing How Water Changes to Ice*: The work of the physical structure of snow led to discussions on the difference between ice crystals and snow crystals. After an introductory period of ver-bal discussions and writing attribute lists, the children froze water, checking its progress every hour. They finished by draw-ing this transformation across three timeframes.

12.0 *Drawing Clouds and Machines that Make Snow:* Some of the children during [*11.0*] believed that the melted snow would be retransformed into snowflakes in the freezer. So all of the classes discussed how snow is made, both naturally and artificially. While some children drew snow-making clouds, others decided to invent their own snow-making machines. These drawings were some of the most interesting in the project because they revealed the children's theories about the water-to-snow process.

## CYCLES OF SYMBOLIZATION

The concept of cycles of symbolization was first introduced in Chapter 10 on the Long Jump project in Reggio. The team at Marks Meadow used this concept as a guide to enhance the reflectivity of children as they drew and cycled back to redraw their current assumptions, ideas, and theories. The children were using symbolization, not only to represent what they already know, but also to reflect and question what it is they say they know. They, in essence, rerepresent their knowledge in order to improve its coherence. The drawing, in this sense, is done in order to learn, instead of in order to communicate, what is known.

### Cycle One: Verbal Outpouring

It is appropriate that teachers start out children with their most fluent symbol system, talking [*1.0*]. The ideas flow without being encumbered by the demands of technical skills. Five- to seven-year-olds already know how to talk. What they do not yet do well, however, is know how to reflect on their words, to debug their logic, or to check the evidence. This is where the subsequent cycles and symbol systems come into play.

### Cycle Two: Initial Drawings and Further Discussion

These initial drawings are determined partly by the verbal outpouring and partly by the continuation of ideas that unfold as the children draw. It is the combined source of these ideas that make drawing powerful. The children talk about snowfall and they get new ideas from what they see emerging on their paper. One can hope that these two sources will create small discrepancies. Discrepancies are the engine behind questioning and subsequent problem solving.

Look for the moment at Figure 13.1. The child has drawn deep snow on the ground and on the roof of the house, but no snow on the top of the car. The snowless car resulted from a habit of drawing. The child usually draws cars like this, so that's how it ends up in her drawing. But in the group discussion that follows, inconsistencies such as these are noted. The child artist now explains the discrepancy away by

**Figure 13.1a.   Child from New England recalls snow**

**Figure 13.1b.   Child from Africa imagines snow**

saying that the car just arrived in front of the house. We should not dismiss this as rationalizing a mistake. In fact, the child has probably thought for the first time that the snowless car could be a clever way to figure out how long a car has been parked someplace else.

Other discrepancies were noted between the two drawings (see the differences between Figures 13.1a and 13.1b). The child who drew the thatched hut (Figure 13.1b) was from Africa and had never seen snow. In his drawing, snow was not well distinguished from rain. The children discussed these differences and the child from Africa was filled with excitement and was eager to discover just what real snow does to the objects outside.

## Cycle Three: Simulation

The drawings and verbal discussions by now had convinced the children that snowfall was more complicated than they had first thought. The drawings, in particular, move the children into a closer analysis of the dynamics of falling snow: where it will land, where it will stay. But since we had no snow, we had no means to confirm our guesses. Thus, the third cycle was included to give the children some physical confirmation of their theories.

Before the teacher sifted the flour onto the miniature city of wooden blocks, the children predicted where they thought the "snow" would fall, where it would stick, and where it would not fall. One kindergartner said, in reference to a curved roof, "It will land on the top of the curvey part, but it will not stay here (pointing to the more vertical part of the curving roof)." Another child offered her opinion that the snow would not get under the toy car.

The teacher, Lynda Wrisley in this case, then sifted the flour evenly, over the entire miniature village as the children watched intently (Figure 13.2). This predict-then-observe strategy of teaching enhanced their interest and maximized the opportunity for an observation to be more than an interesting occurrence, but also relevant evidence for an hypothesis.

Children were pleased with their correct predictions (see Figure 13.3) and pleasantly surprised at the unexpected. One boy said, in reference to a tiny ridge of flour on the skyward point of a triangular block, "I did not think that it would land there!" More than one child commented that two identical triangles had noticeably different amounts of snow on their skyward facets. Through some guided discovery they learned that this difference was caused by differences in grain textures between the two wooden blocks; one was smooth and the other rough.

Figure 13.2. Flour is sifted over miniature village

Figure 13.3. The car, once removed, shows where the snow did not fall

Thus, the simulation cycle adds physical confirmation to the guesses and theories defined in the two previous cycles. Now the children are even better prepared for the actual snowfall that is certain to arrive, soon, we hoped. In one class, Cindy Weinberg's kindergarten class, the children did yet another activity before the snow actually came—a large mural across the entire back wall of the room.

## Cycle Four: Using the Drawing as the Referent

The children in Cindy Weinberg's class spent several days filling up a huge mural with drawings and paper cutouts of houses, cars, trucks, people, trees, streets, and buildings [4.0]. Then they waited and thought about this drawing as the place where snow will one day fall. Thus, the drawing itself was the referent, the "real object" so to speak. After a week of looking at the completed cityscape, they now returned with white paint to add the snow. Yet, unlike the flour sifted on wooden blocks, the drawing would not give the children physical confirmation. Knowing that they could do anything, since the medium allows it, caused the children to talk even more about how to add the white paint. One might rightly assume that by contrasting simulation with drawing, children would be more reflective when drawing how they think the system behaves. That is, the simulation confirms that the system is not capricious or fanciful, and the freedom to say anything in drawing places more responsibility on thinking to figure out what would really happen. With the simulation alone, children might

Figure 13.4.  Snow envelops the house on all sides

have a tendency to say, "I don't know," and just wait for the teacher to sift the flour. Thus, it is useful to have both these cycles: simulation and drawing as referent.

Figure 13.4 shows how one child added white paint (snow) to a house. The white paint enveloped the entire house, including the vertical walls, instead of resting only on the upper surfaces of the house. Perhaps we should have cycled again through the simulation to generate discussion about differences in their predictions in the simulation and their drawings in the fourth cycle. As you will see, the field trip, perhaps in combination with the simulation, did sensitize children to the functional differences in vertical and horizontal surfaces. Notice, however, that this child had been sensitized to an in-between case, the slanted roof. She had drawn some snow on the roof, itself drawn in perspective. We felt that this awareness, that the roof has a horizontal "footprint" to the open sky, was a major breakthrough for several children.

### Cycle Five: The Experience

Finally the snow arrived. The children were primed to seek answers to questions raised in the verbal outpouring [1.0], during their initial drawings [2.0], during the simulation with flour [3.0], and as they added white paint to the mural [4.0]. They went out into the snow to inspect the fall of the snow on the seesaw, the way the snow slowed you down on the slide, and the crystal structure of an individual flake frozen on the fabric of the teacher's coat.

We would like to caution ourselves and others about the use of the word "experience." Not all experiences are equally educational. Once again we draw on the distinction between the occurrence of an event and an event that serves as evidence for a theory, answer to a question, or satisfaction of curiosity. The prior cycles of symbolization make the field experience more a case of evidence than the less reflective case of an occurrence. In fact, it is the *hands-off* activities that make the *hands-on* activities more educational.

### Cycle Six: The Postexperience Drawings

What we said about the importance of representations prior to the field experience can also be said for representations subsequent to the field experience. Granted, the children make discoveries in the field, but their excitement and physical movements make it difficult for them to synthesize their discoveries at some higher level. During this postex-

**Figure 13.5.   Emphasis on the lay of the snow**

perience round of drawings [6.0] the children learned that their discoveries are shared (or debated), and they then tried to represent the revisions of their knowledge.

As shown in Figure 13.5 it becomes clear that the same children who drew the cityscape mural are no longer placing snow along the vertical walls of the buildings. They are also aware that the snow will fall on any edge that is at least as wide as an individual snowflake. This attention to dynamics of falling snow, as a powdery medium coming to rest on horizontal edges, broadened and deepened the children's interest and curiosity and lead to activities [7.0] through [12.0].

## Cycle Seven: Broadening

Instead of asking what happens when the snow makes contact with objects, they began to ask what happens when an object comes into contact with the snow. For example, what sound does a shovel make when removing snow? The teachers decided to help children think about these object-to-snow questions by *drawing* these sounds.

The teachers brought in audiotapes of several such sounds; the children discussed what they might be; all agreed and then they tried to make graphic representations of these sounds. Making a visual representation (picture) of a nonvisual experience (sound) is called *cross-modal representation*. The graphic rendering of sounds encourages the child to think in more creative ways about sound. This is true because the cross-modal representation has few clichés and because the activity is clearly metaphorical. In addition, the children listen to the sounds through their eyes and thereby hear different aspects of

**Figure 13.6.   One child's graphic rendering of snow sounds**

sounds, such as intervals of silence, continuous tones, and other attributes that have spatial analogies. Children often listen to the less formal and more content-based attributes when they are preparing to give a verbal description. That is, the cross-modal graphic picks up attributes of continuity and discontinuity as you see in Figure 13.6, while the verbal description will orient the child to the source of the noise or other noises that are similar, for example, "snow shoveling sounds like sanding wood." Thus, the cross-modal representation has a metasymbolic cast, compared to the verbal account.

### Cycle Eight: Deepening

The children had already made many comments about the snow as a medium of particles. This naturally led to activities that focused on the particle level of snow, the individual snowflake. Activities [8.0], [9.0], and [10.0] dealt with the look and growth of the individual snowflake. These three activities represent a type of spiral with the cycles of symbolization because the children are using representation, experience, rerepresentation within this special topic: the growth of a crystalline structure. The spiral is a recapitulation of this cycle sequence, but is at the same time an advance because these activities deepen the children's world view of the snow.

The children laid out their rendering of snowflakes [8.0], watched a time-lapsed video [9.0] of a growing snowflake, and then rendered these stages of growth themselves [10.0]. Figure 13.7 shows four theories of growth from four different children, all who had watched the same time-lapsed video. Note that these four children, from left to right, view growth as a process of (a) enlarging, (b) layering, (c) adding unit elements, and finally (d) growth by differentiation of parts.

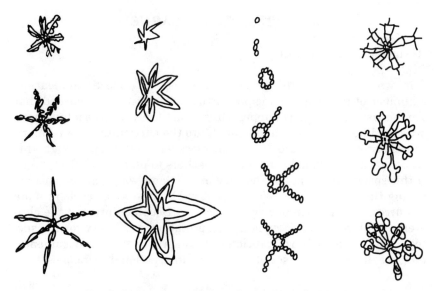

**Figure 13.7.   Four versions of a growing snowflake**

This spiral of cycles impressed upon us that even the best video presentation [9.0] does not give the facts away. The children still have to reconstruct these facts into a set of relations that make sense to the children themselves. Drawing their theories on paper helps each child see the other child's thoughts and to rework one's own thoughts during the small group discussions. The video without the cycle of representation would let these diverse theories remain unexpressed and thereby provide no constructive conflict among the students. The video alone could also encourage mental passivity and the acceptance of superficiality that comes when children are not asked to communicate their thinking to others.

## Final Cycles: More Broadening and Deepening

The activities that followed, and they could have been continued indefinitely, continued to broaden and deepen the children's interest and understanding. The children both drew the ice to water transformation and performed empirical experiments [11.0]. The children made drawings of clouds and snow-making machines [12.0], and they observed these systems outdoors and on area ski slopes. The snow-making machines were quite fascinating, and actually led to our next annual project, simple machines, carried out the following year.

## WHAT THE TEAM LEARNED

### Resources for Success

Our own reflection on this project continues. The project team learned a number of important principles. Broadly speaking, we learned that the multisymbolic project approach, at least the version that we have presented here, can be implemented into the curriculum of an American classroom. It should be noted, however, that even though this school system provided time for all teachers to plan and reflect, much of this special planning for the City in the Snow was done by teachers during their spare time. We are still working to give teachers more resources for this form of project teaching. Documentation of the children's thinking and subsequent interpretation is primary for the success of this approach. In addition to this appreciation for documentation, we did develop a set of important instructional principles.

### Representation and Rerepresentation

It is important to have children cycle back through a first draft of a representation after they have had practical or simulated experience. The rerepresentation, as part of our cycle of symbolization, helps the child consolidate knowledge or improve the definition of their misconceptions. Both objectives are laudable.

### Using Ready-Made Symbols as Catalysts

The teacher can serve as a resource to help the child enter the system under study. The photographs of the snowflakes and the videotape of how the snowflake forms were ready-made symbols. These ready-made symbols are complex. Therefore, the reproduction of these symbols require high-level thinking about the referent and the referent processes.

The teacher does not directly teach drawing by focusing on graphic details. Rather, the teacher asks the children to reflect on the meaning of these ready-made symbols in order for the children to reinvent the geometric rules of structure or the dynamics of particles forming clusters. The ready-made symbols serve as a frame, a delimitation of the system. The ready-made symbols are hints at latent patterns, patterns that could be interesting to know. But a pattern needs to be constructed by the child to be known. Patterns do not exist in the ready-made symbol. Patterns exist in the cognitive order the child brings to the stimulus array. The drawing presents a window to this cognitive order for both the child him/herself, for the teacher, and for other children to whom the child is communicating.

## Open Media Versus Simulation

Instruction is a two-phase process: the phase of generating questions followed by a phase of testing questions. If teachers only use graphic art to stimulate the imagination, the instructional value of art has been truncated. Thus, we came to value media that has consequences: media that is not so open-ended that anything can happen. This is why we shifted to sifting and why we used the videotape of the growing snowflake.

## Representations as a Platform for Asking Questions

Once drawn, the graphic representation becomes a platform on which the children and the teacher can play out their interpretations. The finesse comes in how to both affirm the child's thinking, while at the same time challenge the child to think more deeply (see Forman, 1989).

Let's take the case of a child who drew an elegant but superfluous snow-making machine, a machine that made snow from an ample supply of existing snow (Figure 13.8). The machine would suck in the

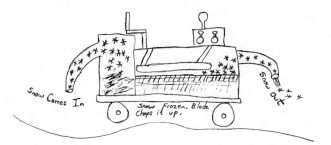

**Figure 13.8.   Snow in, melted, frozen, and chopped**

snow, melt it, chop it up, and spit out the "snow" (the chopped ice). The proper platform for instruction in this case is to deal with the child at his level. We would question the child from the higher perspective about machines in general. We would not immediately head the child to consider work as the production of something finished from something raw. We would ask the child to give a verbal rendering of the process *as drawn*, hoping to hear him describe both the nature of the snow that comes in and the nature of the snow that goes out. From his own reflections on his own verbal descriptions he might well become aware that he has invented a snow-moving machine, not a snow-making machine. The illogicality of the snow-in/snow-out redundancy would be one level higher and attained further on; and the fact that chopped ice is not really snow could also eventually come to his consciousness. These broader questions about purpose and exact products often came into consciousness during small group discussions among four to five children.

## Building on Intuitive Knowledge

This is a difficult principle to implement, because it presupposes that teachers have sufficient time to learn what their students know and have time to continually update the transition from intuitive to more objective knowledge structures. But this City in the Snow project made it perfectly clear that knowing what the children believe is essential for a successful project.

Building on the child's intuitive knowledge is important for two reasons. One is motivation. When children have some intuitive theories about process, it means they are interested in the subject matter. They have gone beyond an attitude of "that's just the way it is." It validates the source of these initial theories to use them as departure points for instruction and this, in turn, heightens the children's motivation.

The other reason for building on the children's intuitive knowledge concerns continuity of instruction. Much has been written about the value of developmental education, but unfortunately these guidelines have been taken too literally. The child's development has to be gauged by general stages rather than by phases of domain-specific learning. This project, this chapter, and indeed this book speak more to the use of domain-specific phases of understanding a content system. For example, look once again at the various theories of snowflake growth. The theory of growth as a simple case of getting larger is more elementary than a theory that notes the changing location of a unit element. The project approach, combined with documentation of children's thinking, helps each teacher become knowledgeable about the developmental phases within a content domain. We can let the general stages take care of themselves.

### Shifting from Static Patterns to Dynamic Systems

As is consistent with existing literature on early learning (see Forman & Hill, 1984), teaching children to ask good questions requires that they be presented with rich problem-solving environments. A rich problem-solving environment is more causal than descriptive. Children try to figure out how something happens rather than try to describe how something looks. While close inspection may be an initial step toward understanding, it should not be isolated from the search for cause.

This shift from static patterns to dynamic systems can be a change in the mental attitude one has as they study patterns. Pattern has typically been described with static attributes (symmetrical, planar, linear, differentiated, homogeneous). But the study of dynamic patterns, that is, the relationship of form to function, presents the child with a rich problem-solving environment. Questions, such as what if this pattern were changed by this cause, become relevant for the first time: What if the water molecules were square instead of V-shaped; how then would snowflakes grow?

### The Necessity for Careful Documentation

Documentation and time to study the documentation are essential for a successful project. This is perhaps the first priority in Reggio Emilia, with great emphasis placed on the time to study the documentation. The project team, as a plea to improve education in general, recommend that all schools find ways to provide "documentarians" for classroom teachers. If done properly, good documentation can serve all masters simultaneously, from individual assessment, to curriculum planning, to instructional accountability.

### The Necessity for Long-Term Projects

We were impressed with our own commitment to continue this theme for a long period. In retrospect, we realized that the theme was always changing in its specific form. The children did not feel they were continually rehashing the same concept. The long-term nature of this project was our long-term discussion of how earlier activities specifically related to current activities, how they related in terms specific to content, for example, how snowfall relates to snowflakes, how snow-flakes relate to ice, and how refrigerator relates to snow cloud or snow machine. We needed a long time, several months, to carry this project through. Had we rushed ourselves we would not have been able to use the emergent objectives as they happened because we would not have had the reflection and planning time needed to define these emergent objectives. And to make a project from only one objective is to miss a great opportunity to help children construct whole systems from subsystems.

## REFERENCES

Forman, G. (1989). Helping children ask good questions. In B. Neugenbauer (Ed.), *The wonder of it: Exploring how the world works* (pp. 21–25). Redmond, WA: Exchange Press, Inc.

Forman, G., & Hill, F. (1984). *Constructive play: Applying Piaget in the pre-school*. Menlo Park, CA: Addison-Wesley Publishers.

**"A monstrous monster." Drawing by 3-year-old at the Villetta School.**

# 14

# Connections: Using the Project Approach with 2- and 3-Year-Olds in a University Laboratory School*

## Debbie LeeKeenan and John Nimmo

### INTRODUCTION

Our first encounter with "The Hundred Languages of Children" exhibit left us impressed and excited by the spectacular project work of the children and teachers in Reggio Emilia. Along with many other teach-

---

\* This chapter is an elaboration and extension of an earlier article, "Using the Project Approach with Toddlers," by Debbie LeeKeenan and Carolyn Edwards, in *Young Children*, (1992), *47*(4), 31–35.

ers, we initially wondered how we might begin to see art of this sophistication in the work of our own classroom. Since this time, however, we have come to understand our classroom practice would be better served by focusing on the pedagogy behind these visual products rather than the beauty on the walls of the exhibit. What was the process that was underlying this new vision for children? The Reggio work made us realize there were many more possibilities for children than we had yet explored in our own classrooms. We wondered were our expectations of children too limited? We wanted to reexamine our values and priorities. Because we were intimately involved in the education of both children and preservice teachers, we felt there was much to learn and examine in the educational philosophy and curriculum approach of Reggio Emilia. We were eager to look at some of these influences and see if we could adapt and apply them to our setting at the Human Development Laboratory School, University of Massachusetts at Amherst.

In this chapter we will do several things: (a) clarify some of the aspects of the Reggio Emilia approach that influenced us the most; (b) describe three projects that we implemented in our classroom; and (c) present some guidelines for creating projects with an approach we call "planning curriculum by making connections."

## INFLUENCES OF REGGIO EMILIA

In Reggio Emilia, projects for children involve spiraling experiences of exploration and group discussion, then representation and expression, through the use of many symbolic media, for example, words, movement, songs, drawings, block-building, shadow play, and even making faces in front of a mirror. Art and aesthetics are viewed as a central part of how children perceive and represent their world. Art is not viewed as a separate part of the curriculum, but rather an integral part of the whole cognitive/symbolic learning of the developing child. Children's work is not casually created, but rather is the result of a guided exploration of themes and events that are relevant to the life of the children and the larger community (Gandini, 1984; Gandini & Edwards, 1988; New, 1990).

The Reggio approach uses an organic or emergent model of planning and implementing curriculum. This is different from the typical thematic approach used in many preschools which is often predetermined and laid out by the teacher months in advance. In that case, the use of themes may be merely a kind of external "decorating" in the classroom where materials and props are often superimposed on children and the

**Figure 14.1.    Three-year-olds playing ball, by children of Villetta School.**

classroom to help give some structure and order to the curriculum, such as a fall theme with leaves, pumpkins, and apples. The length of the theme is preset by the calendar or teacher even before the project starts. As a contrast, in the project approach as implemented in Reggio Emilia, there are no time constraints. The projects evolve on their own organic time table, creating a sense of adventure for both children and teachers. The end result of these joint ventures is rarely clear from the start. There is active involvement of the children from the beginning— even to helping suggest the subject for the project. In such an emergent model the teacher starts with careful observations of children's interests and questions, which are then developed into concrete learning experiences. Through documentation, reflection, repetition, and revision, children are guided into deeper experiences. The project approach is based on an integrated model, tying children's experiences together, building connections and relationships within the child's world that helps them make sense of their environment.

In projects at Reggio, we saw a strong connection between process and product. This was particularly interesting to us working with young children of ages two and three. Because children of this age tend to be immersed in the immediate moment and in the process rather than the product of their activity, often teachers, when developing curriculum, tend to put little emphasis on long-range planning and on developing extensive connections between different activities. But through the Reggio ideas we saw a way to bridge this gap. The product and the process seem to merge together. Any piece of work shifts through multiple transitions as ideas are explored, discussed, and revised and new children enter the adventure to offer new elaborations. Through group analysis of the product, the product can become a starting point from which to start something new.

Finally, collaboration by children, teacher, and parents is another major idea that influenced us. Working together on a project is seen as an opportunity to share and comment on ideas, and thus move on to deeper understandings. Negotiation and conflict are important aspects in this collective process that engages feelings and thoughts. The use of representation and documentation in unusual ways (e.g., photographs, music/movement, drawings, clay sculptures, videotapes, tape recordings, story writing) becomes a central way for children to notice each other and eventually communicate ideas in shared endeavors.

## "IN-DEPTH STUDY PROJECTS"

Over the past two years we have conducted "in-depth study projects" in our Two-Year-Old Program at the Human Development Laboratory School. As we describe the projects we created in our classroom, it will be important to understand the dynamics of our program which enabled us to implement the projects. The Two-Year-Old Program not only provides a model preschool classroom for children and parents, but is also a primary training site for early childhood teacher preparation at the University of Massachusetts School of Education. In this classroom there are 18 children and a team of 9 student teachers who are responsible for running all aspects of the classroom from curriculum planning to holding conferences with parents. There is no master teacher but instead a faculty facilitator and graduate teaching assistant who guide the student teachers' work in the classroom and remain on site at all times. The student teachers hold a postsession meeting each day after the children leave to process and evaluate the day's events. These daily meetings became a crucial place to evaluate our in-depth study projects on an ongoing basis.

An "in-depth study project," as we define it, is a project that begins with a germ of an idea that evolves over a long period of time (two to four months) into an extensive, complex study. This organic model of curriculum begins with careful observation of the children's interests, questions, and ideas and then develops those ideas into concrete learning experiences. After reflection on the experience, new ideas are generated and new activities are designed.

While an in-depth study project can last for several months, it is important to note that the project is not the only thing that the children are doing in the classroom during this time. Sometimes the whole group may be involved in a project activity, but other times it may only be a small group of six, four, or even two children involved in a specific project event. Working with small groups simplifies the process of collaboration between such young children as they need only to notice and respond to the words and actions of the few in the group. We also noticed that these small groupings offer the opportunity for "peak experiences" of greater depth that later served to enrich the play in the larger group. For teachers, especially our novice student interns, smaller groups clarified the difficult task of observing and responding to children's words and actions.

Choosing a project topic is the first step. The following description of how to create and develop an in-depth study project is drawn from an earlier article about our work at the Laboratory School (LeeKeenan & Edwards, 1992). It should be something concrete, close to children's personal experience, interesting and important to the children, and "dense" in potential meanings (emotional and intellectual), so that it is rich in possibilities for varied activity during different parts of the day and for sustaining long-term interest. Once a project topic has been selected, there are four basic components that can be repeated more than once during the study. It is important to note that these different components are not presented in a specific sequential plan. Different components can occur as needed to further provoke children's questions or to sprout a new subgroup of study.

- *Exploration*: The project is introduced with a *provocation*, a stimulating event or activity that gets the children thinking about the topic. The initial event should evoke plenty of images and feelings and be inspiring to the children. During this exploration period both the children and teachers should be open to new ideas. Teachers, in particular, must be able to be energized by a fresh and open perspective. They should not only notice carefully children's reactions, questions, comments, and ideas, but be able to "play" and learn alongside the children as they explore these new project experiences.
- *Organization*: Children's ideas and questions are developed into learning activities to provoke further exploration that helps focus and expose new ideas. Their ideas are documented through drawings, construction, photographs, writing, and videotapes. Through reflection and repetition children are guided into deeper experiences on the same topic (Dyson, 1990; Thompson, 1990).
- *Discussion/representation*: Throughout the project, children's solu-

tions, answers, and responses to activities are shared among children and noted by the teachers. The children's current ideas are compared and contrasted to their initial ideas and the ideas of their teachers. Each day's activities build on a previous day's events.

• *Summary Experience*: Finally, a culminating experience takes place. This is a type of celebration; a symbolic way of acknowledging what has been accomplished and learned by the group during the course of this project. Often the culmination may become a springboard for new projects and ideas, an example of merging process and product. Afterwards teachers conduct an evaluation with the children and with other staff. They consider what children learned and accomplished and what they themselves learned and accomplished.

## EXAMPLES OF THREE PROJECTS

### Water Project–Spring 1989

The first in-depth study project we implemented was in the spring of 1989. The weather was getting warmer and the children were interested in being outdoors and playing with water. Water is a basic element in the daily lives of children—they bathe in it, wash in it, drink it, play with it, see it everywhere around them in nature as well as in their homes. Before we officially introduced the project to the children, we began by having the student teachers brainstorm about what was interesting about water to them as adults and what they thought children might want to know and experience about water. They felt children would be interested in "how water feels, how it flows, what will sink or float in it." These initial ideas became a baseline for teachers' entry into the project. Contradicting our expectations, however, we soon discovered that children were much more interested in the color of water (they said, "Water is white" when trying to describe its clearness) and the fact that water can be absorbed by objects (children said, "The sponge ate the water").

We realized that the focus of children's questions and comments could be our only real guidelines for the project. For instance, when one child was interested in how newspaper absorbed water and commented on how it became heavier, we were able to pursue this observation by introducing sponges into other water activities. On another occasion, a child's comment that "water melts sand" was an entry point for the teachers to offer experiences in how water altered other materials such as jello and cornstarch. We put an emphasis on discovering and uncovering children's questions and thoughts, rather than being constrained by teacher expectations and stereotyped ideas.

Over the course of the project certain key ideas began to emerge from the children that became the source for activities that developed. For example, looking at the many functions of water led to activities such as washing dolls, animals, and dishes; painting with water on paper, chalkboards, and the sidewalk; and finally cooking with water to make lemonade and soup. Another idea in which the children were interested was the temperature of water. Experiences with hot water, cold water, and ice led one child to comment while looking at an ice cube melting in a paper cup, "Water comes from inside the ice." (In this example the child was interested in whether ice melts from the inside out or the outside in. A follow-up activity was devised using squeeze bottles filled with hot water to sculpt a bin of ice.) Interest in how water evaporates led to activities such as fanning a wet chalkboard to dry it, and washing and hanging clothes on a clothesline to dry. Interest in the reflection of water led teachers to provide mirrors and aluminum foil for children to use in the water table. (One child became very excited about the sun's reflection on the ceiling above the water table. He jumped up and down pointing to the dancing spot of light on the ceiling. The aluminum foil enabled the child to experience a sense of control over the water reflections.) The culminating activity was an outdoor Water Day in which water was involved in every choice activity from tricycle washing to transporting water down the slide.

By the end of this three-month project, the 2-year-old children were using new vocabulary meaningfully in their everyday play (e.g., soak, clear, absorb, flow, evaporate) (LeeKeenan & Edwards, 1992). We assume increasing vocabulary and language awareness reveals a deepening or broadening of knowledge. In part, our attention to how the children engaged in materials led us to provide appropriate challenges to the children's thinking. For instance, the children's fascination with the color of water led us to offer experiences that enabled them to explore their own ideas. Many children said that "water is white." To further explore this thought the children were presented with white paint and clear water with which to paint. For teachers the project provided a concrete way for us to observe and evaluate children's learning about water. Through observation of children's actions, words, and questions, teachers could sense the shifts and changes in understanding, the evolution of new ideas and questions by the children about water.

## House Project—Fall 1989

The following fall semester, 1989, we began another project: This one was about houses. Children had been interested in construction and the use of woodworking tools. They often built structures with blocks and manipulated tools such as hammers. We commenced with an initial brainstorming of ideas as we had in the previous semester. We created several curriculum "webs" of potential activities about houses that children might be interested in. In a web, the central idea shoots off into multiple directions with each thread offering further connected ideas. This web included diverse activities such as building with cardboard boxes, comparing different types of houses, looking at animal homes, and transportation.

This project never really took off the ground and in evaluating why it didn't work we learned some significant things. While webbing often provokes more creative curriculum ideas, we also found them to be potentially misleading. The smorgasbord of activities shifted the student teachers' focus of attention onto filling the slots in the daily schedule and away from what was interesting, relevant, or connected to the children's world. Moreover, we noticed that the webs led the students into more thematic-style activities, often based on their adult perceptions of what is important to "know" about houses.

Another factor contributing to the project's lack of success was the developmental readiness of the children. As is usual during the fall semester, the group of young 2-year-olds were brand new to the program. We typically spent much time dealing with separation issues and adjustment to school and building group familiarity. The children were not aware yet of each other's interests and personality styles. They did not yet have the ability to communicate with each other about their ideas as much as they did six months later. Moreover, we discovered that children need plenty of time at the beginning of the year for an "exploratory period" of their new environment and materials before projects may emerge. Children cannot be pushed through this exploration time before they are ready. Otherwise children may merely imitate teachers to fulfill their expectations.

Looking back, we also believe there was a lack of sufficient emotional response by the children to this particular topic. In general, particularly when working with very young children, a topic needs to be emotionally meaningful, concrete, and part of the children's immediate experience. The subject of houses and the different types of homes for people and animals did not appear to be highly engaging to our children.

## Looking At Each Other—Spring 1990

The following Spring 1990 semester, with the same group of children and a new group of student interns, we began our third project called,

"Looking at Each Other," which developed from the children's growing interest in peer relations. This project was also intended to integrate elements of antibias curriculum into our work, focusing on similarities and differences within the group (Derman-Sparks & the A.B.C. Task Force, 1989). As in the other projects, we began by brainstorming what we as *adults* were interested in about each other and then thinking about what the *children* were interested in about each other.

The provocative event which introduced the project to the children involved face masks prepared from a 5 × 7 color photograph of each child's face, cut out, laminated, and mounted on a stick (adapted from Forman & Hill, 1984). These "face puppets" were very exciting to the children and allowed them to compare one another indirectly and then interact in nonthreatening ways. On this and subsequent days they traded face masks with each other, drew on them, and used them as props in dramatic play. Unusual and unexpected uses of photography provided continuity and connection to the project and became a central means to carry this project theme forward. Laminated photographs of the children were on different occasions hidden in the sand table and in the playdough, frozen in ice cubes, taped on the bottom of blocks, taped

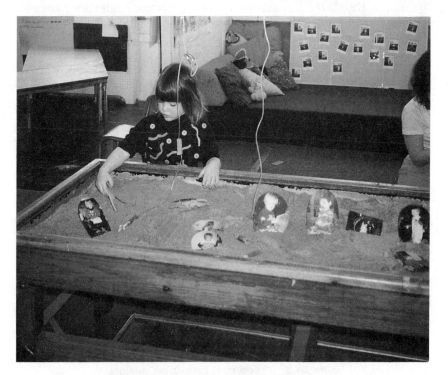

Figure 14.2.    "Looking at Each Other" project.

to doll heads, and so on. We used photographs to make books about each other. Photocopied photographs of the children were made and given to the children to use in different coloring and collage activities over several weeks.

In this project we used more representation and documentation than in previous projects. We realized the importance of documentation: It boosts memory and helps guide children's thinking, particularly with children as young as ours. In one activity in which the children's photographs were buried in the sand box, one of the children discovered that her photo showed her wearing a favorite dress she had worn in dramatic play the previous week. Mei-Lan excitedly insisted on finding the real dress in the classroom and revisiting her experience with that role. Besides photographs we could also look at dramatic play, verbal expression, and body movement as kinds of documentation and ways to understand children's reactions to certain activities.

Making connections with parents was also a priority in this project. Particularly when working with young children we found that parental input is essential to help provide insights into what the children were thinking about and how they were responding to our project themes. At the start, the parents were asked through questionnaires to provide initial input. The parents were asked, "What do you feel your

**Figure 14.3.** "Looking at Each Other" project.

child is most interested in about others? *Who* are they interested in? *What* about them interests them? *How* do they show it? List any specific comments or questions your child has made about others." These data were used to help shape the direction of the project. For instance, two parents commented on their children's keen interest in how they compared with the size and strength of others. These reports confirmed our own observations and we set about introducing the use of a variety of mirrors such as hanging mirrors and flexible mirrors in different activities. Other parents offered the observation that their child had begun to define others in the group (e.g., "Shelly is shy," "Jason is funny," and "Martha has a nice hairdo"). Our response was to begin encouraging children to elaborate their thoughts about others through activities with photos and face puppets.

Weekly letters were then sent to parents about the project, with information on the types of activities being done in the classroom, observations on children's response to the activities, and suggestions for follow-up activities to be done at home. Parents were encouraged to contribute information, pictures, books, objects, and materials to the class about the project and encouraged to talk with the child at home about the project. Documentation (e.g., booklets, photos, drawings) were passed from school to home and home to school. Parents were invited to participate in special project activities at school.

By the end of this project, the children had not only become much more aware of each other but were more able to accurately articulate their similarities and differences (LeeKeenan & Edwards, 1992). For instance, they were particularly interested in the languages other than English spoken in our classroom. When one child, Bill, became aware that he spoke English while some of his peers spoke Chinese or Korean, he started to invent his own (make-believe) language! This anecdote became an opportunity for teachers to respect how a child views his world around him. It wasn't just a "cute thing" Bill did. This was his reconstruction or representation of how he saw other children speaking a language with which he was unfamiliar. Teachers need to respect and extend these generative insights of children.

## PLANNING CURRICULUM
## BY MAKING CONNECTIONS

In this next section we would like to describe what we learned about doing in-depth projects assisted by the guiding principle of "making connections." Malaguzzi, the founding father of the Reggio system, claims, "From the very beginning, curiosity and learning refuse simple and isolated things: they love to find the dimensions and relations of complex situations" (Malaguzzi, 1987, p. 19). In Reggio the process of learning involves making connections and relationships between feelings, ideas, words, and actions. It involves building connections and relations between child, parent, teacher, and community.

The project approach became a way for us to make connections throughout the curriculum and classroom through integration and a continuity of ideas and activities. It gave the classroom a sense of community and wholeness in an organic, meaningful way that developed as the projects progressed. Below we highlight several specific types of connections we made and give examples, based on the projects described above.

## Making Connections Through the Environment of the Classroom

By putting related materials in several areas of a classroom, children can make connections in their environment. For example, finding photographs of children hidden in the sand table, under blocks, and in playdough provides children multiple opportunities to discuss their peers. Young children need repetition of ideas, activities, and concrete materials in order to absorb and process concepts. The use of related materials throughout the classroom allows for continuity of focus from one area to another. It also provides a new context for children's thinking—to see a familiar object in a new context builds new associations.

## Making Connections Over Time: Connecting Yesterday to Today . . . and the Future

Multiple-step activities, extensions, and variations of activities from one day to the next help children tie together events and experiences and provide a memory boost. For example, in one activity we videotaped an infant being washed by its mother in our water table and later played back the videotape for children in the same area, but provided dolls, soap, and towels for the children to wash their "babies" with in the water table. Another way to make connections over time is to connect one part of the day to another. For example, we made snacks during the free-choice play period with children, and later ate them at snack time. We did body tracings of each other on paper on the floor with crayons and markers and then, on another day, did body tracing outside on the cement wall with chalk. Repetition in a new environment offers children a variation on the original experience that encourages children to think about the task in new ways. For example, doing the body tracing outside lets children think about how the light casts shadows on their tracings, and also lets them compare a horizontal to a vertical tracing.

Making connections over time also creates a history of the classroom. Creating a class scrapbook with photographs, drawings, and comments from past events gives children a sense of permanence. Showing photographs of last year's children playing in the classroom to this year's children tells them that this classroom was here before they were here and will be here after they leave. It can also give the children more "possibilities" for them with which to identify—who they were, who they are, and who they are becoming.

## Connecting Children's Outside Experiences to School Experiences

Building strong home-to-school connections should be a part of any quality, early childhood program. But in this context the outside experiences can mean home, family, neighborhood, or culture. In our neighborhood of the university campus, the duck pond is a central focal point for the community at large. Therefore, a visit to the duck pond was a logical beginning point for our Water Project, making a connection to the fact that the duck pond was a meaningful place to the children that they had visited many times before. In the Looking at Each Other Project, we noticed that the children were not only interested in each other, but also noticed which mothers and fathers belonged to which children. Therefore, we videotaped the "arrival time" one morning with parents dropping off the children, then later replayed the tape, letting the children discuss who was who. Other examples of connections to home involved bringing things from home to school and things from school to home. As mentioned earlier the importance of parental input at this age is crucial to understanding the child, since home is so central to the child's life. Outside experiences could also be used to extend projects and develop new variations for other ideas and activities.

## Connecting Children with Each Other by Sharing Emotions, Interests, and Experiences

Providing opportunities for peer feedback, sharing, and discussion are important ways to build ideas as well as a way to build community in a group. Examples include cooperative projects, such as a group mural of underwater sea life, to which children added over a period of time. Each day children would add new materials to the mural—paper fishes, fabric plants, yarn seaweed, gravel and sand, shells, or other drawings and words. A layer of clear vinyl was put on top so children could experience some depth to the ocean. Other collaborative projects included a class poster where children's comments about each other's photographs were written down for all to see. Sharing children's individual face puppets with each other was a way for children to share feelings and emotions. These face puppets were highly personal and emotionally meaningful to the individual children, and it often took an adult to facilitate this connection between children in a sensitive manner. The children's interest in connecting with each other was also evident in their enthusiasm for hugging. We quickly incorporated this greeting ritual into a group-time activity of "musical hugs."

### Connecting Teachers' Interests to Children's Interests

We have spent a lot of time tending to children's interests in this chapter, but teachers are also an integral part of the classroom. Young children, in particular, are very interested in their teacher's lives, almost more than in those of their peers. They want to know what their teachers do outside of school, where they sleep, eat, shop, and so on. Therefore, it is relevant to try and connect teachers' lives and interests to children's interests and experiences as long as teachers don't impose their ideas and interests. Having the student teachers do an initial brainstorm about each project topic was a way to make them feel like they were also a part of the classroom. Teachers have feelings and ideas that may be the same or different from the children. Having teachers share photographs from home was another way for them to bring their lives into the classroom. In mid-March the university had a spring break when many college students went to Florida for their vacation. During the Water Project, one student teacher planned a Beach Day in the dramatic play area with sand, water, bathing suits, and so on, to coincide with her interest in going to Florida.

### Connecting Events, Ideas, and Feelings
### Through Representation and Documentation

The purposes of representation are many: to provide children a way to reflect and interpret their experiences, to evoke memories, to create a sense of history, and to communicate ideas to others. Some forms of representation are more relevant for children, others for teachers or parents. Following the practice in Reggio Emilia, we used much more photographic documentation in our projects than is usual in preschools. It served to validate the children's self-esteem, and more importantly, provided a systematic way for children to revisit their experiences (with attendant thoughts and feelings) and then reconstruct and reinterpret them in a deeper way. Given the very young age of our children, such a concrete spark to memory was absolutely essential to sustain the momentum of the project over time. Types of documentation included children's drawings, paintings, constructions, stories, poems, or writings that were made into classroom displays or books that were posted around the room. They also included photographs, videotapes, and slides made by teachers and shown to children. Documentation also benefited the adults in the classrooms. Anecdotal records and notes made by teachers were used to prepare short written quotations (of things children did or said that pertained to the project) that were hung on the walls to remind the teachers of the children's insights. These methods of documentation not only let the project theme "permeate the classroom," but also preserved and communicated ideas and curricula to parents and other staff.

For children ages two to three, however, we found that we needed to go beyond the typical recording of children's actions to allow children to represent their ideas in different ways. We feel these children are in transition from a sensory exploration of their concrete world to communicating and interpreting their world through representation. Teachers need to think widely and creatively to provide children with many opportunities to represent and interpret their experiences. For example, let the children rather than the teachers take photographs so that the pictures more accurately reflect the children's perspective of the world. Use tools, such as puppets, dramatic play, or flannel board manipulatives, with which the children are comfortable and adept, as a way to represent the children's ideas and thinking. These types of representations document children's play by creating stories to be retold. In the Looking at Each Other Project, children used photographs of each other that were hung on a clothesline as props to act out stories about each other or themselves. Another type of representation in the Water Project involved having the children create their own Duck Pond with sticks, twigs, mud, dirt, leaves, and plastic ducks in a big clear basin in the classroom, after a visit to the campus duck pond.

## CONCLUSION

We learned much as teachers of teachers and teachers of children from creating these in-depth study projects in our Two-Year-Old Program.

However, while we highly admire the work in Reggio Emilia, we wondered if there are obstacles here in the United States that prevent us from fully implementing projects as they do in this northern Italian community. How much is the success of the Reggio approach due to the high value placed on art and aesthetics in the Italian culture? In the evaluation of our projects by our teachers, they wondered how the outside curriculum requirements, which are often superimposed on teachers, might prevent them from having the time and freedom to truly slow down and get involved in complex studies, prevent them from, as David Hawkins said, not "covering" curriculum but "uncovering" it? Other teachers were concerned about the lack of physical space and teacher power to document and carry out the projects in a typical classroom with 20 children and one teacher.

Upon reflection, though, we realize our intent was never to transplant or duplicate exactly what is done in Reggio Emilia to our classrooms here. Instead, Reggio Emilia became a way to inspire new "possibilities" not only for children but for us as teachers. As we adapt ideas, we find new solutions that fit our own needs, thinking, context, and perception of children. For the student teachers in our program there were important insights that came from drawing their attention away from the ease of prepackaged curriculum and into the worlds that children experience. Attending to the words and actions of children as the source and inspiration of curricula is often more difficult than simply designing "creative activities."

In all, we found the project approach to provide rich insights into designing curriculum for very young children. We viewed both content and process as critical to sustained and joyful learning. Through careful and detailed documentation, we raised children's ability to reflect on their own and others' ideas and to make connections over time. By taking the lead from the children's interests and questions, we joined them in their desire to understand a world of great complexity and adventure.

## REFERENCES

Derman-Sparks, L., & the A.B.C. Task Force. (1989). *Anti-bias curriculum. Tools for empowering young children.* Washington, DC: National Association for the Education of Young Children.

Dyson, A. (1990). Symbol makers, symbol weavers: How children link play, pictures, and print. *Young Children, 45*(2), 50–57.

Forman, G., and Hill, F. (1984). *Constructive play: Applying Piaget in the preschool.* Menlo Park, CA: Addison-Wesley.

Gandini, L. (1984). Not just anywhere: Making child care centers into "particular" places. *Beginnings: The Magazine for Teachers of Young Children, 1*, 17–20.

Gandini, L., & Edwards, C. (1988). Early childhood integration of the visual arts. *Gifted International, V*(2), 14–18.

LeeKeenan, D., & Edwards, C. (1992). Using the project approach with toddlers. *Young Children, 47*(4), 31–35.

Malaguzzi, L. (1987). The hundred languages of children. In *The hundred languages of children: Narrative of the possible* (Catalog from the Exhibit of the same name). Prepared by the Department of Education, City of Reggio Emilia, Region of Emilia Romagna, Italy.

New, R. (1990). Excellent early education: A city in Italy has it. *Young Children, 45*(6), 4–10.

Thompson, C. (1990). "I make a mark": The significance of talk in young children's artistic development. *Early Childhood Research Quarterly, 5*(2), 215–232.

**"Elephants," drawn by child of the Michelangelo School.**

## 15

# Another Way of Seeing Things: We're Still Learning

**Baji Rankin, Nora Cannon, Pat Corsaro, Betsy Damian, Eunice Perry, Diane Rollo, and Irene Rochwarg**

"These must be gifted children to be doing this kind of work. It couldn't happen in my school!"

"Teachers must do a lot of the work for the children. It just couldn't happen if you let the children do it themselves!"

These and similar comments are often heard when people first experience Reggio Emilia's educational approach. In this chapter, as educators from the Early Childhood Educational Exchange (ECEE), who have visited the schools in Reggio Emilia and who organized the exhibit, "The Hundred Languages of Children," in Boston in 1989, we

**Figure 15.1. Playing hopscotch, Diana School**

share our experiences in working with children, parents, teachers, and one another, striving to apply Reggio Emilia's inspiration, principles, and ideas.

We do not intend to duplicate the Reggio experience; it would be foolish and impossible to do so. Yet, we want to use certain principles and ideas suggested by the Reggio experience. For example, just as the Reggio approach bases itself on listening to children and observing their work, so we can constantly guide ourselves with our observations of children. Our strength consists in the fact that we are working in a variety of settings and roles, including as a teacher in an urban day care center, a kindergarten teacher in a large urban public school, an arts education specialist in a public school, an arts specialist in a suburban day care center, a director of a laboratory preschool at a college, and an instructor of a college course on curriculum planning.

Although we work in separate situations, the ECEE provides a sense of community among us, a forum in which we can talk about our developing ideas. This community is essential to our growth, as individuals and as a group. Although that was true before eight of us went to Reggio, our visits reinforced and intensified the importance of our ongoing interaction and communication. Here are several of our stories.

## DIANE'S STORY

### Improving Parent Participation and the Classroom Environment

**Baji:** Diane, what did you find most striking about the Reggio Emilia experience?

**Diane:** The order and aesthetics of the classroom environment, the special relationship between parents and school, and most importantly, the emphasis on listening to the children as a guide to curriculum planning were the key elements that stand out in my mind. Viewing the schools in Reggio Emilia provoked new ideas and ways of thinking about children.

Too often in our materialistic society, our classrooms and homes become cluttered with possessions and objects. We seem to lose the beauty of simplicity and overstimulate ourselves and our children. The Reggio classrooms, in contrast, are simply beautiful. They contain a variety of materials, displayed and ordered in an articulate fashion. They are also rich in materials related to the children's culture and family life, for example, family photos, regional foods, and personal mementos from home. Animating the classrooms with symbols of family life is vital here in the United States, too, considering the diverse cultural and socioeconomic backgrounds of children.

**Baji:** Tell me about some of the changes you made at your center after visiting Reggio Emilia.

**Diane:** The Reggio classrooms are open, airy, and bright with splashes of color. My child care center, in contrast, is located in an old, dark converted building. The first change I made was to paint the drab yellow walls of the classroom white, giving a more open and spacious look to a small space. In the spirit of Reggio, I turned to the parents for help in painting the classrooms. It was important that they participate from the start, to feel that the school belongs to them, and to know they actually have a voice in their child's school environment. The turnout for the painting party was outstanding.

I believe, as do the educators in Reggio Emilia, that when parents participate directly in the classroom experience, a stronger relationship among teachers and parents develops. Parents and I met together at the beginning of the 1990–1991 school year and discussed curriculum ideas for the new year. A monthly report was designed to keep parents informed about ongoing classroom experiences. The report also gave parents a list of possible activities to do with their child as a way of extending classroom experiences into the home. Parents felt that they had a better understanding of what was going on in the classroom and had a chance to participate in that experience. Implementing a program that made parents feel like insiders instead of outsiders resolved many conflicts and tensions between teachers and parents and increased parental involvement.

In Reggio Emilia, all materials in the classroom are displayed in an aesthetic manner. Art materials are placed on shelves in a noncluttered arrangement in transparent containers accessible to the children. Objects are displayed on lighted shelves at children's eye level. For example, children might find sea shells ordered by size, color, or texture. I felt it important to improve the arrangement of materials in my small classroom, to create more focus and less confusion for both children and adults.

To make shelves more attractive, I kept only a few items on each shelf and rotated them periodically. Everything had its place. The children were still provided with enough choices of materials to use, but the choices were displayed in a more appealing and less over-stimulating way.

The bathrooms were also made more attractive by placing bottles of colored sand in order of size on the shelves. Unsightly supplies stored in the bathroom were removed. I lined the walls with mylar mirrors at children's eye level. For children to really learn about themselves, they need to look at themselves in different ways.

The Reggio classrooms have a wonderful addition rarely found elsewhere, an *atelier*, or studio/laboratory, to assist children in the discovery process. Although it was impossible for us to devote a room solely to this purpose, we wanted to dedicate some special space to enhancing creative expression. In the United States, teachers emphasize children's verbal skills and often ignore or undervalue children's other forms of expression and representation. Providing a particular place to help children discover many forms of self-expression returns value and respect to these other symbolic languages.

I set aside a portion of the classroom, therefore, and provided a large table and two shelving units that separated this area from others. The shelves were stacked in an uncluttered way with recycled materials in transparent, accessible containers. Different types of paper, paints, brushes, clay, markers, and so on, were also available in this area. To further eliminate clutter in the classroom, I created a recycle center in the upstairs conference room. Making these materials accessible and aesthetically appealing encouraged optimal use and nonverbal expression.

Finally, I wanted to improve my teaching by listening more to the children, then leading them in creating their own solutions to their questions. I was greatly struck by Reggio Emilia's philosophy of using children's words as a guide in planning curriculum. Tape-recording children's conversations has become indispensable to me in assessing children's interests and planning curriculum. For example, I taped a conversation of a group of children playing with Ninja Turtle figures, during which I mentioned that the Turtles were named after famous artists who lived a long time ago. Later, listening to the tape, I noticed that these questions arose: "What's an artist?" "What did they do?" "What do they look like?" These questions led to a project that included a series of visits to the Boston Museum of Fine Arts, where we studied different artists and their techniques, as well as explored colors, shape, and line. Many of the children brought sketch pads to the museum and copied their favorite painting or sculpture. Back in the classroom, they recopied their sketches on a larger scale. This is just one example of how recording classroom conversations helped provoke a series of rich experiences and reexperiences, for children, initiated by children.

## BETSY'S CHALLENGE

### Bringing It Home to the Urban Classroom

**Diane:** Betsy, what is your classroom like, and how are you dealing with its particular challenges?

**Betsy:** I teach kindergarten in an urban public school system. My classroom is diverse, consisting of 20 children from various ethnic backgrounds. Half speak English as a second language, some have no English at all. One-third have serious emotional or behavioral problems. Some children come to school ready to learn, with the beginnings of reading and writing and a strong self-image, while others cannot name a color or a shape. Children meet for the first time early in September and are with me for one short year.

I really want to emphasize the striking contrast between the cohesive, coherent approach found in Reggio Emilia and the situation here. I work in a school that houses three different programs. Each program has a separate director with its own goals and guidelines. Neighboring classrooms embrace opposite educational philosophies, and teachers seldom have the leisure time to visit or exchange ideas during the school day. Within this fragmented framework, I am striving to develop a space and working style which reflect the influence of Reggio Emilia. The most important thing to keep in mind is that any small change has value.

My materials may be similar to those available in Reggio Emilia, but what the children can do, and what I expect, are very different. In my classroom early this year I put out watercolors and ordinary paint boxes from the five-and-dime store. I thought that I would discover the skill levels of my students so I could then go on to enhance their knowledge and learning in an appropriate way. In this way I was applying my understanding of how Reggio teachers approach problems by choosing media that will most directly address a question.

As the children used the watercolors, I found myself chanting, "Water, paint, paper . . . water, paint, paper," to help some children understand how to get the color from the paintbox onto their paper. One little boy was working at the table, paint brush in hand. He moved his brush happily from water to paint box and made some initial markings on his paper. Then, when he replaced his paint brush into the water, he was shocked, and then scared. He looked up at me with large, frightened eyes and said anxiously, "Teacher, my water is getting dirty."

I learned quite a bit from this experience. This child had never seen or used watercolors before. He was frightened about something. Could it be he thought the teacher would be angry because he dirtied the water? How did he think the teacher would react? If he had never used watercolors before, how many of the other classroom experiences would be new to him? How could I expect him to express himself with unfamiliar materials?

Events like this happen every day in my classroom as I continue to translate an Italian educational philosophy into my own language and integrate it with my understanding of children and schooling. I share some of the children's anxiety as I, too, cross into unknown territory. I can see that some of the peaceful contentment I felt in Reggio Emilia's classrooms must come from the comfort and security children gain from repeated use of the same symbolic media, as well as from their secure relationships with adults.

I feel very strongly that in my case the best approach seems to be to introduce materials slowly and carefully to the children, to study and document their progress and experimentation, and to observe the direction of their interests.

My shelves are stocked with materials open to exploration. Countertops are kept clear and clean. The space is open and inviting, well lit, with curtained windows and fresh flowers on the playhouse table. I want the children to experience this beautiful, safe, comfortable, and predictable environment as a place for them to relax and enjoy life, discover their potential, and build strength and happiness.

Playdough has been available daily at one table for over a month. Certain children have definitely chosen this as their preferred medium. They have already worn out four batches of my best recipe! Yet what each child has discovered at the table is highly individual.

One child, for example, has mastered the skill of sitting down at the table and keeping the playdough off his clothes. He is learning to concentrate and focus. Eventually, he will be able to complete a successful construction and express himself with playdough; in the process, he will understand that his ideas are valuable and interesting.

Another child makes balls and coils with the playdough; she can sit and work with an idea for an extended period of time. I have shown her additional ways to work: how to pinch the playdough to make certain shapes, or how to use a carving tool for more delicate designs. She often helps other children by demonstrating her techniques. She may even work directly on their playdough, helping them develop ideas without the frustration and isolation of having to do it all independently.

The more experience the children have with materials, the more they are able to understand it and develop it as one of their languages. Carlina Rinaldi taught me that the material has to belong to the children in order for them to use it as a tool for communication. It has to have a history with them. In time they will be able to express themselves clearly in order to solve a particular problem.

Skills learned with watercolors and playdough transfer easily to other classroom activities. They affect the whole child in solving problems, understanding particular strengths, working hard and long with another person toward a mutual goal, compromising, arguing, laughing, sharing, and feeling strong and good inside. The same is true of myself as a teacher. I am looking at things through new eyes, thinking about projects and materials that would present the right challenge. Where could we gather, make, or find some things that the children can "own"? Our walks to the local playground provide us with much material to discuss and use. But why not also gather leaves, rocks, sand, or gravel at the park? What stories would the children tell working with these natural objects? How would they incorporate them into their developing playdough expertise? What problems would arise? What new understandings would develop? All of these moments lie ahead for us, and I look forward with anticipation.

## NORA'S PROBLEM

### Getting Started in an Elementary School Art Classroom

**Betsy:** Nora, how did you become interested in the Reggio Emilia approach?

**Nora:** It all started as I stood within the "Hundred Languages of Children" exhibit at Boston City Hall in the winter of 1989. I had been struggling with what I experienced as too much distance between one side of myself, the artist, and the other, the one who teaches art to elementary school children. The role of *atelierista* allows for convergence of these sides. The coupling of these two simple words, "artist educator," may be easily said but is much more difficult to put into practice.

**Betsy:** How are you applying the concept of *atelierista* here in your work?

**Nora:** I work as an art education specialist in afterschool programs, public schools, and a summer camp. How do I integrate aspects of the Reggio experience into these different settings? It happens the moment I walk in the door, talk to another teacher, set up my supplies, and start working with the students.

For example, I came in once a week for eight weeks to work at an afterschool program in a local inner-city school. Many of the students no longer had a designated art period because of budget cuts, so my top priority was to keep open an expressive channel for them. Paint was plentiful at this site, so this became our point of departure. Every student was able to start working from his or her own comfort level.

The project was kept open-ended as we started with the familiar— homes and faces—painted in expected ways. Paints were placed on palette trays, paper was supplied, and the students worked away, making piles and piles of paintings. I noticed that they started taking as much joy in mixing all the paints together and painting the tray as they did in painting their pictures. I took this as my cue. In the spirit of Reggio Emilia, I felt that the natural progression for this project would involve experimentation in mixing the paints.

Black and white paints were introduced, and students learned how one color can have many hues. The familiar became the unfamiliar, and students made large shapes with these newly discovered colors. The result was abstract paintings using tints and shades. The students' experimentation guided the project and my work with the students.

At a suburban public elementary school, I worked to expand the art experience beyond the students' weekly, 40-minute time period in the art room. I was completing my student-teaching practicum at this site, and a part of my assignment was to design the curriculum prior to meeting with the students.

I had chosen what, according to my supervisors and cooperating teacher, was an ambitious project for fourth and fifth graders: making banners to be stitched in burlap. Many of the children had never threaded a needle before, let alone designed a banner. But in a way surprising to all of us, boys and girls alike eagerly dived into the project.

As our time together was limited, I knew the students would need additional time outside the art class. Here I was inspired by the model of the Reggio *atelierista* involving the classroom teachers. At the coffee machine, over lunch, and while on playground duty, I sought them out. We discussed ways they could help students keep their momentum during the week. Teachers agreed, rather reluctantly at first, to keep the banners in their classroom, not promising that the students would accomplish much. Over the following weeks, however, very positive progress was made. Some teachers allowed the students to work on the banners after completing their other work. "A great quiet activity," one teacher later commented to me. Other teachers let the students take the banners home. What a wonderful way for grandparents and parents to assist in something for which they have expertise!

Back in the classroom, students shared stories about their at-home stitching lessons. Thus, the art activity did successfully overflow beyond our weekly meeting. The students drew all of us in with their excitement, and everyone (in the spirit of Reggio Emilia) worked to keep the motivation going. In the end, we all took pride in the students' achievements, but they themselves were the real stars, with the banners as their medals. I gained a new sense of meaning for my dual role as artist and art educator.

## PAT'S AND IRENE'S ADAPTATION

### Creating an *Atelier* in a Day Care Center

**Nora:** Pat, you work as an *atelierista* in a day care center. How did this come about?

**Pat:** Over a period of three years, Irene and I have moved from the initial excitement of our first exposure to the ideas of Reggio Emilia, to a more focused exploration of how we might establish an *atelier* with an *atelierista* in our center. We are still discovering and learning how to do this.

We have strong memories of our Reggio experiences, especially of visiting the school, La Villetta. "We must become the child and think as the child" ring the words of Amelia Gambetti, a teacher, and Giovanni Piazza, the *atelierista*. These words remind us to constantly observe the children. Some days they will just mess about playfully with the materials, and other days they will work intensely. We value and reinforce all of their processes of experimentation.

In 1989, we introduced into our program an Arts Specialist (our name for *atelierista*) to provide more exploratory and open-ended experiences for children. All children, regardless of age grouping, attended these special self-expressive sessions weekly. Yet, acceptance of the change was not easily accomplished that first year, by either staff or children. Teachers expected more instructive and prescriptive activities from the Arts Specialist. However, through giving support and seeking input from the staff about projects, timing, and mechanics, the program was established.

After some initial trial and error, we found an effective structure to be one of working with small groups of four to six children for extended periods, in a corridor area lit by skylights. The children seemed to enjoy a change from their usual environment and also found pleasure in the smaller group size. We often paired different combinations of children together, in hopes of their forming new relationships and making joint discoveries. In most instances, the experience seemed calming and relaxing for both staff and children.

The majority of our art materials were recycled ones. Parents brought in materials from their workplaces, ranging from discontinued upholstery fabrics to obsolete paper from print shops.

In November 1989, several "specialists" combined their talents of movement, music, and art to lead the children in a holiday production of "The Nutcracker." Children learned their parts and stenciled their costumes on pillowcases. Parents became involved in set design and helped draw scenery in chalk on queen-size sheets. When opening night came, all of the parents showed up to share this evening with their children. The children, who had been shy and reserved during rehearsals, burst with enthusiasm at the chance to perform and display competence in another symbolic language. The entire production was videotaped, and the children were able to enjoy viewing their efforts long after the last curtain call.

In 1990, we established a permanent *atelier* at the center by redefining the space in the same skylit corridor. We set up two large tables, metal shelving stocked with materials, and a light table. In the past, perhaps at times, we rushed the child to manufacture a piece of art work, even hoping that it would look like all the others, perfect in the tradition of the assembly line. Now we have begun seeing the children as artisans, who slowly ply their craft. We have found that as children explore at their own pace, they take much time to play with paint, color, and different size brushes, rather than painting a picture of "something." Such experimentation leads to unexpected rewards both within and outside of these sessions.

For example, one afternoon last fall, teachers decided to put leftover, multicolored, sequin materials into an indoor sandbox, rather than throwing them away. The next morning the children began to play with the sand and discovered the beautiful, shiny, metallic circles they had used to make Halloween masks the day before. They each took a drinking cup and eagerly began to collect them. Some children asked for glue and paper from their teacher and began to create a multitude of different pictures. Carlina Rinaldi, during her October 1990 visit, had suggested mixing materials in unexpected ways; and the combination of sand and sequins is an example of how we applied her advice. Some children used wallpaper scraps to cut out faces and then used the sequins to create facial features and jewelry. All were excited to show their friends and teachers the treasures they had found in the sandbox.

Facilitating children's expression in any of the "hundred languages" of children now happens in a hundred ways. From time to time, children will come to the *atelier*, start to work with the materials, and spontaneously talk about problems bothering them. Children have begun to feel comfortable in a small-group setting, surrounded by others who are listening, observing, and examining their expressions. Such an experience fosters mutual respect for one another's work, opinions, and reactions. Our program values these ideals.

## EUNICE'S IDEA

### Pairing an Early Childhood Teacher with an Art Educator

**Pat:** Eunice, you work as the director of a college laboratory school where you have a multiage program for children aged 3–5. What aspect of the Reggio experience was most valuable to you?

**Eunice:** There are many aspects that interested me, but what I wanted most to adapt to my program was the staffing pattern that I observed there. Even before going to Reggio, I felt that our program could benefit from some changes. While we had an excellent curriculum and teaching staff, I felt that our approaches were quite predictable. An area that I wanted to develop was the further exploration and understanding of children's symbolic expression. I felt that the combined skills of an early childhood trained person and one with a strong background in developmental psychology and art would be just the pairing for this change. When such an opportunity for hiring new staff came about, it was possible to realize this change. Although all of us at the school agreed that this was a good idea, we did not realize the challenges that would ensue. But I have learned that similar challenges happened in Reggio too, when they altered their traditional models by introducing the co-teaching team as well as the role of the *atelierista*.

Bringing people into such close, novel working partnerships had caused people to have to work through many disagreements and conflicts in Reggio. This was our experience as well. When our two new teachers began their work together, they did not realize how much they had to offer to each other, and, especially to the children. Their combined skills are an important part of the balance that is needed in good program planning. Now, four years later, our program reflects the efforts that were made through the collaboration of these professionals. It is clear to me that the unique and innovative ideas of the early childhood educators here have always been a sustaining force in building this new approach. Like the Reggio educators, we have had our arguments, disappointments, and provocations, all of which has led us to a wider view and a different way of working with young children. The elements of both tradition and change can coexist, bringing a richer and more diverse program to everyone.

**Pat:** How does this reveal itself in your classroom?

**Eunice:** The integrated use of curriculum materials, coupled with careful documentation of the children's work, has provided us with

**Figure 15.2.    Loris Malaguzzi speaks with a foreign delegation visiting the Diana School.**

new ideas and ways to offer both the individual child and the group the creative challenges they enjoy and are capable of accomplishing. Additionally our planning has its own built-in management features, as seen in the children's social interactions and learning experiences.

For example, we introduced a drawing table, now an integral part of our program. The table is actually a table top that we bring out daily and use exclusively for drawing. The children use a variety of mark-making tools: pens, pencils, conte crayons, cray pas, as well as wax crayons and magic markers. We see much more skill and mastery when just these few simple tools are combined with adequate time to work and play. The children had drawn before, but we did not know what an impact this new approach would have on the direction of our program.

**Pat:** Have you seen changes only in the children's drawings?

**Eunice:** No, another dimension that we have developed is the use of clay. Previously, we primarily used playdough, and we still use it occasionally. It is a wonderful material for children. However, we have now given more emphasis to clay, which allows for more elaborated and extended construction of ideas and a greater variety of steps in processing, including molding, glazing, firing, and preserving the material. The ideas and messages that come from work with clay have provided the children with yet another important means of personal expression. Children have greatly strengthened their skills and competence in the use of clay; like the drawing table, it is available every day.

In sum, through the collaboration of early childhood teacher and arts educator, we have seen children gain more concentrated, independent, and self-regulated use of materials. One particular experience has confirmed to me that this kind of staffing pattern benefits the children. One day I observed a child who was working at the clay table for quite a long period of time. He played with the clay, shaped it, molded it, and finally created a piece that pleased him. When he was finished, he said to me, "Now I'm ready to have my clay fired in the kiln. I want my blue glaze to look real good. I did a lot of work; I used the slip; I shared the clay; I made a project. I can't wait to see what it looks like after it's fired! I guess I'll go to circle time now." In just those few moments, this child had displayed to me his motor skills, his capacity for creative expression, an extensive use of new words, an ability to share with others, and a high level of self-esteem. The child was satisfied. So was I.

**Diane:** Certainly we could not take the Reggio Emilia approach, created over 30 years in another culture, and simply replicate it in the United States. But our reflections on our experiences in Reggio helped us focus anew on concepts—beauty and order, the multiple languages of children, letting go of the clock, listening and observing as a basis for teaching—that have often been forgotten or deemphasized in our society and classrooms. If Reggio does nothing else but help us return and remember what is really important for our children, then the approach has been applied successfully.

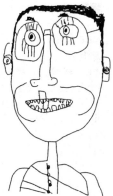

"Self-portrait," by 5-year-old boy of the Pablo Neruda School.

# 16

# A Backward Look: From Reggio Emilia to Progressive Education

## Meg Barden

[T]he problem of the education of children cannot be set apart from history: it depends on many variables that are never independent of the universe of reasoning on which it is based.—Loris Malaguzzi

When I visited "The Hundred Languages of Children" exhibits in Boston and Amherst, Massachusetts and read the accompanying booklet, it was like coming back to my childhood hometown to find that the houses, fields, and trees I'd known as a child were still there. Just as I'd wandered about the neighborhood of my early years delighted at the silver maple tree, the big boulder in the front yard, and the short-cut path to the school all remaining after 60 years, so I felt delight at the descriptions of the day care centers at Reggio Emilia and their curriculum. The ideas, concepts, and even phrases—although they had an Italian slant—were reminiscent of my own elementary school days in the 1920s and 1930s, and much later, during my teacher-of-teacher days in the early 1970s.

Now, as a college professor and supervisor of student teachers, I visit day care classrooms in America where all too often the wall is dominated by a commercial alphabet of cartoon figures along with a calendar with weather or holiday symbols made by a teacher. Children's work, if displayed at all, imitates a given example—orange pumpkins at Halloween, green shamrocks in March. Thus, at the exhibits I found it inspiring and comforting to not only see children's original work, but also photographs detailing the children's involvement in such intriguing activities as Harvesting Grapes With Farmers, Shadowiness, and In Pursuit of a Plane Tree Leaf. The children's work and the photos remind parents and visitors that children's creations and activities are not only important but also delightful to see. For me, the exhibits and later my visit to Reggio also brought back memories of the past.

**Figure 16.1.** "Harvesting Grapes." (Drawings from the exhibit catalog, *The Hundred Languages of Children*, 1987. Reprinted by permission.)

**Figure 16.2.   "Harvesting Grapes."**

Let me start with some of the similarities in the buildings. Carla Rinaldi, speaking at the Boston exhibit, stated that in every Reggio Emilia Center,

> . . . the building is the result of many meetings among teachers, educators and architects who together decide on the floor plan and the selection of materials, toys and equipment. . . . The environment created in every building is the container or place where the impact of teachers, children, their families and the history of their culture is tangible and visible. Every building therefore is an original, a custom made place fit for a particular group of children and adults. (Rinaldi, 1989, p. 2)

As I listened to this my mind turned back to the progressive elementary school I attended from 1929 to 1932 in a suburb of New York City.

The first years of Hessian Hills School were in a parent's garage. As more families became involved with the school they purchased a wonderful old farmhouse which the parents helped remodel. In 1931 a fire destroyed this building. The teachers, children, and their families, just as in Reggio, then worked to build a new school especially designed for themselves—a particular group of children and adults. Katherine

Moos Campbell, granddaughter of the founder of Hessian Hills School, gives us the following glimpses of the spirit of progressive education at that time. The fire, she writes,

> . . . brought parents together in an effort to rebuild. Six parents of Hessian Hills School families administered the School Building Fund. They recruited John Dewey as honorary chairman . . . and their sponsors included notable parents Waldo Frank, Heyward Broun, Stuart Chase, Floyd Dell and Lincoln Steffens; as well as Lewis Mumford, Oswald Garrison Villiard and Edward L. Thorndike. For all these people, the small isolated experiment in creative child centered education was worth saving, even in the midst of the depression" (Campbell, 1984, p. 132). Dell and Chase commented that Hessian Hills School fitted children for "happy lives in the machine age" through "a rediscovery of the human values of culture." (Campbell, 1984, p. 133)

Much thought went into the new school building. The director and staff drew up plans for an ideal new school: "classrooms to house fifteen children each, private toilets, space for both quiet and noisy activities; soundproof walls yet easy access to the fields and woods we use so much. . . . Most of all they needed shops for every form of hand work, a place for a forge, kiln, printing press, a large room for rhythms, dramatic and chorus work (Campbell, 1984, p. 134).

Elizabeth Moos, the Director of the school, stated in 1931:

> There are obvious parallels between the philosophy behind modern architecture and modern education. Modern architects and modern educators are discarding dogmas, taking nothing for granted; they are experimental and flexible. Neither educators nor architects if truly modern, accept tradition unless it justifies its value for their civilization. Our children are to be fitted to take their places in this particular type of civilization; they should grow in a physical harmony with it.
>
> We work with the child as a whole; architects with the whole building. Both must be purposeful and they must function. Each of us works from the inside out and is no longer satisfied with any artificial facades. And above all we are both trying to let in the light. (Campbell, 1984, p. 135)

As I explored my memories and the writings of progressive educators of the past and moved among the charming Reggio schools, it became clear that both were aware of the need to "let in the light"— both sunlight and enlightened ideas. The environment surrounding the schools is also important. Compare the following statements from the Reggio Emilia exhibit about Harvesting Grapes With Farmers with that of Caroline Pratt's *I Learn From Children*. Pratt was the Director of City and Country School in New York City which began even before Hessian Hills School and is still operating. Both schools were members of the Associated Experimental Schools. Pratt's book was published in 1948, but was written about her experiences in the 30 preceding years.

> The children and teachers of our schools have participated in this tradition for over twenty years: each school has a longstanding relationship of friendship with farm families of the area. Our September appointment is a meeting with the agricultural ambience, with land that is worked and bears fruit, with vineyards, machinery, tools, the architecture and furnishings of a house, stables, out-buildings, the skills and problems of those who work the land and raise animals, the customs of farm families, the techniques of gathering grapes and the processes involved in transforming them into wine, with both traditional equipment and the Winemaking Cooperatives' modern machinery. The process is then repeated directly in the schools with the help and advice of our farmer friends. (Malaguzzi, 1987, p. 95)

Pratt further describes the surroundings near their school:

> The six children and I spent a great deal of time at the docks. The river traffic, endlessly fascinating, brought good simple questions to their lips, but they were too shy at first to ask the tugboat men and bargemen and the wagon drivers for answers. When they saw that I would not do their asking for them they plucked up courage to make the first move and met with such friendly answers that their diffidence vanished quite away. I explained to the men that these visits were part of their school work. The men liked being asked to contribute to the children's education. They answered the young voices patiently and carefully. We sat for an hour at a time on the tail of a wagon backed up on the dock, watching the boats coming and going, the tugs nudging the laden scows in and the empty one's out. We saw the wagons being loaded with all kinds of things for the city, and asked the drivers where they were taking their loads. (Pratt, 1948, p. 42)

Back at the school Pratt describes how the river and the boats played an important part in the unit block buildings the children made of the city. "Here the children put to use the facts they had acquired, some by asking questions, but most through their eyes and ears" (Pratt, 1948, p. 42).

In both Reggio Emilia and in New York City the experiences the children had "in the field" were recapitulated in the classroom. The children were able to show themselves what they had discovered and thus provide continuity between school and the real world. As the Exhibit book comments: "their identity as children is rooted in a longer history, in diverse yet always contemporary worlds" (Malaguzzi, 1987, p. 96).

At Reggio and in the early progressive schools there was deep respect for children and obvious pleasure in listening and learning from them. "The schools are not places for lectures, but places where teachers actively listen so they can with the children 'adventure' in the world of knowing" (Rinaldi, 1989, p. 5).

> If the child's own play-work was to be his learning method, as I insisted it should be, then he must get his inspiration for it in his own way, by knowledge gained with his own eyes and ears, questions asked by him about things *he* wants to know, answers found by him within the limits of his own ability to find and understand them. A teacher or parent or sympathetic adult can help and encourage him in his researches but the original impulse comes from him. (Pratt, 1948, p. 10)

The teachers in both Reggio Emilia and the progressive schools were committed to research and experimentation with young children. Their enthusiasm and commitment resulted in worldwide dissemination of both the concepts and the content of their projects with children. The Progressive Education Association had a booth at the World's Fair in the summer of 1939. Reggio Emilia preschools started receiving delegations of foreign visitors in 1979 and has continued to play host to them ever since.

## THE RISE AND FALL OF PROGRESSIVE EDUCATION

There had been attempts in the 1930s to establish a public progressive school in New York City. Known as the Little Red School House, classes contained 30–35 children and the budget was no larger per capita than that provided by the city to public programs (DeLima, 1943, p. 7). Earlier attempts to incorporate progressive ideas in the public schools at such places as Winnetka, Illinois and Gary, Indiana had been much hailed in the early 1900s, but did not always persist. After only a few moths, New York City withdrew its funds from the Little Red School House. However, it has continued as a private school.

There are several interpretations concerning the rise and fall of progressive education and the extent to which it did influence American public education. Campbell stated that Hessian Hills School and progressive education as a whole declined during World War II. After 1938,

> ... attacks on social reconstructionist methods, anti-communist attempts to remove individual left wing teachers, to stop the use of progressive social studies text books began in 1938–40, but accelerated during and after the war. Many progressive schools adapted to the war time pressures as Hessian Hills did by adopting wartime patriotism, down playing their differences with the public schools, toning down experimentalism and radicalism. (Campbell, 1984, p. 338)

Lawrence Cremin, writing in 1961, attributes the collapse of progressive education to schisms in the movement, negativism in all social reform movements, inordinate demands on teachers' time and ability, a general swing towards conservatism in post-war political social thought, and a failure to keep pace with the continuing transformation of American Society (Cremin, 1961, pp. 348–351).

Patricia Albjerg Graham, writing about the Progressive Education Association, which published a journal and held conferences from 1919–1955, gives most of the same reasons for its demise (Graham, 1967). In a review of her book in the *Harvard Educational Review* (1967), James Wallace, Director of Teacher Education at Reed College, argues that Graham "concedes too much to the critics of progressive education. She puts substantial stress on the internal squabbles of the progressives as elements in weakening the movement and not enough emphasis on the massive resistance of American power groups to any radical reform of the schools" (Wallace, 1969, p. 191). Wallace closes his review with a quote from John DeBoer, a one time president of the Progressive Education Association: "In the long run no education system can be better than the society in which it operates, and . . . therefore progressive education demands a progressive society" (Wallace, 1969, p. 191).

This bit of wisdom applies as well to the education system which followed progressive education. Commenting that by the early 1950s some progressive methods had entered the public schools, Campbell writes,

> But much of the essence . . . was not copied in public education. Social reconstructionism, the idea that children should experience cooperation rather than compete with each other, creative approaches to student-written drama, science and dance did not transfer into the mainstream of public education in America. Experimental methods flourished in Great Britain, and it was not until the 1960's and 1970's that American educa-

tors rediscovered them and brought them back to this country as "open education." (Campbell, 1984, pp. 331–332)

## POST-PROGRESSIVISM

Campbell describes open education as an,

> . . . indirect descendant of progressive education in the sense that the European New Education which had close connections with American progressive education nurtured the British "integrated day" movement of 1945–65. Progressive education and open education both concentrate on learning by doing, on letting the child develop to his own schedule, on "integrating" art, science and social studies. (Campbell, 1984, p. 351)

President Johnson's War on Poverty, announced in 1965, created a climate conducive to a humane and progressive society and thus encouraged American educators to create more humane and progressive schools.

Many Americans were seeking ways to reform the schools. The President's Science Advisory Committee published *Innovation and Experiment In Education* in 1964, a report of a series of panels of influential scientists and educators who had been meeting in 1962 and 1963 to consider how educational research and development can learn "to provide for all students the education an exceptional teacher provides for a few" (Panel on Educational Research and Development, 1964, p. vii). Although claiming to support no particular method of pedagogy, the Report does favor "a particular approach to teaching, an approach called 'inductive teaching' or the 'discovery method.' The plan is to get students to discover things for themselves" (1964, p. 6).

In 1967, the Central Advisory Council for Education in England published *Children and Their Primary Schools*, part of the Plowden Report, after Lady Bridget Plowden who chaired the Council. American educators, still dissatisfied with American schools, welcomed its recommendations. American educators visited schools in England. Many books on open education were published in America, and one of the models of the national "Follow Through" experiment was based on these British ideas. These ideas differed little from progressive education of the 1920s.

Harvard professor, Courtney Cazden, visited the Gordonbrook Infant School in 1967 and published an interview with the headmistress. Speaking about English teachers, the headmistress stated:

> [Y]ou really know your children. Not only are you aware of their needs, intellectually and physically, you also have the opportunity to

stand back and observe. It's only in observing children that you really do know your children. If you're sitting there and you've got all the little ones all doing the same thing at the same time, what opportunity have you really to know your children? But if they can select what they want to do, and you can find the thoughts that are going on in the child's mind, you really do begin to know your children. Couple that with the fact that you can see the parents . . . At the end of 2 years, or 3 years in the case of some children you really do know them. (Cazden, 1969, p. 10)

Compare the above with Rinaldi's statement about Reggio Emilia: "The schools are not places for lectures, but places where teachers actively listen so they can, with the children, 'adventure' in the world of knowledge" (Rinaldi, 1989, p. 5).

Leaders of progressive education, open education, and Reggio Emilia show again and again in their writings their similar understandings of how children learn, and planning a curriculum could be based on children's interests. Recall Caroline Pratt's tugboats and the description of Grape Harvesting in Reggio Emilia. The British *Plowden Report* also detailed a "Use of the Environment" project:

Rural schools have an abundance of material on their doorsteps. Crops and pastures, wild flowers and weeds, farm animals, wild creatures of every kind, roads and footpaths, verges, hedges, ditches, streams, woods, the weather, the season, the stars, all provide starting points for curiosity, discussion, observation, recording and inquiry . . .

Teachers in town schools can make use of railways and other transport systems, and the local shops and factories, all of which can provide suitable material. Building sites are almost ubiquitous and can provide an approach to geography, mathematics and science. We have heard of children doing 'traffic counts,' discovering from shop keepers the source of their goods and even in one case exploring unofficially the sewage system of the area. (Plowden, 1967, p. 200)

In England, as in the earlier progressive schools, there was recognition of the teaching power of firsthand experience with the local environment, whether it be a river, a city street, or a country road.

Scientists, professors, teachers, and students visited British Infant and Primary schools throughout the 1960s and 1970s. Among these visitors were David and Frances Hawkins who then opened the Mountain View Center for Environmental Education in Boulder in 1970 where teachers could take short courses taught by visiting scientists. Advisors were available to go out to schools where requested. The Hawkins also published a journal, *Outlook*, from 1970 ,to 1987. The national "Follow Through" program adopted Open Education as one of its models. With headquarters at the Education Development Center in Newton, Massachusetts, the Open Education model, supported by grants from the federal government and the Ford Foundation, adopted an advisory system of helping classroom teachers based on a model from Leicestershire. From about 1967 to 1976 advisors swooped into classrooms in public schools in such diverse places as Paterson, New Jersey, Rosebud, Texas, Smithfield, North Carolina, and Philadelphia, among others. Advisors attempted to help principals and teachers bring about Open Education from preschool through third grade. I was one of those advisors. Although we did help implement some wonderful open classrooms, our success overall was rather limited. This was a richly funded educational experiment. We not only went to far away school systems by plane and rent-a-cars, but we paid for teachers to come to EDC for workshops. All advisers had been sent to England for a few weeks to experience Open Education first hand.

However, the principals and teachers of the schools chosen for making the change to Open Education often had little input in choosing the Open Education model. Some teachers welcomed new ideas and were hungry for advice about how to make learning more meaningful for their pupils. Some teachers saw us as threats, and some had real problems in trying to figure out "open education." I recall one bewildered teacher in a Paterson kindergarten telling us, "If I could just get it into my head I think I could do it."

I have often recalled that Paterson teacher's remark when I attended meetings of Americans who visited the Reggio Emilia schools. Some members of these groups suggest that the way to work toward better day care centers in this country is to adopt some small aspect of the Reggio programs, such as having the child's teacher remain with the group for three years or trying some specific curriculum project based on a Reggio project. I think the Paterson teacher knew better. In order to have attractive, humane centers where both children and teachers are actively involved in learning, there must be first teachers and parents and community leaders who know "in their heads" that this kind of care and education is important for little children. Once we know that, we can devise our own techniques and curriculum to bring it about. Reggio Emilia should be used as an inspiration, not as a model.

## THE RISE AND FALL OF OPEN EDUCATION

One of the many visitors to Leicestershire was Professor Schafftel of Stanford University. A letter of hers sent back to England after her visit is quoted in Phillip Sherwood's article, "The Leicestershire Myth," in *Outlook* (1974).

I left England feeling that the schools I had visited had a concern for children as persons, not just learners, that American schools have lost. We had it in our progressive schools of the thirties. We buried it under the pressure of scientism and post-sputnick frenzy. It is my hope that efforts like yours will stimulate a new movement in our country. Certainly the number of American visitors to English schools suggests a new quest. (Sherwood, 1974, p. 9)

In that same article students from Wheelock College who had visited Leicestershire were also quoted: "Each Leicestershire school is a creation of the people of its town, its staff, its children and its history. They have taken a long time to become what they are" (Sherwood, 1974, p. 9).

This same comment might well be said today about each Reggio preschool. On my visit there I found that just as intriguing as the curriculum and the wonderful art work of the children were the words of pride about the history of the school, whether spoken by teachers, parents, or pedagogista.

Writing in 1974, Vito Perrone reflected on "Open Education. Where Has It Been? Where Is It Going?" He traced the literature on Open Education through four phases: First, it drew heavily on the English experience. Next, greater attention was paid to the work of Jean Piaget and after 1971 there was less emphasis in the literature on the English experience. The third phase drew on the literature of the progressive movement, and the fourth phase was a literature on "How to do it."

Although still hopeful at that time that schools would become more responsive to children, Perrone cautioned that,

> In spite of the growing movement toward open classroom practice, with its emphasis on community resources, there remains a narrow use of community . . . The community itself needs to see itself as integral to the entire process of education, not separate from it. Bringing about an intersection of the school and the community is necessary if the strengths of each are to be made a part of children's education. I am not at all optimistic that progress in this arena will be rapid. (Perrone, 1989, p. 85)

Perrone ends this chapter pointing out that the funding for Open Education, both federal and from foundations, is declining, that decline has continued. Mountain View Center closed in *1983*. *Outlook* stopped publishing in *1987*.

In the 1920s and 1930s, educators and other professionals concerned with making schools responsive to children visited progressive, private schools in and around New York City. In the 1960s England's Open Schools were the place to go; now it's to Italy. Educators clearly feel a need to see good programs for children in action and to listen to their leaders. Two of these leaders, Malaguzzi in Italy and Perrone in the United States, urge us to look at the history of programs that are responsive to children. Vito Perrone, now a Harvard professor, ended a talk in 1982 with the suggestion that we read again Agnes DeLima, Caroline Pratt, Frances Hawkins, and so on.

> I view these descriptions as more than grist for challenge to contemporary formulations of education; I view them also as an important base for the long term progressive struggle for better schools, as part of an ongoing effort to assure that what is learned is retained, as capable of informing the next generation of progressives who might be even more successful because of our efforts now when conditions appear so unsympathetic and complex. (Perrone, 1989, p. 99)

These comments seem just as true, if not more so, for the 1990s, as they did in 1982.

As the United States and Great Britain both became less concerned with children and schools and more concerned with individualism, materialism, and defense spending, Open Education languished in both countries. DeBoer's prophetic remarks about Progressive Education could now be applied to Open Education: "No education system can be better than the society in which it operates."

In order to learn from the Reggio Emilia preschools, we need to heed the political and social setting which surrounds them. Diane Rollo visited the schools in 1990; quoting Rinaldi:

> Reggio Emilia is a city with rich and deep cultural, economical and political heritage in a region where the ideas of socialism and cooperation for the well being of all took root long ago. These concepts of cooperation and shared work to promote the common good are principles underlying the Reggio Emilia preschool experience. (Rollo, 1990, p. 3)

Later, Rollo makes this observation:

> In Italy you can not help but notice the Italians deep appreciation for beauty and aesthetics. It can be found in every nook and cranny. Cleanliness and order always surround you. There is an aesthetic order to the environment. It can be seen in the grandeur of the art and architecture to the way flowers are arranged in a vase, or how pasta is displayed on your plate. (Rollo, 1990, p. 8)

In the 1990s, after Americans have been inspired by visits to Italy and informed by reading about similar programs in America in the past, they need to turn their creative energy not only to educational reform, but also to the social and political scene in whatever community they reside. A humane society appears a necessary prerequisite to bringing about humane schools, where teachers are able to "learn from children" and their environment and where they will tear up those stencils of pumpkins and shamrocks with our blessing.

## REFERENCES

Campbell, K.M. (1984). *An experiment in education: The Hessian Hills School, 1925–1952*. Doctoral Dissertation, Boston University.

Cazden, C. (1969). *Infant school*. Newton, MA: Education Development Center.

Cremin, L.A. (1961). *The transformation of the school*. New York: Alfred A. Knopf.

DeLima, A. (1943). *The little red school house*. New York: Random House.

Graham, P.A. (1967). *Progressive education: From arcady to academe*. New York: Teachers College Press.

Malaguzzi, L. (1987). *The Hundred Languages of Children*. A catalog of the exhibit, "The Hundred Languages of Children," published by the Comune di Reggio Emilia, assessorato all' Istruzione, Regione di Emilia Romagna.

Panel on Educational Research and Development of The President's Science Advisory Committee. (1964). *Innovation and experiment in education*. Washington, DC: U.S. Government Printing Office.

Perrone, V. (1989). *Working papers*. New York: Teachers College Press.

Plowden, Lady B., et al. (1967). *Children and their primary schools: A report of the Central Advisory Council for Education* (Vol. 1). London: Her Majesty's Stationery Office.

Pratt, C. (1948). *I learn from children: An adventure in progressive education*. New York: Simon and Schuster.

Rinaldi, C. (1989). *The role of the environment: The third educator*. Unpublished extracts from Workshop at the Conference "Exploring the Hundred Languages of Children." Boston, MA.

Rollo, D. (1990). *"Non facciamo niente senza gioia. The Reggio Emilia preschool experience for children*. Unpublished graduate field study article.

Sherwood, P. (1974). The Leicestershire myth. *Outlook, 13*, 5–13.

Wallace, J.M. (1969). Review of *Progressive education: From arcady to academe*. *Harvard Educational Review, 39*(1), 187–191.

"Zebra." Drawing by child of the
Diana School.

# 17

# Poppies and the Dance
of World Making

## Paul Kaufman

### SCENE ONE: FELLINI WOULD APPROVE

The warm, honeyed breath of the Italian spring hangs in the air. A line
of children moves quietly into the poppy field. Parting the long
grasses—like Moses and the Israelites—they make their way through
a blazing sea of red. "You may pick a few flowers," says the *atelierista*,
a handsome woman with Botticellian hair and a 35mm camera.

A boy holds a poppy up to the sunlight, scrutinizes it with obvious
discernment, and blows at it. "This is better than ice cream," he
murmurs. In the sweetest of primeval rituals, two girls groom each
other.

"Let me try to put the flower in your hair," one says. She inserts the stem of the poppy delicately into her friend's hair and pats it approvingly. The other girl responds in a soft, husky voice, "I want to make a cross of flowers in your hair."

Eeeeee! Shrieks and squeals. A zebra has entered the far end of the field: Some of the children have spotted it. Head vigorously bobbing up and down, a bouquet of poppies clenched in its foam rubber mouth, its stark black and white formal attire clashes deliciously with the country reds and greens. A boy shouts: "It's the Diana School zebra and *I* know *who* it is!" The children hurry across the field to greet the beast and the teacher's aides crazy enough to bob and sweat under the zebra's skin.


### SCENE TWO: "AH . . . NO . . . AND PLEASE PASS THE ACQUA MINERALE."

Flashback. In the lunchroom of a Reggio Emilia school several days earlier, founder Loris Malaguzzi and staff eat with the American television crew. The Americans want to capture the essence of the Reggio Emilia approach to early education for a new television series on creativity. The Italians are polite but appropriately cautious. There is much cross-talk between them about possible arrangements.

"We'd like to shoot the poppy project."

"But you're here for only five days. There are a number of stages. It will take much more time than you have, to show the whole process."

"But, we don't have a lot of time! Believe me, we wish we had more."

"Yes, but first the children do individual drawings. Then, they begin to work with each other. Finally, the whole group creates a work."

As he listens and savors the delicate pasta, the American producer recalls that his old school lunchroom in San Diego was never like this. He drifts. He becomes momentarily disoriented and imagines he sees an evanescent shape release itself from the corporeal Malaguzzi, who is listening intently to a discussion about just what should be put on television. An apparition of Malaguzzi himself rises from the table and, wine glass in hand, wanders over to the American. The spirit lays a translucent paw on the producer's shoulder. "Look here, my friend, you Americans come over here a lot these days. Especially the scholars—oh, they're some bunch—a few of them have made a cottage industry of studying us—but now also the media has discovered Reggio Emilia. After you leave, there's another television crew heading in. One day we'll be in *Newsweek*. Ehhhh . . ." The phantom takes a sip of wine. "Here's my point: Nothing changes back there. You come. You look. You go back. You come, you look . . . "

The producer snaps back to reality. Malaguzzi is arguing with the teachers.

"The zebra should come into the poppy field," he says. "It will be a surprise."

"Ah . . . No . . . Malaguzzi!" a teacher demurs with a dramatic flourish of her hands. "The zebra is *not* part of the project. It will only distract the children." Malaguzzi will not back down. "The children need surprises." She pleads. "But Malaguzzi, the children will get too excited."

Someone asks for the acqua minerale. Eating and talking and eating and talking, the producer relaxes into the feeling of being part of a big, loving, quarrelsome family to which he has belonged all of his life.


## SCENE THREE: SHOOTING AT DIANA SCHOOL

The video crew's Director of Photography shoulders the heavy video camera. She needs to frame Malaguzzi better as he walks through the schoolroom, pointing to the artwork done by the children. The producer back-peddles awkwardly to stay out of the shot but still maintain eye contact with Malaguzzi. They converse in French. The sound engineer, grappling with a swaying fish-pole microphone, scuttles about like Quasimodo on a bad day. Malaguzzi pauses before a collage. "This is the final part of a project exploring one word only. The word is 'crowd.' As you can see, the crowd is made up of children, of old people . . . of adults, of little dogs, of smells, of sounds. It's a very complex picture. Here, what children are doing is taking apart the word 'crowd' and drawing out all of its separate meanings."

The children's drawing shows a woman walking in one direction, while a man walks in another. A mother pushes her child along in a stroller. A dog is held by the collar. "The problem is this. To give a visual meaning to a word as complex and explosive as 'crowd' can be. Children have the ability to put many images in their minds. One image can even become a crowd of images and a crowd of images can create a *dialogue* between children. This dialogue is not only a means of conveying something. It is also the child's way of inventing new directions, of enlarging the possibilities of speech, of enriching one another," says Malaguzzi. Malaguzzi pauses, his eyes shining with the light of informed passion. *"I believe there is no possibility of existing without relationship. Relationship is a necessity of life.* From birth, children are in continuous relationships. They have this need, this desire, to master interaction: to be protagonist one time, to be listener another time. And then, to be a protagonist again. For children, dia-

**Figure 17.1.** Detail from "Summer Fresco." Mural painted by children of the Diana School.

logue opens this game of playing different parts. Children have the great fortune to know how to pull thoughts and meanings from one another's voices. They can speak in images that are close but also images that are remote. To adults, these images may appear out of focus, but they are always close to the sensitivity of children."

## SCENE FOUR: THE CHILDREN PAINT

The former denizens of the poppy field now sprawl on the floor together, painting a large fresco. The poppies and their friends—grasshoppers, frogs, dragonflies—appear in a startling aesthetic that is simultaneously primitive and sophisticated. Flamboyant creatures, expressions of newly awakened little phenomenologies, meld into a vernal dreamscape. As the children paint, they negotiate. "What's this *thing* doing inside the poppy?" asks one girl of another. "*Ma!*" she responds with a gasp of exasperation: "It's a joke!" "Ohhh . . ." says the other with the smile of a six-year-old going on thirtysomething. Malaguzzi comes over to where the children are working and observes, "It's not just the images that come from the hands and imagination of the children that count, but also the fruit of the harmony of all their ideas. To place the colors, to find the right balance in a symphony of colors, means for the child to become the extraordinary instrument of an orchestra."

## SCENE FIVE: WRAP AND BANQUET

The Americans are wrapping up production. Cables are coiled and light stands are trundled away. The crew is especially careful not to leave a mess, even searching for the wads of used gaffer tape that hide under tables and behind desks. On the last night, the school staff and the Americans have dinner together at a country inn. The Americans toast the Italians. The Italians toast the Americans. The producer embraces Malaguzzi. Malaguzzi embraces the producer, "Caro amico." If there is a dry eye in the house, it belongs to the waiter.

Back at the hotel, the Americans are depressed about leaving Reggio Emilia. Their next stop is an innovative factory in Sweden. A colleague who has gone ahead reports by telephone that Sweden is cold and expensive and, besides, she isn't sure how good the story is. The producer is assailed by dark fantasies. The Swedish plant is a chill, gloomy cavern in which a few bearded giants in coveralls move about, occasionally clanking their wrenches. He tries to interview them about creativity, but all they will talk about is why Swedes love to visit sunny Italy.

The producer repairs with a beer to an outdoor table facing onto the grand piazza. It is evening and he watches the men of Reggio Emilia gather as they have gathered for centuries . . . to talk. They stand in little groups just as their fathers and fathers before them stood. He wonders what they are discussing. Politics, no doubt. The producer longs to belong in such a ritual, this communion through communication. He recalls Malaguzzi's words: "*I believe there is no possibility of existing without relationship. Relationship is a necessity of life.*"

A field of poppies, a *piazza* of people—it is all the same. The children dance their dance of world making and the old men also dance. The bells of a nearby church sound and the producer recalls the faces of the children.

"Little saviors of Interpretation," he muses. God knows we need them.

# Conclusion

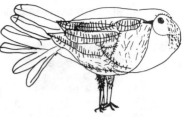

"A bird looking back." Drawing by child
of the Diana School.

# 18

# Conclusion: Where Do We Go From Here?

## Carolyn Edwards and George Forman

This book presented an introduction and overview to the Reggio Emilia approach to early childhood education. The purpose of this educational project, so say the educators in Reggio Emilia (Department of Early Education, 1984), is to produce a *reintegrated child,* capable of constructing his or her own powers of thinking through the synthesis of all the expressive, communicative, and cognitive languages. But this reintegrated child is not a solitary investigator. On the contrary, the child's senses and mind need help from others in perceiving order and change and discovering the meanings of new relations. The child is a *protagonist.*

This book, like the Reggio Emilia system itself, is the product of many collaborations. First of all, it is the culmination—the end of the "first act"—of the ongoing and accelerating drama of dialogue and exchange between educators in Reggio Emilia and the United States, with Lella Gandini serving as original ambassador representing both

**305**

**Figure 18.1.** "Children concluding their story." Photograph placed by children at the end of their photo-story, "Pedinovela." (From the exhibit catalog, *The Hundred Languages of Children*. Reprinted by permission.)

sides. Indeed, cross-cultural understanding always happens best when "cultural insiders" and "cultural outsiders" talk together about the meaning of events and ideas (Edwards & Gandini, 1989; Whiting & Edwards, 1988). Both groups offer necessary perspectives, complementary interpretations, and out of that juxtaposition emerges a more complete "truth-for-now" about the meaning and significance of the Reggio Emilia approach.

Second, this book represents something we would like to encourage: the collaboration—fusion, really—between the liberal arts and the professional discipline of early childhood education. The knowledge base of the arts and humanities is too often used superficially and uninspiringly in classrooms, because teachers feel they are not well-enough prepared or are "not good at" things related to art, music, history, and literature. In contrast, the program in Reggio Emilia demonstrates how teachers can, through documentation and team-work, prepare school environments and activities that awaken in young children powers to perceive, study, and represent the beautiful and orderly worlds of nature and culture surrounding them. As a result, children, through guided exploration, play, and self-expression, are introduced in appropriate ways to the important symbols and knowledge systems of adults. Children early gain a deep sense of their history, heritage, and cultural traditions.

Finally, this book represents a yearning toward the most hopeful kind of collaboration of all, the one between children and adults. As Dean Murray Schwartz said, introducing the 1988 Conference at the University of Massachusetts:

> One of the things we have learned in this century from people who work with children is that play is not only a way of testing reality, but also a way of creating it. The freedom of children to play creatively changes the world! When those children grow to adulthood and teach other children . . . if they can create an adult community, then it will have a profound effect on the way that we perceive, change, and respect the real world.

So then, where do we go from here? The Reggio Emilia approach represents a unique combination of elements, but its basic philosophy and premises about teaching and learning are ones that most American early childhood educators will find familiar and sympathetic. For instance, in spite of our heavy emphasis on autonomy and individualism, most of us are seeking to promote greater cooperation, community, and participation in both schools and American life. Even though we might find situations in which to use sequential or behavioral approaches, we are still basically child-centered and wholistic.

One worthwhile pursuit will be to study in greater depth the work ongoing in Reggio Emilia. We have barely begun to understand, for example, the way in which teachers work there. How different are individual teachers in what they do? How consistently do they maintain a balance between teacher- and child-direction of learning? Exactly how do they turn disagreements and conflicts into problem-solving opportunities? How do they find the time to document children's work and conversations while executing their other responsibilities?

Beyond studying the program in Reggio Emilia, however, we should be looking abroad at other international successes in education (Cochran, in press; Lamb, Sternberg, Hwang, & Broberg, 1992; Olmstead & Weikart, 1989). Certainly, Reggio Emilia is not the only interesting site of innovation in Italy, much less Europe! Because the peoples of Western Europe have moved ahead of North Americans with regard to social services and family policy, we should be studying their experiences as we debate whether and how to publicly finance early childhood care and education, how to design spaces and environments for infants and young children, and what are different possible models for grouping children, organizing the school day and year, defining adult roles, and building decision-making structures.

When it comes to "bringing it home," there are many possibilities. One initial issue has to do with whether it is better to proceed, on the one hand, by setting up demonstration schools or classrooms, embodying as closely as possible all of the important central premises of the Reggio Emilia approach, or on the other hand, by trying to incorporate one or more strands of the approach into ongoing endeavors, in whatever setting or level of education we happen to work. Yet, this is really a pointless debate. All attempts to incorporate the ideas and approaches of others are bound to be more or less partial. Even with all of the money, freedom, and resources wished for, one cannot do everything anew, or import exactly what they do in Reggio; nor would one want to. In the first place, there are 22 municipal preprimary schools and 13 infant-toddler centers in Reggio—each with its own distinct individuality evolving over time—so there is no single, static "it" to model upon. In the second place, as David Hawkins (Remarks) reminds us, importing foreign models wholesale has never worked; each society must solve its own problems. Thus, the question becomes simply how ambitious and complex a project one wants to undertake: how many dimensions to try to consider simultaneously.

In any event, those engaged in adaptation and application immediately find themselves confronting interesting and subtle issues. For some aspects of the Reggio Emilia approach—for example, the use of long-term study projects—one can readily find practical resources (Katz & Chard, 1989) and rationale in terms of developmentally appropriate practice (Bredekamp, 1987). The evident success of incorporating ideas from Reggio Emilia into elaborate project work with American children is attested by Forman, Lee, Wrisley, and Langley (Chapter 13) and LeeKeenan and Nimmo (Chapter 14). Other aspects, however, present much more difficulty, even when they present strong face validity as worthwhile ideas. One such aspect concerns the provision of time to children. The educators in Reggio deplore the way Americans "hurry" children and deny them the long blocks of time they need for project work. Although that criticism seems justified, we have very deep-seated commitments to sticking to schedules and using time efficiently. Perhaps the example of Reggio Emilia can help us to reexamine and modulate the excesses of our American tendency to rush and jam too many activities and transitions into our own and our children's schedules. Another such aspect concerns the three-year continuity of teachers and groups in Reggio preprimary schools—a practice common throughout Italy and other parts of Europe. The immense benefits seem obvious in terms of protecting young children's sense of security, promoting parent–teacher bonds, and making preschools less institutional. Why then is the practice not normative in the United States?

So the question, "Where do we go from here?" raises many provocative possibilities. We hope that your adventures are dense with moments of confusion and illumination, conflict and progress.

## SUMMARY: A MULTISYMBOLIC APPROACH TO TEACHING

The approach to teaching in Reggio Emilia is a large part of what makes the program so unique and interesting. From the manuscript as a whole, we have abstracted a list of principles, or teaching guidelines. This set is not final or exhaustive; they are our best summary for now. We have divided these principles into six categories. Since they have been described fully throughout the book, here they will simply be listed only briefly. Please consider this section a summary of many of the key ideas of the book, as well as a set of reminders for the practicing teacher.

### Staging the Project

- Think in terms of "reconnaissance" rather than "planning"
- Use small groups of two to six children in project work
- Allow themes far removed from everyday experience
- Challenge children to do something large or complicated
- Do not shy away from emotionally laden themes
- Present the project as a need to display and communicate
- Get prepared for anything by brainstorming possibilities
- Anticipate where academic content might naturally emerge

### Representational Strategies

- Ask children to copy the representations of adults, for example, maps
- Let children make cross-modal drawings, for example, pictures of sounds, feelings
- Show children photos of themselves at work; stimulate reflectivity
- Use first drawings as a reference for improving later representations
- Encourage children to make their first sketches hurriedly
- Use the children's drawings to "unpack" their naive theories
- Photocopy child's icons and use them in many contexts

- Substitute children's invented symbols for standard notations
- Ask children to invent notations and syntax, for example, to represent footprints
- Use one symbolic domain to push and challenge another
- Go beyond art as aesthetics; instead see art as a thinking tool
- Integrate drawings from both observation and imagination
- Draw the same object or system from different perspectives
- Represent the same object across time, for example, lengthening shadows, growing plants

## Group Dynamics

- Model on the adult level the kinds of democratic participation, collaborative learning, and conflict-resolution you are trying to teach to children
- Allow children to compare and criticize each other's work
- Help children turn differences of opinion into problem-solving opportunities
- Let the system of group relations be the educational medium
- Experiment with different-sized small groups in project work
- Be sensitive to gender differences in problem-solving styles
- Trust the children to debate among themselves to closure
- Use the sense of "we" to improve social dynamics of project
- Use social constructivism by supporting constructive conflict
- Make use of children's interest in rules as an educational medium
- Have the project culminate as an event for the larger community

## Teaching Strategies

- Dispense occasions that challenge children intellectually and emotionally
- Serve as children's scribe; write what they dictate
- Offer replica props to support children's discourse
- Have children talk about which representation communicates the best
- Let children choose and discuss which media work best
- Teach technical skills directly, for example, when working with clay
- Comment on the work itself rather than on the children's skill level
- Work around children's lack of technical skills and go directly to their thinking, for example, by use of photocopies

- Combine objects and materials in unexpected ways; for example, bring the outdoors in and the indoors out
- Learn from children as they try to learn from you
- Allow children slow, unhurried time

## Cognitive Goals

- Encourage children to think about what something is not
- Encourage children to think about what something could be
- Encourage children to think about reciprocal relations
- Help children reframe the mundane and ordinary
- Emphasize in-depth knowledge of complete systems
- Allow children to discuss the incomplete nature of their work

## Interpretation of Children's Work

- Document, document, document!
- Share your documentation with parents, children, colleagues, the public
- Take the perspective of a researcher
- Find in yesterday's notes the problems to pose today
- Review transcripts and photos of children with children
- Encourage children to work and rework a representation
- Treat all answers as derivatives of a logic to be understood

## REFERENCES

Bredekamp, S. (1987). *Developmentally appropriate practice in early childhood programs serving children from birth through age 8.* Washington, DC: National Association for the Education of Young Children.

Cochran, M. (Ed.), (in press). *International handbook on child care policies and programs.* Westport, CT: Greenwood Press.

Department of Early Education, City of Reggio Emilia, Region of Emilia Romagna. (1984). *L'occhio se salta il muro (When the eye jumps over the wall).* Catalog of the Exhibit, "L'Occhio se Salta il Muro."

Edwards, C.P., & Gandini, L. (1989). Teachers' expectations about the timing of developmental skills: A cross-cultural study. *Young Children, 44*(4), 15–19.

Katz, L.G., & Chard, S.C. (1989). *Engaging children's minds: The project approach.* Norwood, NJ: Ablex.

Lamb, M.E., Sternberg, K.J., Hwang, C.P., & Broberg, A.G. (Eds.). (1992). *Child care in context.* Hillsdale, NJ: Erlbaum.

Olmstead, P., & Weikart, D. (Eds), (1989). *How nations serve young children: Profiles of child care and education in 14 countries.* Ypsilanti, MI: High/ Scope Press.

Schwartz, M. (1988, December). Introduction to the "Hundred Languages of Children" Conference, University of Massachusetts, Amherst.

Whiting, B.B., & Edwards, C.P. (1988). *Children of different worlds: The formation of social behavior.* Cambridge, MA: Harvard University Press.

# Glossary of Terms Used by Educators in Reggio Emilia

*Asilo Nido* **Infant-Toddler Center:** full-day educational child care center for children aged four months through three years.

*Assessore:* Elected official, serving under the Mayor, in charge of all public education for the city.

*Atelier:* Workshop, or studio, furnished with a variety of resource materials, used by all the children and adults in a school.

*Atelierista:* Teacher trained in art education, in charge of the *atelier*; supports teachers in curriculum development and documentation.

*Comune:* Also called *municipio*, the city government and the building where it is located.

*Consiglio di Gestione* **Advisory Council on Community-Based Management:** Elected committee of parents, citizens, and educators serving a preprimary school or infant-toddler center.

*Consulta di Asili Nido e delle Scuole dell' Infanzia* **Municipal Board of Infant-Toddler and Preprimary Education:** Composed of representatives of the Advisory Councils; has governing authority over the early childhood system.

***Direttore* Director of Early Childhood Education:** A civil service professional who oversees the whole infant-toddler and preprimary system and guarantees the quality and integrity of the educational services provided to children and families.

***Educatore* Teacher:** In a preprimary school.

***Gestione Sociale* Community-Based Management:** The system of governance, involving representatives of the different sectors of the local community, used in the Reggio Emilia municipal early childhood system.

***Operatore* Teacher:** In an infant-toddler center.

***Pedogogista* Pedagogical Coordinator:** Acts as consultant, resource person, and coordinator to several schools and centers. The Team of *Pedagogisti* serves under the Director who is responsible for the preprimary schools and infant-toddler centers in the city.

***Scuola dell' Infanzia* Preprimary School:** Full-day educational child care center for children aged three, four, and five years of age (includes the American kindergarten year).

# Additional Published Resources About the Reggio Emilia Approach

Department of Early Education, City of Reggio Emilia, Region of Emilia Romagna. (1987). *I centro linguaggi dei bambini (The hundred languages of children: Narrative of the possible)*. Catalog of the Exhibit, "The hundred languages of children," in Italian and English. Assessorato Scuole Infanzia e Asili Nido, Via Guido da Castello 12, 42100 Reggio Emilia, Italy.

Edwards, C.P., Gandini, L., & Nimmo, J. (1992). Favorire l'apprendimento cooperativo nella prima infanzia (Promoting collaborative learning in the early childhood classroom). *Rassegna di Psicologia*, no. 3. University of Rome.

Edwards, C.P., Shallcross, D., & Maloney, J. (1991). Promoting creativity in a graduate course on creativity: Entering the time and space of the young child. *Journal of Creative Behavior, 25*(4), 304–310.

Forman, G.E. (1989). Helping children ask good questions. In B. Neugebauer (Ed.), *The wonder of it: Exploring how the world works* (pp. 21–24). Redmond, WA: Exchange Press.

Forman, G.E. (1992). The constructivist perspective. In. J.L. Roopnarine & J.E. Johnson (Eds.), *Approaches to early childhood education*. Columbus, OH: Merrill.

Gandini, L. (1992, May/June). Creativity comes dressed in everyday clothes. *Child Care Information Exchange*, No. 85, Summer, 26–29.

Gandini, L. (1984, Summer). Not just anywhere: Making child care centers into "particular" places. *Beginnings*, pp. 17–20. (Reprinted in *Child Care Information Exchange*, No. 78, March/April 1991, 5–9.)

Gandini, L., & Edwards, C.P. (1988). Early childhood integration of the visual arts. *Gifted International, 5*(2) 14–18.

Katz, L.G. (1990). Impressions of Reggio Emilia preschools. *Young Children, 45*(6), 10-11.

LeeKeenan, D., & Edwards, C.P. (1992). Using the project approach with toddlers. *Young Children, 47*(4), 31–36.

Lewin, A.W. (1992). The view from Reggio. *Hand to hand: Youth Museums Newsletter, 6*(1), 4-6.

New, R. (in press). Italian child care and early education: *Amor maternus* and other cultural contributions. In M. Cochran (Ed.), *International handbook on child care policies and programs*. Westport, CT: Greenwood Press.

New, R. (1991). Early childhood teacher education in Italy: Reggio Emilia's master plan for "master" teachers. *The Journal of Early Childhood Teacher Education, 12*(37), 3.

New, R. (1991). Projects and provocations: Preschool curriculum ideas from Reggio Emilia. *Montessori Life, 3*(1), 26–28.

New, R. (1990). Excellent early education: A city in Italy has it! *Young Children, 45*(6), 4–10. (Reprinted in *Early childhood education. Annual editions, 91/92* and *92/93.* Guilford, CT: Dushkin, 1991 and 1992.)

The 10 best schools in the world, and what we can learn from them. (1991, December 2). *Newsweek*, pp. 50–59.

Rankin, B. (1992, May/June). Inviting children's creativity: A story of Reggio Emilia, Italy. *Child Care Information Exchange*, No. 85, 30–35.

## Video Resources

*To Make a Portrait of a Lion (Per Fare il Ritratto di un Leone).* (1987). Comune di Reggio Emilia, Centro Documentazione Ricerca Educativa Nidi e Scuole dell'Infanzia. Available through Baji Rankin, 346 Washington St., Cambridge, MA 02139.

*The Long Jump: A video analysis of small group projects in early education as practiced in Reggio Emilia, Italy.* Forman, G.E., & Gandini, L. (1991). Performanetics Press, 19 The Hollow, Amherst, MA 01002.

*Childhood.* (PBS, 1991). Short segments on Reggio Emilia in Parts 3 (*Love's labors*) and 4 (*In the land of the giants*) of 7. Ambrose Video Publishing, 1290 Avenue of the Americas, Suite 2245, New York, NY 10104.

*The Creative Spirit.* (PBS, 1992). Segment on Reggio Emilia in Part 2 of 4 (*Creative beginnings*). PBS Video, 4401 Sunset Boulevard, Los Angeles, CA 90027. Companion volume: *The creative spirit*, by D. Goleman, P. Kaufman, and M. Ray (New York, Dutton, 1992).

*An Amusement Park for Birds.* By G. Forman, L. Gandini, L. Malaguzzi, C. Rinaldi, G. Piazza, & A. Gambetti. (1993). Performanetics Press, 19 The Hollow, Amherst MA 01002.

## Newsletter

*U.S.-Reggio Emilia Network Newsletter.* The Merrill-Palmer Institute, 71A East Ferry Avenue, Detroit, Michigan 48202. Beginning November, 1992.

# Author Index

# Subject Index